PRESIDENTIAL IMPEACHMENT

PRESIDENTIAL IMPEACHMENT

JOHN R. LABOVITZ

NEW HAVEN AND LONDON
YALE UNIVERSITY PRESS
1978

Published with assistance from the foundation
established in memory of Philip Hamilton McMillan
of the Class of 1894, Yale College.

Designed by Sally Sullivan Harris
and set in VIP Electra type.
Printed in the United States of America by
Vail-Ballou Press, Inc., Binghamton, N.Y.

Published in Great Britain, Europe, Africa, and
Asia (except Japan) by Yale University Press,
Ltd., London. Distributed in Latin America by
Kaiman & Polon, Inc., New York City; in
Australia and New Zealand by Book & Film
Services, Artarmon, N.S.W., Australia; and in
Japan by Harper & Row, Publishers, Tokyo Office.

Library of Congress Cataloging in Publication Data

Labovitz, John R 1943–
Presidential impeachment.

Includes index.
1. Impeachments—United States. 2. Nixon, Richard
Milhous, 1913– —Impeachment. I. Title.
KF5075.L33 353.03'6 77-76300
ISBN 0-300-02213-1

TO MY PARENTS

CONTENTS

PREFACE

As 1974 began the Committee on the Judiciary of the House of Representatives was initiating its investigation to determine whether grounds existed for the impeachment of Richard M. Nixon, only the second president in our history and the first in more than a century whose removal from office through impeachment was more than a theoretical possibility. Seven months later, at the conclusion of its investigation, the Judiciary Committee voted to recommend three articles of impeachment against President Nixon to the House. That recommendation, coupled with the forced release of additional inculpatory evidence by President Nixon a few days later, made his impeachment by the House and his conviction and removal by the Senate a virtual certainty, and Nixon became the first president in our history to invoke another consititutional procedure—resignation from office.

During the seven months of the committee's inquiry, I worked for its Impeachment Inquiry Staff, headed by Special Counsel John Doar. I was a member of a small unit of the staff responsible for constitutional and legal research. Because of its assignment, our group spent much more time on the history and characteristics of the impeachment process than on the particular allegations against President Nixon that were under investigation. While those who were gathering information and preparing the staff's evidentiary presentation to the committee had what John Doar termed a romance with the facts, our group was immersed in the constitutional law of impeachment and the presidency. We had a crash course in the deliberations of the Constitutional Convention of 1787 and the state ratifying conventions, the writings of legal commentators on those subjects, and the records of earlier impeachment investigations and trials.

One purpose of this book is to share some of what we learned. While inspired and heavily influenced by my experience on the Impeachment Inquiry Staff, however, this book is not intended to be an insider's account of the Nixon proceeding. No member of the inquiry staff except John Doar could conceivably provide a full account of what happened. Nor is the book a legal history of the inquiry; none of us has sufficient perspective to undertake that task.

Instead, this book is an analysis of presidential impeachment and the related topic of the president's constitutional duty to "take care that the laws be faithfully executed" in the light of the Nixon impeachment inquiry. The opinions, legal and otherwise, expressed in it are my personal views, based in part on research and reflection after the fact. I neither warrant nor expect that they coincide with those of others involved in the Nixon inquiry, and especially with those of participants whose roles were more significant than mine.

The need for legal analysis of impeachment is, fortunately, less than pressing. No presidential impeachment seems to loom on the horizon, and it may be a considerable time before the use of the constitutional procedure for removing unfit presidents is again seriously contemplated.

Indeed, one of my principal reasons for writing this book was the infrequency with which the impeachment process is employed. Making predictions about presidential impeachment tends to be a hazardous business, as evidenced by the long series of confident assertions between Andrew Johnson's acquittal by the Senate in 1868 and the unraveling of the Watergate cover-up in 1973 that impeachment of a president would never again be attempted. Two predictions, however, seem safe enough. The first, which is merely conservative, is that impeachment will remain in the Constitution as the mechanism for ousting presidents from office. The second, which may be considered pessimistic, is that some day another president will be suspected, rightly or wrongly, of misconduct that seems to warrant or necessitate his removal. When that occurs the Nixon inquiry will be studied for guidance on how to proceed. It is not precedent in the sense that past decisions are for courts, but the Nixon inquiry will influence the next impeachment proceeding. Because I feel a prospective occupational kinship with those lawyers who will have the job, I also feel a sense of obligation to aid them in their struggle with the issues we confronted in 1974. Though our learning—and especially my rendition of it—will hardly solve their problems, this book will achieve its purpose if it points them in some of the right directions.

It is presumptuous, I suppose, to write a book whose primary audience one hopes will not be around for a long time to come. I also hope, therefore, that this book will be of more immediate interest to those who would like to know more about the constitutional procedure that the House of Representatives invoked in 1974. With the abrupt end of the impeachment proceeding as a consequence of President Nixon's resignation, analysis of presidential impeachment seemed to lead to one homily—the constitutional system works—supplemented in some instances by the caveat that it is a deficient system. This caveat, even if valid, will probably be disregarded; there is little likelihood that impeachment will be replaced or even that an acceptable alternative can be devised. The homily, on the other hand, is insufficient; it is instructive to understand what the system is that seemed to work and to examine how it did so.

Presidential impeachment is a remarkable mechanism: a lawyer's solution to a statesman's problem. It is a legal procedure, but one for which there can be very little law because (out of good fortune or otherwise) it is so rarely used. It is not meant to be partisan, but it is directed at a critical political problem and consequently reflects existing partisan divisions and may create new ones. It poses fundamental questions about the nature of our constitutional government, which it forces Congress to address in the midst of a possible governmental crisis. It requires clear-cut choices—to accuse or not, to adjudge guilty or not—by the branch of government most prone to compromise or defer controversial decisions. It involves, in short, a complicated and sometimes contradictory tangle of legal and political considerations.

The interplay between law and politics in presidential impeachment makes it difficult to extricate one from the other. If anything, it might be easier to posit the political preconditions that are required for a presidential impeachment proceeding to be initiated or pursued than to identify the applicable legal standards. The legal issues in an impeachment proceeding are themselves influenced by the political context. To some indefinable extent, an impeachment investigation or an impeachment trial is an elaborate ritual to legitimize a political decision.

Yet there is more to impeachment than politics. Whether viewed as form or substance, legal considerations have an important role in an impeachment proceeding, if for no other reason than that the participants are scarcely likely to acknowledge that the legal rhetoric is but a rationalization for decisions based on their personal or political predilections. And there are instances—I believe the Nixon impeachment inquiry was one—in which decisions do primarily reflect legal judgments rather than political preferences.

In this book I focus on the law of impeachment rather than the politics. Some readers may think there is an overemphasis on legal issues and stratagems, especially in the discussion of the Chase and Johnson impeachments. I recognize, of course, that these cases were not ordinary lawsuits tried in an ordinary forum and that the transcripts of the trials hardly provide the full story of what happened. Nevertheless, I have stressed the legal aspects of these cases both because available historical accounts tend to emphasize their political side and because that is what will be most material in the context of another impeachment proceeding.

I am indebted to Chairman Peter W. Rodino, Jr., the members of the Judiciary Committee during the second session of the Ninety-third Congress, Special Counsel John Doar, and my former colleagues on the impeachment inquiry staff for the ideas that shaped this book. I owe special thanks to John Doar for giving me the opportunity to work on constitutional and legal issues throughout the inquiry and for sharing some of his thoughts both during and after the event. Among those on the staff, I am especially indebted to Joseph A. Woods, Jr., senior associate special counsel, who directed the constitutional and legal issues unit during the first four months of the inquiry. His insights concerning presidential impeachment influenced my thinking about the subject more than those of anyone else. Other former colleagues whose work affected this book are (in roughly chronological order of our work together) Dagmar Hamilton, Paul Goodrich, David Hanes, William Weld, Evan Davis, Hillary Rodham, Alan Marer, Terry R. Kirkpatrick, Robert D. Sack, Richard H. Gill, and Bernard W. Nussbaum. Professor Owen Fiss of the Yale Law School sharpened my thoughts in the process of shortening my prose in the early and late stages of the inquiry. My thanks are due to all for their unintended contribution to this book.

Messrs. Doar, Woods, Sack, Davis, and Marer also made a direct contribution to the book by reading and reacting to manuscript material. In addition, Professor Burke Marshall of the Yale Law School offered a number of valuable suggestions for improving the manuscript.

I am indebted to these readers, none of whom should be considered responsible for any continued persistence in error on my part.

Finally, I am grateful to the Ford Foundation for providing financial support that enabled me to write this book.

1. THE FRAMERS' VIEW OF IMPEACHMENT

The Constitution contains a half dozen provisions referring to impeachment. It provides that the president (as well as the vice president and all civil officers of the United States) "shall be removed from Office on Impeachment for, and conviction of, Treason, Bribery, or other high Crimes and Misdemeanors" (Art. II, §4). It vests "the sole Power of Impeachment" in the House of Representatives (Art. I, §2) and "the sole Power to try all Impeachments" in the Senate (Art. I, §3). It requires that, when sitting for the purpose of an impeachment trial, members of the Senate "shall be on Oath or Affirmation"; when the president is tried, the chief justice shall preside; "no Person shall be convicted without the Concurrence of two thirds of the Members present"; and "Judgment in Cases of Impeachment shall not extend further than to removal from Office, and disqualification to hold and enjoy any Office of honor, Trust or Profit under the United States: but the Party convicted shall nevertheless be liable and subject to Indictment, Trial, Judgment and Punishment, according to Law" (Art. I, §3). The other references to impeachment are exceptions from provisions otherwise applicable to offenses or crimes. Article II, section 2, provides that the president "shall have Power to grant Reprieves and Pardons for Offences against the United States, except in Cases of Impeachment"; Article III, section 2, provides that "[t]he Trial of all Crimes, except in Cases of Impeachment, shall be by Jury; and such Trial shall be held in the State where the said Crimes shall have been committed."

The Drafting of the Impeachment Provisions of the Constitution

The constitutional provisions concerning impeachment were drafted with the removal of the president primarily in mind. The delegates to the Constitutional Convention wished to create an independent, but responsible, executive. They had difficulty, however, reconciling the concept of executive accountability with the principle of separation of powers, which was fundamental to their new scheme of government. To avoid executive usurpation of power, the delegates sought to provide checks upon his conduct, including provision for his removal through impeachment. But to insure the independence of the executive, they sought to avoid his subservience to the legislature. These general concerns were central to their deliberations on the related questions of the composition of the executive, the mode of selection, the length of term, reeligibility, and impeachment.

The Initial Deliberations of the Convention in Committee of the Whole

The Constitutional Convention began its deliberations in committee of the whole, considering the Virginia Plan for a national government, fifteen resolutions drawn up by delegates from that state and proposed to the convention by Edmund Randolph on May 29, 1787. The resolutions called for a national legislature of two branches, a national executive, and a national judiciary. The seventh resolution proposed a national executive "to be chosen by the National Legislature for the term of   years, . . . and to be ineligible a second time; and that besides a general authority to execute the National laws, it ought to enjoy the Executive rights vested in Congress by the Confederation." The national judiciary, proposed in the ninth resolution, was to have jurisdiction over "impeachments of any National officers."[1]

After postponing the question of whether the executive should be a single person, the committee of the whole agreed that the executive should serve for a term of seven years and be elected by the national

1. 1 Max Farrand, ed., *The Records of the Federal Convention of 1787*, 21–2 (1937) (hereafter Farrand; in this chapter all references to Farrand will be given by volume and page number. Footnotes and brackets omitted in all quotations from Farrand).

legislature.[2] One delegate, Gunning Bedford of Delaware, opposed a seven-year term, arguing instead for a triennial election with ineligibility after nine years. Bedford thought a seven-year term too long and impeachment an insufficient remedy. "[A]n impeachment would reach misfeasance only, not incapacity," he said, and it would provide no cure if it were found that the first magistrate "did not possess the qualifications ascribed to him, or should lose them after his appointment." Another delegate from Delaware, John Dickinson, moved that the executive be removable by the national legislature upon the request of a majority of the legislatures of the states. Dickinson agreed that it was necessary "to place the power of removing somewhere," but he did not like the plan of impeaching the great officers of the government and wished to preserve the role of the states. During debate on Dickinson's motion, Roger Sherman of Connecticut suggested that the national legislature be empowered to remove the executive at pleasure. George Mason of Virginia replied that, although "[s]ome mode of displacing an unfit magistrate is rendered indispensable by the fallibility of those who choose, as well as by the corruptibility of the man chosen," to make the executive "the mere creature of the Legislature" would be a "violation of the fundamental principle of good Government." Dickinson's motion was opposed because it would have given the smaller states equal power with the more populous ones. James Madison of Virginia and James Wilson of Pennsylvania argued that it would "enable a minority of the people to prevent ye removal of an officer who had rendered himself justly criminal in the eyes of a majority," open a door to intrigues against the executive in states where his administration was unpopular, and tempt him to pay court to particular states whose partisans he feared or wished to engage in his behalf.[3] The motion was defeated, with only Delaware voting for it.[4]

2. I:64–77.

3. I:69 (Bedford); I:85 (Dickinson, Sherman); I:86 (Mason, Madison, and Wilson).

4. I:87. The New Jersey Plan, later proposed to the convention on behalf of the small states by William Patterson of New Jersey, included a variant of Dickinson's proposal. It provided that the executive (to be elected by Congress, to consist of an unspecified number of persons, and to serve a single term of unspecified length) would be "removable by Congs. on application by a majority of the Executives of the several States." The plan also gave the national judiciary jurisdiction over "all impeachments of federal officers" (I:244). Debate on the New Jersey Plan in committee of the whole concentrated on its preservation of the equality of state representation provided by the Articles of Confederation rather than specific provisions. The plan was rejected by the committee of the whole in favor of the Virginia Plan it had previously considered and amended (I:322).

The committee of the whole then agreed that the executive should be ineligible after a single seven-year term and, without debate, added a clause proposed by Hugh Williamson of North Carolina providing that the executive would "be removeable on impeachment & conviction of mal-practice or neglect of duty."[5]

The delegates next considered whether there should be a single or plural executive. Randolph, who had previously said that he considered unity in the executive to be "the foetus of monarchy," declared "the permanent temper of the people was adverse to the very semblance of Monarchy." In support of a single executive, Wilson argued that this would give the "most energy dispatch and responsibility to the office," as well as provide tranquility to the government. He said that he could see no evidence of opposition on the part of the people; "[a]ll know that a single magistrate is not a King," and every state had a single executive. The committee of the whole agreed to a single executive, leading Mason to comment that the delegates were creating "a more dangerous monarchy" than the British, "an elective one."[6]

Initial Deliberations in the Convention

After it completed consideration and amendment of the Virginia Plan, the committee of the whole reported its resolutions to the convention,[7] which began its deliberations on them. The convention took up the resolution concerning the executive on July 17. It agreed unanimously that the executive should consist of a single person and turned to the method of his selection, his term, and his reeligibility. Gouverneur Morris of Pennsylvania proposed election by the people instead of the legislature, arguing that if the legislature both appointed and could impeach the executive he would be "the mere creature" of it. This proposal, as well as a proposal for selection by electors chosen by state legislatures, was rejected by the convention. Selection by the legislature and a seven-year term were unanimously retained. The delegates then struck the clause making the executive ineligible for reelection, with Morris contending that ineligibility "tended to destroy the great motive to good behavior, the hope of being rewarded by a re-appointment. It was saying to him, make hay while the sun shines."[8]

5. I:88.
6. I:66, 88 (Randolph); I:65, 96 (Wilson), I:97 (single executive); I:101 (Mason).
7. I:228–32.
8. II:29; II:32 (selection by legislature); II:33 (Morris).

By a vote of only four states to six, the convention rejected a proposal that the executive serve "during good behavior"—a motion whose "probable object," James Madison explained in his journal of the proceedings, "was merely to enforce the argument against the re-eligibility of the Executive Magistrate, by holding out a tenure during good behaviour as the alternative for keeping him independent of the Legislature." The seven-year term was again retained, but it was unanimously agreed to reconsider the question of reeligibility.[9]

The following day the convention considered the resolution on the judiciary. Decision on the method of appointing judges was postponed and the clause giving the judiciary jurisdiction over impeachments was struck, principally because of uncertainty about how the executive should be tried on an impeachment. It was contended that the executive should not appoint the judges if they were to try him. On the other hand, it was suggested that trial of the executive before the judges would be improper because they might "be drawn into intrigues with the Legislature and an impartial trial would be frustrated."[10]

On July 19 the convention again considered the executive's reeligibility, a subject that reopened the question of the method of his selection and his term. The debate indicated the extent of the delegates' concern about executive dependence on the legislature. Morris, a proponent of reeligibility, argued:

> One great object of the Executive is to controul the Legislature. The Legislature will continually seek to aggrandize & perpetuate themselves; and will seize those critical moments produced by war, invasion or convulsion for that purpose. It is necessary then that the Executive Magistrate should be the guardian of the people, even of the lower classes, agst. Legislative tyranny.

He advocated a popularly elected executive with a two-year term, who would be eligible for reelection and not removable by impeachment. The impeachability of the executive was "a dangerous part of the plan," Morris said. "It will hold him in such dependence that he will be no check on the Legislature, will not be a firm guardian of the people and of the public interest. He will be the tool of a faction, of some leading demagogue in the Legislature." Morris did "not regard . . . as formidable" the danger from the executive's unimpeachability: "There

9. II:36 (good behavior); II:33 (Madison); II:36 (seven-year term, reconsideration of reeligibility).

10. II:41–6.

must be certain great officers of State; a minister of finance, of war, of foreign affairs &c. These . . . will exercise their functions in subordination to the Executive, and will be amenable by impeachment to the public Justice. Without these ministers the Executive can do nothing of consequence."[11]

Morris was not the only delegate who emphasized the risk of executive dependence on the legislature. Wilson remarked that "the unanimous sense" seemed to be that the executive should not be appointed by the legislature unless he was ineligible for reappointment. The convention voted for selection by electors chosen by state legislatures, rejected ineligibility for a second term, and agreed to a six-year term.[12]

The July 20th Debate on Removal of the Executive by Impeachment

On July 20 the convention considered a motion to strike the provision making the executive removable on impeachment and conviction for malpractice or neglect of duty.[13] This was the major debate on impeachment during the Constitutional Convention; and, because it is so often quoted in discussions of the impeachment provisions ultimately included in the Constitution, it is helpful to consider the context in which it arose. The delegates were concerned about the dependence of the executive on the legislature and had settled upon a method of election—electors chosen by state legislatures—intended to reduce that dependence. This provision was a temporary compromise, which was reconsidered (and discarded) the following week. The delegates had made no decision about the procedure that would be used to impeach and try the executive. The convention had struck the provision for trial by the judiciary and had not yet considered how impeachments would be originated, though impeachment by the popular branch of the legislature was the procedure followed in England and in several of the states. The delegates had also not determined whether impeachment would involve criminal sanctions. English impeachments could lead to criminal punishment, including execution; state constitutions varied on the point, with a few (such as New York's) expressly limiting judgment on impeachments to removal from office

11. II:52–4.
12. II:56–9.
13. This debate appears at II:64–9.

and disqualification from future office and others (such as Virginia's) explicitly providing for the imposition of criminal sanctions.[14]

The motion to strike the impeachment clause was made by Charles Pinckney of South Carolina and Morris. Pinckney initiated the debate by suggesting that the executive "ought not to be impeachable whilst in office." (The Virginia and Delaware constitutions provided that the executive could be impeached only after he left office.)[15] William Davie of North Carolina replied that if the executive were not impeachable while in office, "he will spare no efforts or means whatever to get himself re-elected." Davie considered impeachability to be "an essential security for the good behaviour of the Executive."

Morris repeated his point about the executive's subordinates, arguing that he "can do no criminal act without Coadjutors who may be punished." "In case he should be re-elected, that will be sufficient proof of his innocence," Morris said, and asked "who is to impeach" and whether "the impeachment [is] to suspend his functions." If not, he suggested, "the mischief will go on"; if so, "the impeachment will be nearly equivalent to a displacement, and will render the Executive dependent on those who are to impeach."

Mason, defending the impeachment clause, said, "No point is of more importance than that the right of impeachment should be continued. Shall any man be above Justice? Above all shall that man be above it, who can commit the most extensive injustice? When great crimes were committed he was for punishing the principal as well as the Coadjutors." Mason noted that there had been "much debate & difficulty as to the mode of chusing the Executive." He preferred appointment by the legislature, in part because of the danger that electors might be corrupted by the candidates. This, he said, "furnished a peculiar reason in favor of impeachments whilst in office. Shall the man who has practised corruption & by that means procured his appointment in the first instance, be suffered to escape punishment, by repeating his guilt?"

Benjamin Franklin argued that the clause was "favorable to the executive":

14. New York Constitution of 1777, art. 33, in 5 Francis Thorpe, ed., *The Federal and State Constitutions* 2635 (1909) (hereafter Thorpe); Virginia Constitution of 1776, 7 Thorpe 3818.

15. Virginia Constitution of 1776, *ibid.*; Delaware Constitution of 1776, art. 23, 1 *ibid.* 566.

> What was the practice before this in cases where the chief Magistrate rendered himself obnoxious? Why recourse was had to assassination in wch. he was not only deprived of his life but of the opportunity of vindicating his character. It wd. be the best way therefore to provide in the Constitution for the regular punishment of the Executive when his misconduct should deserve it, and for his honorable acquittal when he should be unjustly accused.

Franklin later mentioned the case of the Prince of Orange, who was suspected of having kept the Dutch fleet from uniting with the French in violation of an agreement between the two nations:

> Yet as he could not be impeached and no regular examination took place, he remained in his office, and strengthe[n]ing his own party, as the party opposed to him became formidable, he gave birth to the most violent animosities & contentions. Had he been impeachable, a regular & peaceable inquiry would have taken place and he would if guilty have been duly punished, if innocent restored to the confidence of the public.

James Madison "thought it indispensable that some provision should be made for defending the Community agst the incapacity, negligence or perfidy of the chief Magistrate." A limited term was "not a sufficient security. He might lose his capacity after his appointment. He might pervert his administration into a scheme of peculation or oppression. He might betray his trust to foreign powers." The executive differed from the legislature or any other public body holding office for a limited period, Madison said; it could not be presumed that all or a majority of an assembly would lose their capacity or be bribed to betray their trust, and "the difficulty of acting in concert for purposes of corruption was a security to the public." But, he said, "[i]n the case of the Executive Magistracy which was to be administered by a single man, loss of capacity or corruption was more within the compass of probable events, and either of them might be fatal to the Republic."

Pinckney, arguing in favor of his motion to strike the clause, asserted that he "did not see the necessity of impeachments," especially because the powers of the executive "would be so circumscribed." And, he asserted, "they ought not to issue from the Legislature who would in that case hold them as a rod over the Executive and by that means effectually destroy his independence." The executive's revisionary (veto) power, in particular, "would be rendered altogether insignificant."

Elbridge Gerry of Massachusetts disagreed with Pinckney, urging "the necessity of impeachments. A good magistrate will not fear them. A bad one ought to be kept in fear of them. He hoped the maxim would never be adopted here that the chief Magistrate could do no wrong."

Rufus King of Massachusetts, who supported the motion to strike, asked the delegates "to recur to the primitive axiom that the three great departments of Govts. should be separate & independent. . . . Would this be the case if the Executive should be impeachable?" Impeachment of the judiciary was appropriate, he said, because judges held their offices during good behavior and it was therefore necessary that "a forum should be established for trying misbehaviour." But the executive was to serve a six-year term, like members of the Senate; "he would periodically be tried for his behaviour by his electors, who would continue or discontinue him in trust according to the manner in which he had discharged it." (King later described "periodical responsibility to the electors" as "an equivalent security" to impeachments of those holding office for life, which "are proper to secure good behaviour.") Like members of the legislature, King asserted, the executive "ought to be subject to no intermediate trial, by impeachment." The executive should not be impeachable unless he held his office during good behavior (a tenure, King said, that "would be most agreeable to him"), and even then only if "an independent and effectual forum could be devised." "[U]nder no circumstances ought he to be impeachable by the Legislature," he argued. "This would be destructive of his independence and of the principles of the Constitution."

Edmund Randolph commented that the "propriety of impeachments" was "a favorite principle with him":

> Guilt wherever found ought to be punished. The Executive will have great opportunitys of abusing his power; particularly in time of war when the military force, and in some respects the public money will be in his hands. Should no regular punishment be provided, it will be irregularly inflicted by tumults & insurrections.

Randolph noted "the necessity of proceeding with a cautious hand, and of excluding as much as possible the influence of the Legislature from the business." He suggested consideration of a proposal made by Alexander Hamilton for a forum composed of state judges and "even of requiring some preliminary inquest whether just grounds of impeachment existed."

Morris, who had cosponsored the motion to strike the clause for impeachment, admitted during the debate that "corruption & some few other offences [were] such as ought to be impeachable; but thought the cases ought to be enumerated & defined." As the debate ended, he acknowledged that his "opinion had been changed by the arguments used in the discussion" and he was "now sensible of the necessity of impeachments, if the Executive was to continue for any time in office":

> Our Executive was not like a Magistrate having a life interest, much less like one having an hereditary interest in his office. He may be bribed by a greater interest to betray his trust; and no one would say that we ought to expose ourselves to the danger of seeing the first Magistrate in foreign pay without being able to guard agst it by displacing him.

Treachery, corrupting his electors, and incapacity were causes for impeachment, Morris said, though for incapacity "he should be punished not as a man, but as an officer, and punished only by degradation from his office." He concluded, "This Magistrate is not the King but the prime-Minister. The people are the King. When we make him amenable to Justice however we should take care to provide some mode that will not make him dependent on the Legislature."

The convention voted eight states to two to retain the clause making the executive removable on impeachment.

The Committee on Detail's Draft Constitution

Four days later the convention reconsidered the method of selecting the executive. Choice by electors was dropped, and the legislature again substituted. A motion to reinstate the one-term limitation led to a variety of proposals about the length of term, including eight, eleven, fifteen, and twenty years. The last was suggested as "the medium life of princes"; it was perhaps offered, according to Madison, "as a caricature of the previous motions." Wilson suggested election for six years by a small number of legislators selected by lot.[16] Debate on the question continued during the next two sessions, and finally the convention reinstated the provisions originally reported by the committee on the whole—a seven-year term, no reeligibility, appointment by the legislature.[17] The resolution on the executive was referred to a five-man Committee on Detail, which was charged with preparing a draft constitution.[18]

The Committee on Detail reported on August 6. Its draft provided that the House of Representatives "shall have the sole power of impeachment," a provision the convention unanimously adopted, without debate, on August 9.[19] It also provided that the president (the name it gave the executive) "shall be removed from his office on impeachment by the House of Representatives, and conviction in the supreme Court, of treason, bribery, or corruption."[20] The jurisdiction of the Supreme Court included "the trial of impeachments of Officers of the United States," but the legislature could "assign any part of the jurisdiction above mentioned (except the trial of the President of the United States) . . . to . . . Inferior Courts."[21] The draft included the provision, which was retained in the final version of the Constitution without debate by the convention, limiting judgment in impeachment cases to removal from office and disqualification from any office of honor, trust, or profit under the United States and stating that the convicted party is nevertheless liable and subject to indictment, trial, judgment, and punishment according to law.[22]

16. II:101, 102, 103.

17. II:120.

18. The committee consisted of John Rutledge of South Carolina, Randolph, Nathaniel Gorham of Massachusetts, Oliver Ellsworth of Connecticut, and Wilson. II:121.

19. Art. IV, §6; see II:231.

20. Art. X, §2.

21. Art. XI, §3.

22. Art. XI, §5. The two other references to impeachment included in the Constitution—the limitation on the president's pardon power and the exception to the criminal trial provision—also first appeared in the draft of the Committee on Detail, though each was subsequently amended by the convention in minor respects. As reported by the committee, the pardon clause provided that the president's pardon "shall not be pleadable in bar of an impeachment" (Art. X, §2, amended II:419–20). The criminal trial provision referred first to the place of trial and then to trial by jury, reading: "The trial of all criminal offences (except in cases of impeachments) shall be in the State where they shall be committed; and shall be by Jury" (Art. XI, §4, amended II:434).

One other provision of the draft should be mentioned because it used a term later to become part of the impeachment clause. The provision for rendition of criminal offenders from one state to another, patterned after a comparable provision in the Articles

Article X of the Committee on Detail's draft, dealing with the president, was taken up by the convention on August 24.[23] Again the delegates were unable to agree upon the method of selecting the executive. On August 27 the impeachment provision was postponed at the instance of Morris, who contended that the Supreme Court was an improper forum for trying the president, especially if (as was then being considered) the chief justice would be a member of a privy council for the president.[24] On August 31 the provisions of the draft constitution that had been postponed were referred to a committee with one member from each state, the Committee of Eleven.[25]

The Committee of Eleven's Proposal on Election of the President and Impeachment

On September 4 the Committee of Eleven reported to the convention, recommending a four-year term for the president as well as for the vice president, a new office it proposed (and which, Hugh Williamson later explained, "was not wanted," but "was introduced only for the sake of a valuable mode of election which required two to be chosen at the same time"). Each state was to choose electors in the manner its legislature directed. The electors (equal in number to the representatives and senators for the state) were to meet in the state and vote for two persons, one of whom could not be a resident of the state. The votes of the electors in all the states would be transmitted to the Senate, where they would be counted. If one person received a majority of the electoral vote, he would be elected president. (If two persons were tied, each with a majority, the Senate would choose between them.) If no person received a majority, the Senate would choose by

---

of Confederation, referred to "[a]ny person charged with treason, felony or high misdemeanor" (Art. XV). The convention substituted "other crime" for "high misdemeanor," "in order to comprehend all proper cases: it being doubtful whether 'high misdemeanor' had not a technical meaning too limited" (II:443).

23. II:401–4.

24. II:427. Morris and Pinckney had proposed a privy council consisting of the chief justice and the heads of executive departments (II:342–4). The proposal was referred to the Committee on Detail, which reported a revised version with an expanded council including the President of the Senate and the Speaker of the House (II:367). The convention never voted on this proposal.

25. Its members were Nicholas Gilman of New Hampshire, Rufus King of Massachusetts, Roger Sherman of Connecticut, David Brearley of New Jersey, Gouverneur Morris of Pennsylvania, John Dickinson of Delaware, Daniel Carroll of Maryland, James Madison of Virginia, Hugh Williamson of North Carolina, Pierce Butler of South Carolina, and Abraham Baldwin of Georgia. II:473.

ballot among the five receiving the most votes. The person receiving the second greatest number of votes would be elected vice president.

The committee also proposed that the Senate, rather than the Supreme Court, should try all impeachments, with a two-thirds vote required for conviction. The vice president would be *ex officio* President of the Senate "except when they sit to try the impeachment of the President, in which case the Chief Justice shall preside," and when he exercised the powers and duties of the president. The committee altered the impeachment clause so that it read, "[The President] shall be removed from his office on impeachment by the House of Representatives, and conviction by the Senate, for Treason, or bribery . . ."—dropping "corruption," which had been included in the Committee on Detail's draft, as well as substituting the Senate for the Supreme Court.[26]

The convention postponed consideration of the proposal for trial of impeachments by the Senate "in order to decide previously on the mode of electing the President." Morris explained the reasons for the committee's recommendation:

> The 1st. was the danger of intrigue & faction if the appointmt. should be made by the Legislature. 2 the inconveniency of an ineligibility required by that mode in order to lessen its evils. 3 The difficulty of establishing a Court of Impeachments, other than the Senate which would not be so proper for the trial nor the other branch for the impeachment of the President, if appointed by the Legislature, 4. No body had appeared to be satisfied with an appointment by the Legislature. 5. Many were anxious even for an immediate choice by the people— 6—the indispensable necessity of making the Executive independent of the Legislature.

He said that "the great evil of cabal was avoided" because the electors would vote concurrently throughout the country at a great distance from each other; "[i]t would be impossible also to corrupt them." He contended that a "conclusive reason" for having the Senate rather than the Supreme Court try impeachments was that the Court "was to try the President after the trial of the impeachment."[27]

The electoral plan encountered opposition, primarily on the ground that the Senate would almost always choose the president (nineteen

26. II:537, 496–9.
27. II:499, 500.

times in twenty, George Mason argued) because no single candidate would receive a majority of the electoral votes. Pinckney asserted that the Committee of Eleven's proposal made "the same body of men which will in fact elect the President his Judges in case of an impeachment." Wilson and Randolph proposed that the eventual selection be referred to the entire legislature, not just the Senate. Morris replied that the Senate was preferable "because fewer could then, say to the President, you owe your appointment to us." He thought "the President would not depend so much on the Senate for his re-appointment as on his general good conduct." Wilson criticized the committee's report as "having a dangerous tendency to aristocracy; as throwing a dangerous power into the hands of the Senate," which would not only have, in fact, the power to appoint the president, but through his dependence upon it would also have the virtual power of appointment to other offices, and would make treaties and try all impeachments. "[T]he Legislative, Executive & Judiciary powers are all blended in one branch of the Government," Wilson observed. The president "will not be the man of the people as he ought to be, but the Minion of the Senate."[28]

To meet this criticism, the convention, after considering a number of alternative proposals, agreed that the House, with one vote per state, should choose the president if no person received a majority of the electoral votes.[29]

The Addition of "Other High Crimes and Misdemeanors" to the Impeachment Clause

On September 8 the convention considered the Committee of Eleven's proposal that the Senate should try impeachments against the president for treason and bribery.[30] George Mason asked:

> Why is the provision restrained to Treason & bribery only? Treason as defined in the Constitution will not reach many great and dangerous offences. Hastings is not guilty of Treason. Attempts to subvert the Constitution may not be Treason as above defined—As bills of attainder which have saved the British Constitution are

28. II:500 (Mason); II:501 (Pinckney); II:502 (Morris); II:522–3 (Wilson).
29. II:527–8.
30. II:550.

forbidden, it is the more necessary to extend: the power of impeachments.[31]

Mason moved to add "or maladministration" after "bribery." James Madison said, "So vague a term will be equivalent to a tenure during pleasure of the Senate." Morris commented that "it will not be put in force & can do no harm— An election of every four years will prevent maladministration." Mason, however, withdrew "maladministration" and substituted "other high crimes & misdemeanors . . . agst. the State," which the convention adopted by a vote of eight states to three. (The provision was later amended, by unanimous consent "in order to remove ambiguity," to read "against the United States," a phrase the Committee on Style and Arrangement deleted.)

Adoption of Trial of Impeachments by the Senate

Madison then objected to a trial of the president by the Senate, "especially as he was to be impeached by the other branch of the Legislature, and for any act which might be called a misdemeanor. The President under these circumstances was made improperly dependent." He stated a preference for trial by the Supreme Court or a tribunal of which it formed a part.

Morris replied that "no other tribunal than the Senate could be trusted. The Supreme Court were too few in number and might be warped or corrupted." He said he was against "a dependence of the Executive on the Legislature, considering the Legislative tyranny the great danger to be apprehended," but contended "there could be no danger that the Senate would say untruly on their oaths that the President was guilty of crimes or facts, especially as in four years he can be turned out."

Pinckney disapproved of trial by the Senate "as rendering the Presi-

31. The references in Mason's remarks were to the impeachment of Warren Hastings, the former governor general of India, then pending in the English Parliament, and to two provisions the convention had previously adopted. The effort to impeach Hastings began in 1785; the House of Commons voted articles of impeachment against him in early 1787. The trial did not begin until 1788 and dragged on until 1795, when Hastings was finally acquitted.

On August 20 the convention had voted to limit treason against the United States to "levying war against them, or in adhering to their enemies, giving them aid and comfort" (II:345–50). Bills of attainder—legislation to punish an individual for past conduct without a judicial trial—had been prohibited by a provision adopted on August 23, as had *ex post facto* laws (II:376).

dent too dependent on the Legislature. If he opposes a favorite law, the two Houses will combine agst him, and under the influence of heat and faction throw him out of office." Williamson observed that "there was more danger of too much lenity than of too much rigour towards the President, considering the number of cases in which the Senate was associated with the President." Sherman commented that the Court would be "improper to try the President, because the Judges would be appointed by him." Madison moved to strike the provision for trial by the Senate. His motion failed by a vote of two states to nine, and the impeachment clause was adopted ten states to one.

The clause was amended to make the vice president and other civil officers removable "on impeachment and conviction as aforesaid." Morris moved to add a provision that members of the Senate should be on oath when trying impeachments, and the amended clause was agreed to, nine states to two.[32]

A five-member committee was appointed "to revise the stile of and arrange the articles which had been agreed to by the House."[33] The committee reported on September 12. Among other stylistic changes, the committee shortened the impeachment clause so that it read in its final form.[34]

Rejection of Suspension upon Impeachment

On September 14 the last issue related to impeachment was brought before the convention. John Rutledge of South Carolina, along with Morris, moved that persons who were impeached be suspended from office pending the outcome of their trials. Madison objected, asserting that the president was already made too dependent on the legislature by the power of one branch to try him on an impeachment by the other. Suspension would "put him in the power of one branch only," which could at any moment, "in order to make way for the functions of another who will be more favorable to their views, vote a temporary removal of the existing magistrate." By a vote of three states to eight, the motion was rejected.[35]

32. II:551–3.

33. Its members were William Samuel Johnson of Connecticut, Alexander Hamilton of New York, Gouverneur Morris, James Madison, and Rufus King. II:553.

34. II:600.

35. II:612–3.

The Role of Impeachment in the Constitutional Scheme

Despite the attention the delegates to the Constitutional Convention had given to the provisions concerning presidential impeachment, supporters of the proposed constitution claimed that it was unlikely that a corrupt man would ever become president of the United States. The method of selecting the president, through electors chosen by the states for that specific purpose, "affords a moral certainty, that the office of President will never fall to the lot of any man who is not in an eminent degree endowed with the requisite qualifications," Alexander Hamilton wrote in *The Federalist* No. 68.

> Talents for low intrigue, and the little arts of popularity, may alone suffice to elevate a man to the first honors in a single State; but it will require other talents, and a different kind of merit, to establish him in the esteem and confidence of the whole Union, or of so considerable a portion of it as would be necessary to make him a successful candidate for the distinguished office of President of the United States.

Hamilton concluded that "there will be a constant probability of seeing the station filled by characters preeminent for ability and virtue."[36]

A "moral certainty" and a "constant probability," however, were not sufficient safeguards to assure that a president would faithfully execute his office, and the framers had also sought to make the president responsible for his conduct. The "two greatest securities" the people have for "the faithful exercise of any delegated power," Hamilton wrote in *The Federalist* No. 70, are "the restraints of public opinion" and "the opportunity of discovering with facility and clearness the misconduct of the persons they trust, in order either to their removal from office, or to their actual punishment in cases which admit of it." Censure was a more important safeguard than punishment, especially in an elective office, Hamilton explained. "Man, in public trust, will much oftener act in such a manner as to render him unworthy of

36. At 444 (Modern Library ed.).

being any longer trusted, than in such a manner as to make him obnoxious to legal punishment."[37]

The president's eligibility for reelection every four years was therefore a major source of responsibility in the office. The framers envisioned that an incumbent president would seek reelection and that the outcome would be a test of his administration of the office. Madison referred to it as "an impeachment before the community, who will have the power of punishment, by refusing to re-elect him." The president, he said, "is impeachable before the community at large every four years, and liable to be displaced if his conduct shall have given umbrage during the time he has been in office."[38]

Unlimited eligibility for reelection was considered to be one of the major inducements to good behavior by the president, for, as Justice Joseph Story wrote in 1833, paraphrasing Hamilton, "A desire of reward is one of the strongest incentives of human conduct; and the best security for the fidelity of mankind is to make interest coincide with duty." If the president were excluded from reelection, he would be tempted "to sordid views, to peculation, to the corrupt gratification of favourites, and in some instances to usurpation," Story contended.[39] An avaricious president, excluded from reelection, might "have recourse to the most corrupt expedients to make the harvest as abundant as it was transitory," Hamilton wrote. If, on the other hand, he were eligible for reelection "[h]is avarice might be a guard upon his avarice."[40] Ineligibility for reelection might be a temptation to usurpation, Story explained, "since the chance of impeachment would scarcely be worthy of thought; and the present power of serving friends might easily surround him with advocates for every stretch of authority, which would flatter his vanity, or administer to their necessities." Exclusion from eligibility for reelection, Story concluded, "would operate no check upon a man of irregular ambition, or corrupt principles, and against such men alone could the exclusion be important."[41]

37. At 460–1, 459.

38. Annals of Congress, 1st Cong., 1st Sess., 498, 462 (Gale & Seaton, eds., 1789) (hereafter Annals).

39. 3 Joseph Story, *Commentaries on the Constitution of the United States* §1437 (reprint of 1833 ed.) (hereafter Story).

40. *The Federalist* No. 72 at 471.

41. 3 Story §§1437, 1441. Story went on to say, "In truth, such men would easily find means to cover up their usurpations and dishonesty under fair pretensions, and mean subserviency to popular prejudices. They would easily delude the people into a

The ultimate check on presidential conduct was not denial of re-election, but impeachment and removal from office. "In addition to all the precautions . . . to prevent abuse of the executive trust in the mode of the President's appointment, his term of office, and the precise and definite limitations imposed upon the exercise of his power," Chancellor James Kent later wrote, "the constitution has also rendered him directly amenable by law for mal-administration":

> If . . . neither the sense of duty, the force of public opinion, nor the transitory nature of the seat, are sufficient to secure a faithful discharge of the executive trust, but the President will use the authority of his station to violate the constitution or law of the land, the House of Representatives can arrest him in his career, by resorting to the power of impeachment.[42]

Without any debate, the Constitutional Convention had vested the power of impeachment in the House of Representatives, as proposed by the Committee on Detail. Although question had been raised in the July 20 debate on the impeachability of the executive about where the power should be placed, once the convention had decided that accusation and trial would be the procedure used to remove the executive, it was effectively settled that the proceeding would be initiated by the popular branch of the legislature. It was not disputed, Hamilton wrote in *The Federalist* No. 65, "that the power of originating the inquiry, or, in other words, of preferring the impeachment, ought to be lodged in the hands of one branch of the legislative body."[43] Impeachment, he explained, is a legislative remedy: "the powers relating to impeachments are . . . an essential check in the hands of that body upon the encroachments of the executive,"[44] "a bridle in the hands of the legislative body upon the executive servants of the government." Vesting the power to originate impeachments in a branch of the legislature was consistent with the English system of impeachment—"the

---

belief, that their acts were constitutional, because they were in harmony with the public wishes, or held out some specious, but false projects for the public good." Story did not explain how, if this were true, eligibility for reelection would provide a check upon misconduct.

42. 1 James Kent, *Commentaries on American Law* * 289 (6th ed. 1848).

43. *The Federalist* No. 65 at 424.

44. *Ibid.*, No. 66 at 430.

model from which the idea of this institution has been borrowed," Hamilton wrote[45]—and with that of several of the states.

The House was the logical branch of the legislature to initiate removal proceedings not only because of its resemblance to the House of Commons, which performed this function in English impeachments, but also because it was the branch of government most directly accountable to the people. In the original constitutional scheme senators were elected by state representatives; the complicated mechanism for electing the president left it to each state to determine how to choose its electors, and, in any case, the framers thought that the choice of a president would often be made by the House of Representatives, with each state casting one vote, because no candidate would win a majority of the votes of state electors.

That the members of the House were direct representatives of the people provided an additional argument in favor of vesting the power of impeachment in the House. The power "is lodged in those who represent the great body of the people, because the occasion for its exercise will arise from acts of great injury to the community, and the objects of it may be such as cannot be easily reached by an ordinary tribunal," James Iredell explained to the North Carolina ratifying convention. "[T]here are no persons so proper to complain of the public officers as the representatives of the people at large," he said; they know the feelings of the people "and will be ready enough to make complaints."[46]

One of the concerns of the convention, in fact, was that the House might be too ready to make complaints, and it was partly for that reason that the method of trying impeachments proved to be a thorny problem. The Senate was ultimately considered a more appropriate forum than the Supreme Court because the Court might try the president on any criminal charge after his impeachment trial, the Court "were too few in number and might be warped or corrupted,"[47] and the issues in an impeachment proceeding did not resemble those in ordinary litigation. Impeachments, James Wilson said in *Lectures on Law*, "come not . . . within the sphere of ordinary jurisprudence. They are founded on different principles, are governed by different

45. *Ibid.*, No. 65 at 425.

46. 4 Jonathan Elliot, *The Debates in the Several State Conventions on the Adoption of the Federal Constitution* 32 (reprint of 1836 ed.) (hereafter Elliot).

47. II:551 (Gouverneur Morris).

maxims, and are directed at different objects."[48] The considerations applicable to judging impeachments, Story reiterated forty years later, "do not properly belong to the judicial character in the ordinary administration of justice and are far removed from the reach of municipal jurisprudence."[49]

The primary reason for giving the Senate the power to try impeachments, however, was that it was considered to be the only body that would be unbiased by an accusation brought by the House. Any other tribunal, Iredell said, might "be too much awed by so powerful an accuser."[50] Only the Senate was "sufficiently dignified" and "sufficiently independent," Hamilton asserted. It was likely "to feel confidence enough in its own situation, to preserve, unawed and uninfluenced, the necessary impartiality" between an accused official and the representatives of the people, his accusers. Members of the Supreme Court were unlikely always to be "endowed with so eminent a portion of fortitude, as would be called for in the execution of so difficult a task"—a deficiency that "would be fatal to the accused." They were even more unlikely to "possess the degree of credit and authority, which might, on certain occasions, be indispensable towards reconciling the people to a decision that should happen to clash with an accusation brought by their immediate representatives"—a deficiency "dangerous to the public tranquillity."[51]

As Hamilton's arguments suggest, it was considered probable that the House, influenced by considerations of faction, would bring unjust or unwarranted accusations against the president. The safeguard for the impeached president was to be derived from the size of the Senate, its independence, the special oath senators would take to try impeachments, and the requirement of a two-thirds vote for conviction. "[T]here could be no danger that the Senate would say untruly on their oaths that the President was guilty of crimes or facts, especially as in four years he can be turned out," Gouverneur Morris told the Constitutional Convention. Instead, Hugh Williamson suggested, there was "more danger of too much lenity . . . towards the President," considering the number of respects in which the Senate was as-

48. 1 Robert McCloskey, ed., *The Works of James Wilson* 324 (1967) (hereafter Wilson). Wilson was explaining why "the trial and punishment of an offense on impeachment, is no bar to a trial of the same offense at common law."

49. 2 Story §764.

50. 4 Elliot 113.

51. *The Federalist* No. 65 at 425 (emphasis omitted).

sociated with him.[52] This turned out to be the major criticism of the impeachment provision in the state ratifying conventions, particularly with reference to the possibility of removing the president for entering into treaties for corrupt or traitorous motives (and, as Edmund Randolph said in discussing the impeachment provisions in the Virginia ratifying convention, treaties are the most common occasions of impeachments).[53] For example, James Monroe asked the Virginia convention: "To whom is he responsible? To the Senate, his own council. If he makes a treaty, bartering the interests of the country, by whom is he to be tried? By the very persons who advised him to perpetrate the act. Is this any security?"[54]

Almost no mention was made in the ratifying conventions of the possibility that the House might be reluctant to impeach the president. One exception was an address by Luther Martin, who had been a delegate to the Constitutional Convention, explaining to the Maryland House of Delegates why he had refused to sign the Constitution and was opposed to its ratification. His lengthy explanation of the Constitution's defects included the argument that it was "contrary to probability" that the House would ever impeach the president, and even less likely that he would be convicted by the Senate, his counsellors. According to Martin, there was

> little reason to believe that a majority will ever concur in impeaching the President, let his conduct be ever so reprehensible; especially, too, as the final event of that impeachment will depend upon a different body, and the members of the House of [Representatives] will be certain, should the decision be ultimately in favor of the President, to become thereby the objects of his displeasure, and to bar to themselves every avenue to the emoluments of government.[55]

52. II:551.

53. 3 Elliot 401.

54. 3 *ibid.* 489. George Mason, the author of the "high crimes and misdemeanor" language of the impeachment clause and an inveterate foe of a strong executive, made a similar argument. Mason also pointed to the danger of the president's continuance in office during the trial. "The President is tried by his counsellors," he told the ratifying convention, and because he is not suspended, "[w]hen he is arraigned for treason, he has the command of the army and navy, and may surround the Senate with thirty thousand troops" (3 *ibid.* 494).

55. Luther Martin's Letter and Address to the House of Delegates, Jan. 27, 1788, 1 *ibid.* 344, 379.

Martin's argument was based on a cynical view of the motivations of those who would serve in the House. He contended that its members would be unduly under the influence of the president because he alone could nominate them to lucrative offices of the government. Neither this misanthropic opinion nor other objections to vesting the power of impeachment in the House are repeated in the available proceedings of the state ratifying conventions.

Indeed, apart from Iredell's contention that the House would be "ready enough to make complaints," the only reported discussion of the role of the House in an impeachment proceeding was a rather backhanded description by Fisher Ames in the Massachusetts ratifying convention in 1788. Ames cited the power of impeachment as one reason why it would be inappropriate to have a one-year term for members of the House. The representatives, he explained, "are the grand inquisition of the Union. They are, by impeachment, to bring great offenders to justice." They could not perform this function if limited to a one-year term. "One year will not suffice to detect guilt, and to pursue it to conviction; therefore they will escape, and the balance of the two branches will be destroyed, and the people oppressed with impunity." If the House were elected annually, the people would "blind the eyes of their own watchmen" and "bind the hands which are to hold the sword for their defence."[56]

The following year Ames, a representative in the First Congress, again adverted to the duration of impeachments, this time in arguing in favor of the power of the president to remove subordinate officers of the executive branch. He criticized "the slow formality of an impeachment," which made it ineffective as a method for preventing crimes. Without suspension pending the outcome of an impeachment trial, Ames said, "we shall find impeachments come too late; while we are preparing the process, the mischief will be perpetrated, and the offender will escape." He referred, as did other members of the House, to the English impeachment of Warren Hastings, then in its third year. The Hastings impeachment was "a transatlantic instance of [the] incompetency" of impeachment, said John Vining of Delaware: "With what difficulty was that prosecution carried on! What a length of time did it take to determine!" Impeachment "was attended with circumstances that would render it insufficient to secure the public

56. 2 *ibid.* 11.

safety, which was a primary object in every Government," Vining said. It was a "circuitous route":

> The dilatory and inefficient process by that mode, will not apply the remedy to the evil till it is too late to be of advantage. Experience has fixed an eternal stigma upon the system of impeachment . . . ; what delays and uncertainty with the forms of trial, details of evidence, arguments of counsel, and deliberate decision!

Impeachment was "tedious and uncertain at best" as a way of removing "bad or obnoxious officers," Vining asserted. Suppose, hypothesized Theodore Sedgwick of Massachusetts, an officer

> grasping at his own aggrandizement, and the elevation of his connexions, by every means short of the treason defined by the Constitution, hurrying your affairs to the precipice of destruction, endangering your domestic tranquillity, plundering you of the means of defence, by alienating the affections of your allies, and promoting the spirit of discord.

"[I]s there no way suddenly to seize the worthless wretch, and hurl him from the pinnacle of power?" he asked. "Must the tardy, tedious, desultory road, by way of impeachment, be travelled to overtake the man who, barely confining himself within the letter of the law, is employed in drawing off the vital principle of the Government?"[57]

There was a massive inconsistency in the argument that Ames, Vining, Sedgwick, and others (including James Madison) were making. On the one hand, they were contending that the president must have the power to remove executive officers partly because of the inadequacies of the impeachment process.[58] On the other, they argued that the president's amenability to impeachment—that "dilatory and inefficient

57. Annals 1st Cong., 1st Sess., 475 (Ames), 373, 465, 571 (Vining), 460 (Sedgwick).

58. Madison suggested that impeachment was "a circuitous operation" for ousting executive officers for whom the president no longer wished to be responsible (*ibid.*, 497); Elias Boudinot pointed out that, if no officer could be removed except by impeachment, "we shall be in a deplorable situation indeed," both because of the difficulty of conducting a prosecution against an officer who resided far from the seat of government and because impeachment would not reach incapacity or disability (at 375). "If the necessity for dismission is pressing," Peter Sylvester asserted, "clearly the mode by impeachment is not likely to answer the purpose" (at 562). Thomas Hartley commented that the principle that impeachment was the only mode of removing an officer "would be attended with very inconvenient and mischievous consequences" (at 480).

process"—was a safeguard to insure that he did not abuse his powers or fail to perform his duties. Vining, the most outspoken critic of impeachment for the removal of inferior executive officers, went on to say that the president was responsible to the people if he does not effectually perform his duty to see the laws faithfully executed. "Have they the means of calling him to account, and punishing him for neglect?" Vining asked. "They have secured it in the Constitution, by impeachment, to be presented by their immediate representatives; if they fail here, they have another check when the time of election comes round."[59]

Whatever the rhetorical uses of the president's accountability through impeachment, it was recognized practically from the outset that it would be neither an easy nor an expeditious method of removal. The consolation, if there was one, was that the electorate could remove the president at the next election and his misconduct would not have to be endured for any longer than four more years.

59. *Ibid.*, 572.

2. *GROUNDS FOR IMPEACHMENT: THE FIRST CENTURY*

When George Mason responded to James Madison's criticism that "maladministration" was too vague by substituting "other high crimes and misdemeanors" as his proposed addition to treason and bribery in the impeachment clause of the Constitution, he laid the foundation for a continuing argument about the constitutional standard for impeaching and removing the president and other civil officers. If "maladministration" was vague, "other high crimes and misdemeanors" proved to be ambiguous, or at least arguably so. It was a term used in English impeachments, where it was applied to offenses against the system of government that were not necessarily criminal in the ordinary courts. But impeachments in England were themselves criminal prosecutions, in the sense that conviction could lead to the imposition of criminal sanctions. Their function and scope were different from what the framers envisioned for American impeachments. Impeachment in England could be directed at ordinary citizens—for high crimes—and not just government officials. In the case of high officers of the government, impeachment was a substitute for trial in the criminal courts—reaching ordinary, as well as high crimes—and not just a political remedy. The law of impeachment in England, including the meaning of "high crimes and misdemeanors," was part of a separate parliamentary law of crimes, a branch of common law developed and applied in impeachment cases.[1]

1. For a brief history of English impeachments, see 93d Cong., 2d Sess., House, Comm. on the Judiciary, *Constitutional Grounds for Presidential Impeachment: Report by the Staff of the Impeachment Inquiry* 4–7, 26–7 (Feb. 1974) (hereafter Impeachment Inquiry Staff Grounds Memo). The memorandum is reprinted in 93d Cong., 2d Sess., House, Comm. on the Judiciary, *Impeachment Inquiry: Hearings . . . Pursuant to H. Res. 803*, Book III, Appendix II, 2159–218 (1974) (hereafter Impeachment Inquiry).

No parliamentary common law of crimes existed in the United States (and, after 1812, no federal common law of crimes existed at all).[2] Impeachments under the Constitution did not result in criminal punishment. The Committee on Detail had introduced a clause in its draft constitution, retained in the final version without debate, that limited the judgment upon conviction to removal from office and disqualification from future office. As a result, it little mattered to the framers whether "high crimes and misdemeanors" might also be ordinary crimes. They may very well have thought that most impeachments would involve criminal charges, just as they appear to have thought that treason and bribery (particularly by a foreign power) would be the most common causes of impeachment, especially after they devised the complicated electoral scheme that minimized the likelihood that a president would corrupt his electors. It does not follow, however, that the framers thought all impeachments would involve criminal offenses, much less that "high crimes and misdemeanors" were limited to ordinary crimes or that impeachment was a criminal prosecution. The purpose of the impeachment process, as the framers envisioned it, was clearly not the same as the purpose of a criminal prosecution or of an impeachment in England. There is no reason to infer that, having adopted impeachment primarily as a method for removing an unfit president from office, the framers then provided a substantive standard that permitted his removal only for conduct for which he could be criminally punished by the courts. Impeachments in the United States, James Wilson wrote soon after the Constitution was ratified, "are confined to political characters, to political crimes and misdemeanors, and to political punishment."[3] It would be incongruous to suppose that they were further restricted to political wrongdoing that was also criminal and could lead to personal as well as political punishment.

The argument that impeachment is a criminal proceeding and that grounds for impeachment are limited to ordinary crimes (or at least intentional violations of known law) was first advanced in a federal impeachment in the 1805 trial of Justice Samuel Chase of the Supreme Court. Like the impeachment of President Andrew Johnson in 1868, the Chase impeachment is generally considered to have been a partisan proceeding. Chase, the most outspoken of the Federalists who

2. United States v. Hudson & Goodwin, 11 U.S. (7 Cr.) 32 (1812).
3. 1 Wilson 426.

dominated the judicial branch, was impeached and tried by a Congress controlled by the Jeffersonian Republicans on charges that he had displayed partisan bias on the bench. His impeachment was part of an attack on Federalist judges that had the support of President Thomas Jefferson. Chase's defense counsel stressed the political motivations behind the impeachment and the risk that it posed to the independence of the judiciary. As part of their argument his attorneys contended that "high crimes and misdemeanors" had a limited meaning and that impeachment was a criminal proceeding. Only if removal from office required proof of criminal wrongdoing (or wrongful acts in violation of law committed with wrongful intent), they argued, could partisan abuse of the impeachment power be prevented and the independence of the judicial branch maintained.

The framers had been well aware of the danger that impeachment might be used as a partisan weapon, although they had not foreseen the rise of permanent political parties and had focused on the threat to the independence of the executive rather than the judiciary. In *The Federalist* No. 65 Alexander Hamilton wrote of the "delicacy and magnitude of a trust which so deeply concerns the political reputation and existence of every man engaged in the administration of public affairs" and commented:

> The difficulty of placing it rightly, in a government resting entirely on the basis of periodical elections, will as readily be perceived, when it is considered that the most conspicuous characters in it will, from that circumstance, be too often the leaders or the tools of the most cunning or the most numerous faction, and on this account, can hardly be expected to possess the requisite neutrality towards those whose conduct may be the subject of scrutiny.

The prosecution of impeachments, he wrote,

> will seldom fail to agitate the passions of the whole community, and to divide it into parties more or less friendly or inimical to the accused. In many cases, it will connect itself with the preexisting factions, and will enlist all their animosities, partialities, influence, and interest on one side or on the other; and in such cases there will always be the greatest danger that the decision will be regulated more by the comparative strength of parties, than by the real demonstrations of innocence or guilt.

The reason, Hamilton explained, is that the subjects of impeachment "are those offences which proceed from the misconduct of public men, or, in other words, from the abuse or violation of some public trust"—offenses that are "of a nature which may with peculiar propriety be denominated POLITICAL, as they relate chiefly to injuries done immediately to the society itself." Impeachment, "designed as a method of NATIONAL INQUEST into the conduct of public men," inevitably has divisive political implications.[4]

The solution is not to attempt to make impeachment a criminal proceeding. "[T]he nature of the proceeding . . . can never be tied down by such strict rules, either in the delineation of the offence by the prosecutors, or in the construction of it by the judges, as in common cases serve to limit the discretion of courts in favor of personal security," Hamilton wrote. A court of impeachments "must necessarily have" the "awful discretion . . . to doom to honor or to infamy the most confidential and the most distinguished characters of the community."[5] The safeguard "against the danger of persecution, from the prevalency of a factious spirit" in either the House or Senate was the division of the powers relating to impeachment, "assigning to one the right of accusing, to the other the right of judging." And, Hamilton asserted, "[a]s the concurrence of two thirds of the Senate will be requisite to a condemnation, the security to innocence, from this additional circumstance, will be complete as itself can desire."[6] Given the nature of the government and the purpose of the impeachment remedy, no other solution was possible; any remaining risk of partisan abuse of the impeachment power was simply unavoidable.

Nevertheless, Chase's counsel argued that criminalization of the impeachment proceeding was another, and necessary, step to avoid partisan excesses. Chase was acquitted, whether because of these arguments or other factors. (There is never an adequate explanation of a decision not to impeach or a judgment of acquittal in an impeachment trial.) In 1867, when the House first considered (and rejected) the impeachment of President Andrew Johnson, and in the following year, when he was impeached and tried, many of the arguments offered in Chase's defense were made again on behalf of President Johnson. His impeachment, too, was based upon deep political differences.

4. *The Federalist* No. 65 at 424, 423–4.
5. *Ibid.*, at 425–6.
6. *Ibid.*, at 430.

Johnson, a Democrat who succeeded to the presidency upon Lincoln's assassination and stubbornly followed a reconstruction policy that the Republicans bitterly opposed, was impeached and tried by a Republican Congress. He was acquitted by a single vote, with seven Republicans and all twelve Democrats in the Senate voting not guilty and thirty-five Republicans voting guilty. The result has generally been acclaimed as a triumph for the independence of the president against an aggrandizing Congress, a victory for law and justice over political passions and expediency. By the time of the Nixon impeachment inquiry, the common perception of the Johnson impeachment was that it had been a vicious misuse of the power of presidential impeachment. It had discredited the constitutional method for removing the president and helped prevent any consideration of its use, or even mention of it in polite political discourse, for more than a century.

Popular reaction to the Johnson impeachment makes objective analysis of it difficult, and the same is true of the Chase impeachment. But they are the two leading impeachment trials in our history, the only ones to involve great men and great issues, the only instances before the Nixon inquiry when impeachment was used in circumstances of remotely comparable importance. Other impeachment proceedings—there have been some seventy investigations by House committees, eleven other impeachments voted by the House, eight other trials, and one dismissal by the Senate—were relatively insignificant episodes, in which the awesomeness of the constitutional weapon was hardly commensurate with the objective to which it was applied. (Over the years, as a matter of fact, a series of metaphors have been devised to describe the application of impeachment to officers or offenses that are too trivial, among them: "charging a cannon to shoot a mosquito,"[7] "employing an elephant to remove an atom too minute for the grasp of an insect,"[8] "rig[ging] up a trip-hammer to crack a walnut,"[9] "making available a nuclear bomb . . . to bring down a

7. District Judge Richard Peters on the possibility of his own impeachment, quoted in 1 Charles Warren, *The Supreme Court in United States History* 289, n. 1 (1922).

8. Joseph Hopkinson in defense of Justice Chase, 2 Samuel Smith and Thomas Lloyd, *Trial of Samuel Chase, An Associate Justice of the Supreme Court of the United States, Impeached by the House of Representatives for High Crimes and Misdemeanors Before the Senate of the United States* 14 (reprint of 1805 ed.) (hereafter Chase Trial).

9. William S. Evarts in defense of President Andrew Johnson. 40th Cong., 2d Sess., Senate, *Trial of Andrew Johnson, President of the United States, Before the Senate of the United States, on Impeachment by the House of Representative for High Crimes and Misdemeanors*, vol. II, at 336 (reprint of 1868 ed.) (hereafter Johnson Trial).

pheasant."[10]) And there is an element of circularity involved in the criticism of the Chase and Johnson impeachments for being partisan. The magnitude and nature of the issues involved, especially in the Johnson case, necessarily aroused political passions, as Hamilton had predicted such a case would. The partisanship was excessive, it might even be suggested, only in retrospect and only because the impeachments failed in the Senate.

Because the Chase and Johnson impeachments involved the use of the impeachment power in a charged political atmosphere, they most clearly demonstrate the underlying tension between the political and legal aspects of the impeachment remedy. Analysis of them, and particularly of the legal arguments made by the House managers prosecuting the impeachments in the Senate and by the lawyers defending against them, helps to illuminate the problem of defining grounds for presidential impeachment and removal. As will become evident, that problem is not simply one of deciding whether "high crimes and misdemeanors" need be criminal. The criminality argument, as used in these impeachments, was but one part of a more complicated defense strategy intended to establish that impeachment must be based on serious wrongdoing, determined in accordance with an objective legal standard and without regard to political considerations. In the Johnson trial, in fact, the criminality argument was much less important than other aspects of this strategy, for a number of the charges against Johnson involved conduct that was putatively criminal. The fundamental issue in that case—the issue of lasting significance, in terms of the presidential impeachment power—was whether Johnson's offenses, even if proved, were serious enough to justify removing him from office. In addition to encountering technical problems along the way (the "criminal" statutes upon which they relied were not well adapted to the use they sought to make of them), the House managers ultimately failed—though just barely, in terms of the vote—to establish that Johnson's wrongdoing was sufficiently egregious to warrant this extreme step.

The Impeachment and Trial of Justice Samuel Chase

Justice Chase was the second Federalist judge to be impeached by the Republican-dominated House of Representatives. District Judge John

10. National Treasury Employees Union v. Nixon, 492 F.2d 587, 615 (D.C. Cir. 1974).

Pickering of New Hampshire was impeached in 1803[11] and tried and convicted by the Senate in 1804. The constitutional standard for impeachment was very much an issue in Pickering's case, but there was no one to argue the point on his behalf. Pickering's son had requested a postponement of the trial and offered evidence of his father's insanity (showing, among other things, that he had a morbid fear of crossing rivers by ferry that would prevent him from traveling to Washington[12]). The Senate rejected the request, and the trial proceeded with no defense. At the conclusion of the managers' case on behalf of the House, the Senate agreed to vote whether Pickering was guilty "as charged" by the House in each article, rather than whether he was guilty of a high crime or misdemeanor upon the charge in each article—the form of the question used in the Hastings case (the most-recent and best-known English impeachment trial) and subsequently adopted in American impeachments. The unusual form of the question on which the Senate was voting was criticized by Jonathan Dayton of New Jersey, who, along with four other senators, withdrew instead of voting on the articles. Dayton explained:

> [T]here were numbers who were disposed to give sentence of removal against this unhappy judge, upon the ground of the facts alleged and proved, who could not, however, conscientiously vote that they amounted to high crimes and misdemeanors, especially when committed by a man proved at the very time to be insane and to have been so ever since, even to the present moment.

Three articles against Pickering charged that he had made procedural errors, prejudicial to the United States, in an admiralty action for nonpayment of duty, and a fourth charged that he was intoxicated and used profane language on the bench during this proceeding. He was found guilty on each by a vote of 19 to 7.[13] The case could be argued to be a precedent for a noncriminal view of grounds for impeachment or even for the removal of judges for errors of judgment without corrupt intent. Its precedential value, however, was undermined by the lack of a defense, the method in which the Senate voted for Pickering's removal, and the practical necessity of removing an insane judge from the bench.

11. Annals 7th Cong., 2d Sess., 642 (1803).
12. *Ibid.*, 8th Cong., 1st Sess. (App.), 340–1 (1804).
13. *Ibid.* (App.), 364–7.

At the time, however, the Pickering conviction was considered a political triumph for the Jeffersonian Republicans, and the House voted to impeach Justice Chase immediately after the Senate had convicted Pickering.[14] Chase was charged, in the words of one of the House managers at his trial, with "perverting the high judicial functions of his office for the purposes of individual oppression, and of staining the pure ermine of justice by political party spirit."[15] Said another manager, "[I]f the holy sanctuary of our courts is to be invaded by party feeling; if justice shall suffer her pure garment to be stained by the foul venom of political bigotry, we may indeed boast that we live in a land of freedom, but the boast will be vain and illusory." "It is our duty to prevent party spirit from entering into our courts of justice"; the trial of Chase gave the Senate an opportunity to "nip the evil in the bud," before it could "grow to an enormous tree, bearing destruction upon every branch."[16]

The Articles of Impeachment

The specific charges against Chase arose out of four events, all of which involved his conduct while sitting as a circuit justice: the treason trial of John Fries in Philadelphia; the seditious libel trial of James Callender in Richmond; Chase's charge to a grand jury in Delaware to investigate a local printer for sedition; and a charge to a grand jury in Maryland, urging defeat of a proposed state constitutional amendment and criticizing the repeal by the Republicans of the Judiciary Act of 1801. The first three events occurred in 1800, while the Federalists were still in power; the last in 1803. The articles of impeachment were drafted—"every word and tittle," he acknowledged in his closing argument in the trial[17]—by John Randolph of Virginia, the Republican leader in the House.[18]

In the Fries trial Chase had prepared a written charge to the jury on the definition of the crime of treason by levying war against the United States, which he gave to defense counsel and the district attorney before the jury was empaneled. He told defense counsel that they could neither cite English treason cases (in an attempt to cast doubt

14. *Ibid.*, 1880.
15. 1 Chase Trial 322 (Early).
16. 2 *ibid.* 332, 364 (Nicholson).
17. 2 *ibid.* 473.
18. The articles appear at 1 *ibid.* 5–8.

upon his legal definition) or the Sedition Act (in an effort to argue that Fries's offense was the lesser crime of sedition, not treason) nor address their legal arguments to the jury rather than the court. Outraged by these rulings—or, depending on the interpretation of the facts, in the hope of strengthening Fries's case for a presidential pardon—his lawyers withdrew from the case. Fries was tried without counsel, convicted, and sentenced to death. He was subsequently pardoned by President Adams.

Randolph's Article 1 charged that Chase had conducted himself "in a manner highly arbitrary, oppressive, and unjust" during the Fries trial. It specified the delivery of the written opinion on the definition of treason, the restriction on the defense counsel against citing English cases and the Sedition Act, and the denial to the defendant of his constitutional privilege of arguing the law to the jury, thereby "endeavoring to wrest from the jury their indisputable right to hear argument, and determine upon the question of law, as well as the question of fact, involved in the verdict which they were required to give." In consequence of this "irregular conduct . . . , as dangerous to our liberties, as it is novel to our laws and usages," the article concluded, Fries was deprived of his sixth amendment right and condemned to death without having been heard by counsel in his defense, "to the disgrace of the character of the American bench, in manifest violation of law and justice, and in open contempt of the rights of juries, on which, ultimately, rest the liberty and safety of the American people."

The "indisputable right" on which Randolph based Article 1 could be—and was—much disputed by Chase's defense counsel. It may be seriously doubted that even in the early days of the Republic juries were considered to have the right to decide the law as well as the facts. It might also be doubted that judges were thought to have as little authority in the courtroom as the article suggested. In any case, the defense was able to offer a lengthy exposition on the responsibilities of judges and juries in criminal cases, confounding the issue of Chase's possible bias against Fries in this broader jurisprudential issue. The defense was also able to argue that the charge was stale, since the trial had taken place five years earlier. (There were, in addition, a welter of factual issues, involving the motivation for the withdrawal of Fries's counsel and their conduct before they withdrew.)

The next five articles dealt with the trial of James Callender, who was charged with a misdemeanor under the Sedition Act for writing and publishing a book alleged to be libelous of President Adams. Here the managers had evidence—in the form of his statements before trial—of Chase's bias against Callender and his desire to see him successfully prosecuted. Indeed, Chase all but admitted his prejudgment of the case in his answer to the articles of impeachment. In denying "indecent solicitude" for Callender's conviction, Chase acknowledged that his "indignation was strongly excited, by the atrocious and profligate libel" charged against Callender. And he admitted that he shared "the general wish natural to every friend of truth, decorum, and virtue, that persons guilty of such offences . . . should be brought to punishment, for the sake of example."[19] Again, however, the articles raised a number of technical legal questions, including the authority of a judge to control the manner in which a trial is conducted in his courtroom, standards for determining bias in a juror, and Virginia procedural rules. Chase's attorneys were able to dwell on these technical questions, obscuring the underlying issue and raising doubts about Chase's intentions and the culpability of his conduct.

Article 2 charged that Chase, "prompted by a similar spirit of persecution and injustice," with intent to oppress and procure Callender's conviction, overruled the objection of a prospective juror, who wished to be excused because he had made up his mind that the publication was libelous. Article 3 charged that Chase, with intent to oppress and procure Callender's conviction, refused to permit a defense witness to testify, on the pretense that his testimony did not go to the whole of one of the twenty counts in the indictment. In response to these articles, Chase's counsel offered lengthy arguments that Chase had behaved properly—arguments sufficient, at a minimum, to suggest that the charge of improper motive was not clearly proved. For example, Chase answered Article 2 by asserting that his decision not to excuse the juror was based on sound legal reasons and added, "But if the reasons should be considered as invalid, and the decision as erroneous, can they be considered as so clearly and flagrantly incorrect, as to justify a conclusion that they were adopted by this respondent, through improper motives?"[20]

Article 4 was the central charge dealing with the Callender trial. It alleged that Chase's conduct during the trial was marked by "manifest injustice, partiality, and intemperance." The article included five

19. 1 *ibid.* 79.
20. 1 *ibid.* 56.

specifications. The first specification charged Chase with compelling defense counsel to reduce to writing and submit to the court all the questions they meant to propound to the defense witness. The third specification charged that Chase used "unusual, rude, and contemptuous expressions" toward defense counsel and falsely insinuated that they wished to excite public fears and indignation and insubordination to law; the fourth charged "repeated and vexatious interruption" of defense counsel, which induced them to abandon the case. Each of these specifications involved questions of the authority of the presiding judge to control the behavior of defense counsel. The second specification in Article 4 charged Chase with refusing to grant a continuance to the next term of court (when he would not be presiding); the defense was again able to raise a technical legal question: the sufficiency of the affidavit requesting the continuance. Finally, the fifth specification charged "an indecent solicitude . . . for the conviction of the accused, unbecoming even a public prosecutor, but highly disgraceful to the character of a judge as it was subversive of justice"; this invited Chase's lawyers to argue that the specification charged no conduct, but merely a state of mind.

Articles 5 and 6 involved technical points of law. Article 5, which omitted any allegation of improper intent or partiality, charged that Chase, contrary to law, had a warrant issued for Callender's arrest rather than a summons for his appearance. Article 6 charged that Chase, with intent to oppress and procure Callender's conviction, brought the case to trial during the term of court in which the presentment and indictment were returned, contrary to law. To support these articles, the managers had to show, first, that a Virginia statute was applicable to a misdemeanor case in a federal court in that state and, second, that Chase's decisions were contrary to the Virginia statute. Both of these propositions rested on questionable interpretations of the relevant federal and state law, as the defense argued at length.

Article 7 concerned the charge to the Delaware grand jury. It alleged that Chase, "disregarding the duties of his office, did descend from the dignity of a judge and stoop to the level of an informer" by refusing to discharge the grand jury and by charging it to investigate the printer for sedition and (with intent to procure the printer's prosecution) authoritatively enjoined the district attorney to examine the printer's papers to find a passage on which he might be prosecuted. The article charged Chase with "thereby degrading his high judicial functions, and tending to impair the public confidence in, and respect for, the tribunals of justice, so essential to the general welfare." This article, too, raised a debatable question of law—the extent to which a judge has the power or duty to supervise a grand jury.

Finally, Article 8 dealt with the political charge to the Baltimore grand jury. It alleged that Chase, "disregarding the duties and dignity of his judicial character," "pervert[ed] his official right and duty to address the grand jury . . . for the purpose of delivering . . . an intemperate and inflammatory political harangue" with intent "to excite the fears and resentment" of the grand jury and the people of Maryland against their state government and constitution. This was, the article charged, "a conduct highly censurable in any, but peculiarly indecent and unbecoming" in a Supreme Court justice. The article further charged that Chase, "under pretence of exercising his judicial right" to address the grand jury, "did, in a manner highly unwarrantable, endeavor to excite the odium" of the grand jury and the people of Maryland against the federal government

> by delivering opinions, which, even if the judicial authority were competent to their expression, on a suitable occasion and in a proper manner, were at that time and as delivered by him, highly indecent, extra-judicial, and tending to prostitute the high judicial character with which he was invested, to the low purpose of an electioneering partizan.

On this article, the defense again argued that there was no rule forbidding Chase's charge to the grand jury; it may have been improper, but it was not illegal. In his answer Chase contended that it had been the practice in the United States since the revolution for judges to express "such political opinions as they thought correct and useful" to grand juries in their charges; by not forbidding this practice, the legislature had given it "an implied sanction" and "virtually declared [it] to be innocent."[21]

The Legal Issues in the Chase Trial

In order to convince the Senate to remove Chase for using the powers of his judicial office for partisan purposes, the House managers had, in effect, to argue that the removal power could be used in a par-

21. 1 *ibid.* 96–7.

tisan manner. The arguments about the law of impeachment offered by the defense appear to have been designed to keep this inconsistency constantly before the Senate, to make the point that for the Senate to use the judicial process of impeachment for partisan purposes was no better than the judicial misconduct charged against Chase. Part of the defense argument, and perhaps the most lasting portion, was that impeachment would lie only for indictable crimes, or at least violations of known law committed with a criminal or corrupt intent. There was more to the argument, however, than criminality; the basic contention the defense made was that there must be some ascertainable standard, known in advance, lest impeachment become merely a political weapon.

Chase and his defense counsel professed to find a criminality restriction in the provisions of the Constitution. Chase himself contended in his answer to Article 1:

> [A]ccording to the constitution of the United States, *civil officers* thereof, and no other persons, are subject to impeachment; and they only for treason, bribery, corruption, or other high crime or misdemeanor, consisting in some act done or omitted, in violation of some law forbidding or commanding it; on conviction of which act, they *must* be removed from office; and may, after conviction, be indicted and punished therefor, according to law. Hence it clearly results, that no civil officer of the United States can be impeached, except for some offence for which he may be indicted at law; and that no evidence can be received on an impeachment, except such as on an indictment at law, for the same offence, would be admissible. That a judge cannot be indicted or punished according to law, for any act whatever, done by him in his judicial capacity, and in a matter of which he has jurisdiction, through error of judgment merely, without corrupt motives, however manifest his error may be, is a principle resting on the plainest maxims of reason and justice, supported by the highest legal authority, and sanctioned by the universal sense of mankind.[22]

22. 1 *ibid.* 47–8. This statement is the very first appearance of the indictable crime argument in a federal impeachment. It should be observed that it is based on fallacious reasoning. Chase appears to have been relying upon the constitutional provision limiting judgment in cases of impeachment to removal and disqualification and providing that the convicted party may nonetheless be indicted, tried, and punished according to

If he made a mistake, Justice Chase asserted, it "cannot be imputed to him as an offence of any kind, much less as a high crime and misdemeanor, . . . unless it can be shewn by clear and legal evidence, that he acted from corrupt motives."[23]

The "indictable crime" restriction for which Chase and his counsel argued was not necessarily limited to federal statutory crimes, for they acknowledged that there were federal common law crimes, a position the Supreme Court rejected in 1812. The key point in the criminality defense was that impeachment required a violation of known law, committed with criminal intent; it could not be invoked simply at the pleasure of the House. While there are some inconsistencies among their arguments, the same themes recurred repeatedly. In the initial closing argument for the defense, Joseph Hopkinson asserted that an impeachable offense must be an indictable offense evincing a corrupt heart or intention:

> The power of impeachment is with the House of Representatives—but only for impeachable offences. They are . . . not to

---

criminal law (Art. I, §3, cl. 7). That clause, however, more readily bears the interpretation placed upon it by James Iredell in the North Carolina ratifying convention: the person convicted on impeachment "is further liable to a trial at common law, and may receive such common-law punishment as belongs to a description of such offenses if it be punishable by that law" (4 Elliot 114). In other words, impeachment for an indictable crime does not bar later punishment, but this does not establish that only indictable crimes are impeachable. Iredell's construction is supported by the antecedent provisions for the clause, found in the New York Constitution of 1777 (Art. 33, 5 Thorpe 2635), the Massachusetts Constitution of 1780 (Art. 8, 3 Thorpe 1897–8), and the New Hampshire Constitution of 1784 (4 Thorpe 2461). The grounds for impeachment under these constitutions—"mal and corrupt conduct" in office in New York, "misconduct and maladministration" in office in Massachusetts and New Hampshire—do not appear to have been limited to indictable crimes.

Ironically, Chase was himself accused of being too quick to point out the illogic of legal arguments. One of the incidents relied upon in support of the third specification of Article 4—the use of "unusual, rude, and contemptuous expressions" toward defense counsel in the Callender trial—involved Chase's reply to a proposition that a defense lawyer had said was a "perfectly syllogistic" conclusion to his argument. Chase said, with a bow, "A *non sequitur,* sir" (1 Chase Trial 172 [testimony of George Hay]). In Chase's defense, Luther Martin contended that this was "the correct answer to a syllogism, which is rather lame in its conclusion" (2 *ibid.* 215–6).

Iredell's legal acumen, moreover, was relied upon in defense of Chase, for Iredell had given a definition of the law of treason in an earlier trial of Fries, over which he presided as circuit justice, similar to the opinion delivered by Chase. In defending Chase against Article 1, Martin described Iredell as "a gentleman of great legal talents" (2 *ibid.* 161).

23. 1 *ibid.* 48.

> *create* the offence, and make any act criminal and impeachable at their will and pleasure. What is an offence is a question to be decided by the constitution and the law, not by the opinion of a single branch of the legislature.

The Senate, Hopkinson suggested, does not sit "to scan and punish paltry errors and indiscretions too insignificant to have a name in the penal code, too paltry for the notice of a court of Quarter sessions." Basic questions of fairness and notice were involved. "Nothing is so necessary to justice and to safety as that the criminal code should be certain and known. Let the judge, as well as the citizen, precisely know the path he is to walk in, and what he may or may not do." A judge should not be exposed to punishment without knowing his offense, Hopkinson argued; the criminality or innocence of his conduct should depend upon the laws existing at the time, not "upon the opinions of a body of men to be collected four or five years after the transaction." He should not be subject to impeachment and removal from office "for an act strictly legal, when done, if any House of Representatives for any indefinite time after, shall for any reason they may act upon, choose to consider such act improper and impeachable." The Constitution "never intended to lay the judiciary thus prostrate at the feet of the House of Representatives, the slaves of their will, the victims of their caprice." "We have read . . . in our younger days, and read with horror," Hopkinson said, "of the Roman emperor who placed his edicts so high in the air that the keenest eye could not decypher them, and yet severely punished any breach of them." The power claimed by the House was ten thousand times more dangerous, more tyrannical, and more subversive of all liberty and safety. At least the Roman code could, with extraordinary pains, be understood;

> but here to be safe, we must be able to look into years to come, and to foresee what will be the changing opinions of men or points of decorum for years to come. The rule of our conduct, by which we are to be judged and condemned, lies buried in the bosom of futurity, and in the minds and opinions of men unknown, perhaps unborn.

Hopkinson contended that if the tenure of judges depended on "propriety and impropriety of demeanour" the independence of the judiciary was at an end.[24]

24. 2 *ibid.* 11 (emphasis in original), 13–4, 15–6, 17–8, 20–1.

Luther Martin, the leading advocate for Chase and a delegate to the Constitutional Convention, as he reminded the Senate, argued that impeachment must be for indictable crimes relating to the office or tending to cover the person who committed them with turpitude and infamy, showing there can be no dependence on his integrity and honor to secure the performance of his official duties. Impeachment, he asserted, "cannot change the law, and make that *punishable* which was not *before criminal*." Government cannot punish acts antecedently done, he argued, citing the *ex post facto* clause of the Constitution. If the House could impeach and the Senate remove "for acts which are not contrary to law, . . . you leave your judges, and all your other officers at the mercy of the prevailing party." A judge, Martin contended, "should always consider himself safe while he violates no law, while he conscientiously discharges his duty, *whomever* he may displease thereby."[25]

In the final argument for the defense, Robert Goodloe Harper conceded that there might be cases where a judge ought to be impeached for acts that conceivably were not indictable. Nonetheless, "some wilful violation of a known law" was required; he could not be removed for "some reason of policy or expediency."[26] In defending Chase against Article 8, Harper admitted that it might be "ill-judged, indiscreet, or ill-timed" for a judge to give a political speech or argue against a public measure to a grand jury. But, while Congress could legislatively prohibit political charges to grand juries, it must declare in its judicial capacity

> that an act, however improper in itself or dangerous in its tendency, shall not, if forbidden by no law, be punished as a crime; that the prevalence of this custom [of political charges] for twenty years, the countenance which it received from some governmental authorities, and the acquiesence of all, are sufficient evidence of its legality; and that the criminal intent which constitutes an essential ingredient of the offence . . . can never be inferred from the act itself, when done in compliance with a custom so long established, and so highly sanctioned.[27]

In reply for the managers, Caesar Rodney suggested that "[t]he independence of the judiciary, the political tocsin of the day, and the

25. 2 *ibid.* 140–1 (emphasis in original).
26. 2 *ibid.* 254–5, 265.
27. 2 *ibid.* 327, 329.

alarm bell of the night, has been rung through every change in our ears"; the defense "have played upon this cord until its vibrations produce no effect." In this country, Rodney continued, "I am afraid the doctrine has been carried to such an extravagant length, that the judiciary may justly be considered like a spoiled child." He did not wish "to see them the slaves of any administration; but the faithful and impartial executors of justice." The purpose of the Chase impeachment was "to teach a lesson of instruction to future judges, that when intoxicated by the spirit of party, they may recollect the scale of power may one day turn, and preserve the scales of justice equal." The managers adjured the Senate, Randolph said in his closing argument, "to exorcise from our courts the baleful spirit of party—to give an awful momento to our judges."

A subsidiary question was whether impeachment was a criminal prosecution or an inquest of office. George Washington Campbell contended for the managers that impeachment was "more in the nature of a civil investigation, than of a criminal prosecution"; it "may fairly be considered a kind of inquest into the conduct of an officer, merely as it regards his office; the manner in which he performs the duties thereof; and the effects that his conduct therein may have on society." Removal and disqualification, Campbell asserted,

> cannot be considered a criminal punishment; it is merely a deprivation of rights; a declaration that the person is not properly qualified to serve his country. . . . [W]e are not bound to make out such a case as would be punishable by indictment in a court of law. . . . We need not hunt down the accused as a criminal, who had committed crimes of the deepest die.

According to Campbell, it was sufficient to show that Chase had "transgressed the line of his official duty, in violation of the laws of his country; and that this conduct can only be accounted for on the ground of impure and corrupt motives."

Harper attacked this argument. If impeachment was a mere inquest of office, he asked, "why this formality of proceeding, this solemn apparatus of justice, this laborious investigation of facts?" If the conviction of a judge on impeachment is to depend not on his guilt or innocence of some crime alleged against him, but on some reason of policy or expediency that the House and Senate think requires his removal, "why the solemn mockery of articles alledging high crimes and misdemeanors, of a court regularly formed, of a judicial oath administered to the members, of the public examination of witnesses, and of a trial conducted in all the usual forms?" No, Harper asserted, "this desperate expedient, resorted to as the last and only prop of a case . . . unsupported by law or evidence; this forlorn hope of the prosecution, pressed into its service, after it was found that no offence against any law of the land could be proved, will not, cannot avail."[28]

Ultimately, the managers retreated from the position that impeachment was not a criminal prosecution, a contention Campbell himself had undercut by suggesting impeachment was not available for indictable offenses because this would involve the "palpable absurdity" of double punishment. Said Joseph Nicholson, in his closing argument:

> We do contend that this is a criminal prosecution, for offences committed in the discharge of high official duties, and we now support it, not merely for the purpose of removing an individual from office, but in order that the punishment inflicted on him may deter others from pursuing the baneful example which has been set them.

And Rodney, also in closing, said, "[W]e rely in supporting this as a criminal proceeding."[29] The managers continued to argue, however, that no indictable offense need be proved.

One of the apparent objectives of the defense in seeking to establish that impeachment was a criminal prosecution was to put the burden on the managers of proving corrupt intent. The mangers had argued that the corrupt intent should be inferred from the conduct. Campbell said of the first article that "when a man violates a law, or commits a manifest breach of his duty, an evil intent, or corrupt motive must be presumed, to have actuated his conduct"; the burden was on the defense to establish "pure motives, and unintentional error" by "satisfactory and incontestible evidence." On Articles 2–4, Campbell argued:

> How could any judge with upright intentions commit so many errors, or hit upon so many mistakes in the course of one trial . . . ? They must have been the result of design, and a predeter-

28. 2 *ibid* 371 (emphasis omitted), 375–6 (Rodney); 481 (Randolph); 1 *ibid.* 352, 353 (Campbell); 2 *ibid.* 251 (Harper).

29. 1 *ibid.* 370 (Campbell); 2 *ibid.* 335 (Nicholson), 402 (Rodney).

mination to bear down all opposition, in order to convict and punish the defendant.

On Articles 5 and 6, Manager Christopher Clarke argued that Chase's conduct could only be accounted for by supposing that he intended to act in conformity to his previous declarations of bias against Callender and "this was one of the means he had determined to pursue in order to convict Callender."[30]

The defense strongly attacked these assertions. Philip Barton Key commented that the managers seemed to be reversing the presumption of innocence and to be contending that "whenever an infraction of a law is committed by a judge, he is to be presumed guilty, unless he establishes his innocence." Even when a judge decides against law, Key contended, the legal rule was that "his errors shall be ascribed to the head, and not to the heart" unless there is proof of his guilt.[31]

In his opening for the managers, John Randolph had urged the Senate

> to consider the facts alleged against the respondent in all their accumulated attrocity; —not to take them, each in an insulated point of view, but as a chain of evidence indissolubly linked together, and establishing the indisputable proof of his guilt.

Chase's "acts of injustice," Randolph said, were "a series of misconduct so connected in time and place and circumstance, as to leave no doubt, in my mind at least, of intentional ill."[32] Especially in support of the charges dealing with the Callender trial, the managers sought to have the articles considered as a whole, as Campbell's argument shows.

The defense argued that the articles must be considered independently. Corrupt intent, Key argued, could not be inferred from "the general mass of the transactions attending the trial of Callender"; the evidence could not be taken accumulatively, but each article "must be taken by itself, and one can derive no force from the rest." If this were not so, Key said, "a hasty word, uttered in an unguarded moment, might be construed into a crime, and a number of small offences, individually of the most trifling nature, be made to constitute a great

30. 1 *ibid.* 367, 383 (Campbell); 2 *ibid.* 4–5 (Clarke).
31. 2 *ibid.* 88–9 (Key).
32. 1 *ibid.* 124, 125.

one." Harper, too, attacked Randolph's general proposition, which he construed to mean that

> although no single act alledged in the articles, should be considered as an impeachable offence, and a sufficient ground of conviction, yet all the acts taken together may constitute such an offence. That is, in other words, that many nothings may make something; that many noughts may make a unit: that many innocent acts may make a crime.

This, Harper argued, was but another form of "the absurd and monstrous doctrine, that judges may be removed on impeachment for reasons of expediency, without the proof of any specific offence." This "last subterfuge" would be of no avail; the Senate, "adhering to the principles of the constitution, the positive rules of law, and the plain dictates of justice and common sense," would require for conviction "the clear proof of a criminal intent, manifested and carried into effect, by some act done in violation of the laws."

The accusation, Harper said in summation for the defense, had "dwindled into nothing. It has been scattered by the rays of truth, like the mists of the morning, before the effulgence of the rising sun. Touched by the spear of investigation, it has lost its gigantic and terrifying form, and has shrunk into a toad." After surveying every part of Chase's conduct, Harper contended, "the ingenuity and industry of the honorable managers have proved unable to detect one illegal act, one proof, or one fair presumption of improper motive."[33]

Four major themes emerge from the arguments in defense of Justice Chase. The first is that there must be an ascertainable standard for determining what is an impeachable offense, known in advance. Second, the infraction (whether an indictable crime or a violation of positive law) must involve corrupt or criminal intent. Third, the burden is on the House of Representatives, as the prosecutors, to prove the intent as well as the act. Finally, each charge in the impeachment must be considered separately, not cumulatively. Impeachment, the defense argued, is a criminal prosecution, and the normal rules of judicial proceedings must apply or else officeholders will be at the mercy of the dominant political party for the time being.

33. 2 *ibid.* 81–2 (Key); 2 *ibid.* 330–1 (Harper).

Chase was acquitted on each of the eight articles. Article 8 failed by a vote of 19 guilty, 15 not guilty; Articles 3 and 4 by votes of 18 guilty, 16 not guilty. The other articles failed to obtain a majority—Article 1 failed, 16–18; Articles 2 and 7, 10–24; Article 6, 4–30; and Article 5 gained the dubious and unique distinction of obtaining a unanimous not guilty vote.[34] Like all acquittals on an impeachment, the result of the Chase trial established no proposition of impeachment law; it is not possible to say which, if any, of the defense arguments persuaded the Senate.

Perhaps because it was the first full-blown impeachment trial, perhaps because of the reputation and skill of Chase's counsel, or perhaps because the result did end the immediate threat of the political use of impeachment against the judiciary, the Chase trial became a leading precedent for the criminality view of impeachment. The arguments that were made by Hopkinson, Martin, and Harper were repeated time and again in later impeachments; the indictability issue, in particular, became a staple in impeachment proceedings. Much of the historical writing on the case has tended to establish a too facile and misleading dichotomy: either impeachment was a partisan proceeding, governed by no law, or it was a criminal proceeding, requiring proof of a crime. The first position was rejected with Chase's acquittal, the analysis runs, so the second must have been adopted.

In fact, as this brief description of the defense suggests, the issue was more complicated, and the "indictable crime" argument something of a smokescreen. Chase's defense counsel skillfully played on every element of weakness in the case, arguing lack of illegal conduct, lack of corrupt intent, lack of evidence, lack of seriousness. They divided, ridiculed, and thereby conquered the charges. They engaged in lengthy expositions on the legal questions raised by the articles, to prove (if nothing more) that Chase's errors were not flagrant and therefore improper motive could not be presumed. While it is difficult to judge from the distance of 170 years, it would appear that their strategy was much more coherent than that of the managers; there can be little doubt that they were more artful advocates.[35] The strength of the defense case was the apparent reasonableness and judiciousness of the position they were asserting; the weakness of the prosecution was that

34. The vote appears at 2 *ibid.* 485–93.

35. Randolph's performance was particularly weak; among other things, he lost his notes for his final argument, for which he apologized to the Senate (2 *ibid.* 463).

the managers espoused inconsistent positions and ultimately seemed to be using a judicial proceeding for partisan purposes, the very offense that lay at the heart of their case against Justice Chase. The articles themselves were a blend of doubtful legalisms and conclusory accusations, a point the defense was able to exploit. Key, for example, said of Article 2, "If we extract . . . the epithets it contains nothing will remain; and epithets fortunately do not constitute crimes."[36] Similarly, the defense lawyers went out of their way to correct immaterial errors of the managers, such as Campbell's assertion that an impeachment for an indictable crime would involve the possibility of double punishment, thereby implying that their entire position was fallacious.

The criminality debate, then, arose in the context of a highly political impeachment; the argument for restricting impeachment to indictable crimes was part of a larger effort to undermine the prosecution case against Justice Chase. That effort was so skillfully performed—and the managers so unprepared to meet it—that the Chase trial has provided the doctrinal arguments in opposition to impeachment ever since.

An afterword on the Chase trial: Luther Martin appeared as counsel in a case before his old friend Justice Chase in the federal court in Baltimore in 1810. Chase said to Martin, "I am surprised that you can so prostitute your talents." Martin replied, "Sir, I never prostituted my talents except when I defended you and Col. Burr," adding to the jury, "[A] couple of the greatest rascals in the world."[37]

The Impeachment of President Andrew Johnson

Between the Chase trial in 1805 and the trial of President Andrew Johnson in 1868, there were only two impeachments, both involving district judges. In 1830, after a series of House committee investigations that had begun in 1826, Judge James H. Peck was impeached and charged in a single article with misusing his contempt power to oppress an attorney who wrote a newspaper article critical of one of his

36. 2 *ibid.* 75.

37. P. S. Clarkson & R. S. Jett, *Luther Martin of Maryland* 280 (1970), quoted in Raoul Berger, *Impeachment: The Constitutional Problems* 244 n. 95 (1973) (hereafter Berger, *Impeachment*). Martin had represented Burr (who, incidentally, as vice president had presided at the Chase trial) in his trial on charges arising out of the Wilkes plot on which Burr was ultimately acquitted.

decisions.[38] The arguments at Judge Peck's trial echoed those in the Chase impeachment. His counsel contended that Peck had not exceeded his authority and, even if he had, there was no wrongful intent. The managers acknowledged that impeachment required a violation of law, but argued that wrongful intent could be inferred from Peck's conduct. Peck was acquitted by a vote of 21 guilty, 22 not guilty.[39] The next impeachment, of Judge West Humphreys in 1862, was not a debatable case. Humphreys was impeached for joining the Confederacy. He did not appear, and no defense was offered on his behalf. The trial took only five hours, and Humphreys was convicted on all the charges in seven articles of impeachment, with the exception of a single specification. The gravamen of the charges was treason, although at least some of the articles did not allege criminal acts.[40]

The leading precedent when the House took up the impeachment of Andrew Johnson therefore was still the Chase case, and it figured prominently in the debates, especially in the initial effort to impeach Johnson in December 1867, which the House rejected.

In considering the Johnson impeachment, it is important to discount the folklore that has grown up about it. Mythology has it that the case was based on trumped-up political charges, that it was a contest between constitutional government and congressional dictatorship, that if Johnson had been removed future presidents would have become lackeys for Congress. That interpretation is partly true. What can be seen in retrospect and with the help of revisionist historians,[41] however, is that the case was not entirely one-sided, Johnson not entirely in the right and the Radical Republicans not totally in the wrong. His impeachment cannot be dismissed as simply an ill-directed

38. See 3 Asher Hinds, *Hinds' Precedents of the House of Representatives* §§2364–7 (1907) (hereafter Hinds'). The sections of Hinds' and its continuation, Clarence Cannon, *Cannon's Precedents of the House of Representatives* (1936) (hereafter Cannon's), concerning impeachment were reprinted during the Nixon inquiry by the Judiciary Committee, 93d Cong., 2d Sess., House, Comm. on the Judiciary, *Impeachment: Selected Materials on Procedure* (Jan. 1974).

39. The published record of the trial, A. Stansbury, ed., *Trial of James H. Peck* (1833) is apparently quite rare, though the Library of Congress has a copy. Some of the legal debate can be gleaned from 3 Hinds' §§2368–84.

40. See Impeachment Inquiry Staff Grounds Memo 46–7 for a description of the articles. The trial appears in Cong. Globe, 37th Cong., 2d Sess., 2943 (1862).

41. An excellent historical account of the case is Michael Les Benedict, *The Impeachment and Trial of Andrew Johnson* (1973).

act of political passion. The outcome may have been correct, even beneficent, but it should be recognized that it was a close case—close both in the vote resulting in acquittal and in the legal questions it involved.

The arguments against the impeachment of Johnson in the House in 1867 and against his conviction in the Senate trial in 1868 involved the criminality question, but they also and more importantly built upon other themes first developed in the Chase trial. The following description of the Johnson impeachment and trial focuses on these legal arguments rather than the politics of the case. Its purpose is to show what can happen when the House seeks to base an impeachment, founded on irreconcilable political differences, on a "specific crime." The Johnson case is the prime example in our history of an impeachment based on a pretextual issue. Like the Chase impeachment, it was politically motivated; like that impeachment, it failed. The legal reasons for its failure illustrate the difficulty of defining grounds for the impeachment of a president.

The 1867 Attempt to Impeach President Johnson

After a wide-ranging investigation that lasted ten months, the House Judiciary Committee in November 1867 reported a resolution of impeachment against President Johnson. The committee had voted 5 to 4 to report the resolution, with five Radical Republicans favoring impeachment and two moderate Republicans and two Democrats in opposition.[42] Debate in the House in early December was limited to speeches on behalf of the Radical Republican majority and the two-man Republican minority.[43] The House voted to reject the impeachment resolution, 57 to 108,[44] and the usual interpretation is that the resolution failed because Johnson was not charged with a specific crime.

The two Republicans on the committee who opposed the resolution had argued in their minority report that impeachment requires proof of an indictable crime or misdemeanor and that, because common law crimes are not indictable in the federal courts, only federal statu-

42. 40th Cong., 1st Sess., H. Rept. No. 7 (Nov. 25, 1867).

43. The speeches appear in Con. Globe App., 40th Cong., 2d Sess., 54–62 (Dec. 5 and 6, 1867) (George S. Boutwell for the majority) and 62–5 (Dec. 6, 1867) (James F. Wilson, committee chairman, for the Republican minority).

44. Cong. Globe, 40th Cong., 2d Sess., 68 (Dec. 7, 1867).

tory crimes could serve as the basis for an impeachment.[45] In presenting the majority case for impeachment, George S. Boutwell conceded to the House, "If the theory of the law submitted by the minority of the committee be in the judgment of this House a true theory, then the majority of the committee have no case whatever."

Boutwell made a lengthy argument against the minority's theory. It assumed, he began, that Congress had the authority to enlarge or restrict the scope of the impeachment power by legislation. But Congress had no such authority; it could neither lay the foundation for impeachment by declaring an act that would not be criminal under the principles of the English common law to be a crime nor limit the impeachment power by declaring acts that "by the common judgment of mankind are crimes" to be "relieved from all taint and impurity" and officers guilty of them "free from responsibility." And it would be impossible for Congress "to anticipate by specific legislation all cases of misconduct which will occur in the career of criminal men" even if it had the authority. There were bound to be omissions. If Congress were to legislate for a century to declare what officers could not lawfully do, nonetheless

> the President of the United States may examine and avoid all statutes of restraint and inhibition, and then fearlessly and successfully usurp power, oppress the people, encourage discord, promote rebellion, corrupt public officers, humiliate and disgrace the nation by multitudinous acts of wrong, and there will be neither redress or relief.

The Constitution did not require this restriction on the scope of the impeachment power, Boutwell contended. The history of the government showed that the founders did not entertain the theory that impeachment reached only federal statutory crimes. The framers of the Constitution served in the government for a quarter of a century and "never took one step or suggested that one step should be taken" to enact the legislation that would be required to make the power of impeachment of any practical value under this theory—an omission that "would have been criminal in character" if they considered the theory to be true. And Boutwell attempted to explain why the 1812 Supreme Court opinion holding that the federal courts had no common law

45. 40th Cong., 1st Sess., H. Rept. No. 7 at 78.

criminal jurisdiction had no bearing on impeachment. Statutes are needed to give federal courts jurisdiction over particular offenses because the Constitution did not directly confer jurisdiction upon them. But all the conditions the Supreme Court held necessary to give courts jurisdiction over a crime are satisfied by the impeachment provisions of the Constitution itself, Boutwell argued. Furthermore, the language of the Constitution indicates that "bribery or other high crimes and misdemeanors" are to be interpreted by the rules of common law. If this were not so, these terms would have been defined in the Constitution, as treason was, or Congress would have been given specific authority to act on the subject.

On behalf of the Republicans opposed to impeachment, James F. Wilson, the chairman of the Judiciary Committee, abandoned the argument that federal statutory crimes are required for impeachment. This part of the minority report, he said, "might be stricken from the record without affecting the case in the remotest degree." The minority believed the doctrine to be correct, but stated it in the report only as a suggestion, which might be important in future cases, rather than as an affirmative declaration of the law. The minority did not expect that "any determination of the present proceeding will either approve or disapprove it," Wilson said. "It is immaterial what opinions members may have of it."

The exchange between Boutwell and Wilson narrowed the ground of their disagreement on the law of impeachment. Wilson, however, was not conceding that an indictable offense was unnecessary for impeachment. Rather, he contended that the case against President Johnson had to be "tested by the principles of criminal law" to determine if high crimes and misdemeanors were disclosed. "[N]o civil officer of the United States can be lawfully impeached except for a crime or misdemeanor known to the law," he asserted, including "the range of both statutory and common law impeachable crimes."

For the committee majority advocating impeachment, Boutwell argued that "bribery or other high crimes and misdemeanors" was used in the Constitution "in accordance with and subject to the rule of reason, which lies at the foundation of the English common law." That rule provided that "no person in office shall do an act *contra bonos mores*, contrary to good morals." Neither the president nor any other officer "can lawfully do any act, either official or otherwise, which in a large, a public sense is contrary to the good morals of the office he holds." The scope of the rule of common law, he contended, is not to be ascertained simply by reference to past cases, for the rule furnishes not only a foundation for these cases but for others that may arise. The security for an officer against impeachment and removal lies first in his own conscience and judgment and then in the reason and conscience of his judges, the Senate.

Especially impeachable, Boutwell said, are acts that "affect the welfare or existence of the State, or render the officer unfit for the discharge of his duties." Not every crime at law is impeachable, nor are impeachable offenses necessarily indictable. He referred to Story's view that impeachable offenses are of "a political character," including not merely legal crimes, but "what are aptly termed political offenses, growing out of personal misconduct, or gross neglect, or usurpation, or habitual disregard of the public interests in the discharge of the duties of political office." These offenses are "so various in their character and so indefinable in their actual involutions that it is almost impossible to provide for them by positive law," Story had written; they "must be examined on very broad and comprehensive principles of policy and duty." Story's description, Boutwell said, "clearly set forth in its general language the offenses of which the majority of the committee complain."

Boutwell also adopted Blackstone's definition of a crime or misdemeanor—"an act committed or omitted in violation of a public law either forbidding or commanding it." In the American system the Constitution and statutes are public law, he said, and "any act done by the President which is forbidden by the law or by the Constitution, or the omission by him to do what is by the law or the Constitution commanded" is a high crime and misdemeanor. The "vital part" of the Constitution with reference to the public affairs of the country is that the president shall take care that the laws be faithfully executed, and "he violates that great provision . . . especially when he himself disregards the law either by doing that which is forbidden or neglecting that which he is commanded to do."

Early in his argument Boutwell had reminded the House of its discretion in the exercise of the impeachment power. Because its action was not subject to revision, the House, "in the exercise of its best judgment and conscience," could give heed to the rule that the law takes no notice of trifles. Although the committee had no such discretion and might feel compelled to report a conclusion based upon unimportant, technical violations of law, the House could decide that they were too unimportant to warrant impeachment. And the House could go still further. Despite evidence that the president was guilty of impeachable offenses of so high a character that under other circumstances it would be compelled to impeach, the House could conclude that "the evil of attempting to correct them in the manner appointed by the Constitution is greater than submission to the continued evil of his administration" and decline to prosecute. The House "acts in its judgment upon the evidence first, but upon its conscience in its regard to public policy whether it will proceed or not." Although he professed to doubt "the power of this House to censure the President as an independent proposition," Boutwell said, "I cannot doubt its power to declare, if it choose so to do, that the President is guilty of impeachable high crimes and misdemeanors, but that upon considerations of public policy it is not for the present wise to prosecute those charges to trial and final judgment."

In his speech against impeachment Wilson was particularly critical of Boutwell's reliance on the "conscience of the House" to guide the exercise of the impeachment power. It would, he said, prevent the Senate from determining "the presence or absence of those elements which alone can constitute any act a real crime." While the House was currently directed by a Republican conscience, it might in the future be directed by a Democratic conscience. "Does he desire us to intrust the character, extent, and uses of this power to the shifting fortunes of political parties? What could be more dangerous to the peace and safety of the Government than this?" The doctrine might carry this case to the determination Boutwell desired, Wilson said, but "can he not see that it may return to plague him and the country?" Boutwell's argument that Congress could not make criminal an act lacking the elements of a crime under common law was "fatal to his argument and destructive of his case," Wilson asserted:

> [T]he conscience of the House is as much bound by [this doctrine] when exercising the impeaching power as it is in matters of ordinary legislation. You cannot bind the ordinary legislative power of this House by the principle . . . and then, when you come to exercise the impeaching power, brush it out of the way

> in order that the obnoxious officer may be removed without the presentation of some act involving the well-known elements of crime.

Wilson also criticized Story's contention, adopted by Boutwell, that the House could impeach for "political offenses":

> What is a "political offense?" Is it the doing of something that the dominant political party in the country do not like? . . . We did not like the removal of our own friends from office by the present President. Are we to impeach for that? He has done many acts of political littleness, meanness, and treachery. Are these impeachable political offenses? . . . [I]t is unsafe for us to wander into the field of political or party action for offenses upon which to rest the impeaching power of this House. Disaster alone could result from such a course of procedure.

The position of the minority, he said, was that "this body must be guided by the law, and not by that indefinite something called its conscience, which may be one thing to-day and quite a different one to-morrow." If there were high crimes and misdemeanors in the record, Boutwell was right in demanding impeachment; if not, "no amount of conscience in House and Senate can justify us in proceeding further with it."

With respect to the facts, Boutwell conceded on behalf of the majority advocating impeachment that "[t]he country was disappointed, no doubt, in the report of the committee, and very likely this House participated in the disappointment, that there was no specific, heinous, novel offense charged upon and proved against the President of the United States." But this was "in the very nature of the case." There were "a series of acts, . . . a succession of events," pointing to the offense with which he was charged—

> that he used as he had the opportunity, and misused as necessity and circumstances dictated, the great powers of the nation with which he was intrusted, for the purpose of reconstructing this Government in the interest of the rebellion, so that henceforth this Union . . . should be merely the continuation of the [Confederate] Government.

Boutwell acknowledged that the particular acts were not of "any great enormity." But,

> [w]hen you bring all these acts together; when you consider what he has said; when you consider what he has done; when you consider that he has appropriated the public property for the benefit of rebels; when you consider that in every public act, as far as we can learn, from May, 1865, to the present time, all has tended to this great result, the restoration of the rebels to power under and in the Government of the country; when you consider all these things, can there be any doubt as to his purpose, or doubt as to the criminality of his purpose and his responsibility under the Constitution?

"It may not be possible, by specific charge, to arraign him for this great crime," Boutwell said, "but is he therefore to escape?" He contended that the individual acts were themselves impeachable and were "the subordinate crimes, the tributary offenses to the accomplishment of the great object which he had in view." He urged the House to impeach if satisfied of Johnson's purpose and that "these tributary offenses were committed as the means of enabling him to accomplish this great crime," even if the charges "appear to be of inferior importance," knowing that "in this way, and in this way only, can you protect the State against the final consummation of his crime."

"We have not yet seen the end of this contest," Boutwell asserted. Only two days earlier, in his annual message to Congress, Johnson had declared that in certain circumstances the executive could resist unconstitutional laws and had stated his opposition to black suffrage. Boutwell asked,

> Are we to leave this officer, if we judge him to be guilty of high crimes and misdemeanors, in control of the Army and the Navy, with his declaration upon the record that under certain circumstances he will not execute the law?

President Johnson controlled the army; "a single soldier at each polling place in the southern country, aided by the whites, could prevent the entire negro population from voting" in the next election. "[I]f it is for the interest of the President to do so have we any reason to anticipate a different course of conduct?" Boutwell asked. If Johnson followed the logic of the propositions in his annual message, Boutwell asserted, the presidential election would be "heralded by civil war," the next inauguration "the occasion for the renewal of fratricidal strife."

For the Republican minority of the committee, Wilson denied that the House could impeach to prevent future misconduct by Johnson:

> Are we to impeach the President for what he may do in the future? Do our fears constitute in the President high crimes and misdemeanors? Are we to wander beyond the record of this case and found our judgment of it on the possibilities of the future?

The House, Wilson said, "must be guided by some rule in this grave proceeding—something more certain than an impossibility to arraign the President for a specific crime." He asked the House,

> If we cannot arraign the President for a specific crime for what are we to proceed against him? For a bundle of generalities such as we have in the volume of testimony reported by the committee to the House in this case? If we cannot state upon paper a specific crime how are we to carry this case to the Senate for trial?

The Republican majority and minority also differed on their interpretation of the facts and of the illegality of the particular acts alleged against Johnson. The legal issues, however, basically boiled down to two: (1) Was it the broad "principle" of common law, which would permit impeachment for nonindictable conduct, or the common law of crimes that governed? (2) In the absence of a single serious offense, could the House impeach for an aggregation of smaller acts? Wilson, in opposition to impeachment, seemed to endorse the view that it would be available if there were a specific offense meeting the indictability criterion he advocated. And both the majority and the minority agreed that the political preconditions for impeachment were present; indeed, Wilson described Johnson in his speech as "the worst of the Presidents." In its report the Republican minority had characterized the case against Johnson as a political success. "Rest the case upon political offences," the minority wrote, "and we are prepared to pronounce against the President, for such offences are numerous and grave." While acquitting him of impeachable crimes, they "pronounce[d] him guilty of many wrongs." But, the minority concluded, "the day of political impeachments would be a sad one for this country. Political unfitness and incapacity must be tried at the ballot-box, not in the high court of impeachment."[46]

46. *Ibid.*, 105.

The Impeachment of President Johnson

On February 21, 1868, some two and one-half months after the House had rejected the impeachment resolution reported by the Judiciary Committee, President Johnson ordered the removal from office of Secretary of War Edwin M. Stanton and authorized Major General Lorenzo Thomas to act as interim secretary. That evening the Senate adopted a resolution stating that "under the Constitution and laws of the United States the President has no power to remove the Secretary of War and to designate any other officer to perform the duties of that office *ad interim*."[47] The Committee on Reconstruction reported a resolution of impeachment against Johnson to the House the following day.[48] The next day it met, February 24, the House voted, 126 to 47, to impeach.[49]

Johnson's actions were argued to be in violation of the Tenure of Office Act,[50] which had been passed primarily to prevent Johnson from removing Republican officeholders. The act provided that any officer appointed with the advice and consent of the Senate would hold office until his successor was similarly appointed. Cabinet officers were the subject of a proviso (the meaning and effect of which became one of the crucial issues of the impeachment trial) stating that they "shall hold their offices . . . for and during the term of the President by whom they may have been appointed, and for one month thereafter, subject to removal by and with the advice and consent of the Senate." The act also provided that, when the Senate was in recess, the president could suspend an officer and appoint a temporary replacement until the Senate met again and decided whether the officer should be removed. President Johnson had suspended Stanton in August 1867 and notified the Senate when it reconvened in December. In January the Senate had refused to concur in the suspension. (Whether this suspension was under the Tenure of Office Act was another issue litigated in the impeachment trial.) And the act carried a criminal penalty for violations, which it said "shall be deemed and are hereby declared to be high misdemeanors."

Those who believed a criminal offense was necessary for impeach-

47. 1 Johnson Trial 156–7.
48. Cong. Globe, 40th Cong., 2d Sess., 1336.
49. *Ibid.*, 1400.
50. Act of March 2, 1867, ch. 102, 14 Stat. 430.

ment were now satisfied. Wilson said that the considerations that caused him to oppose impeachment in December "are not to be found in the present case":

> The logic of the former case is made plain, not to say perfect, by its sequence in the present one. The President was working to an end suspected by others, known to himself. His then means were not known to the law as crimes or misdemeanors, either at common law or by statute, and we so pronounced. He mistook our judgment for cowardice, and worked on until he has presented to us, as a sequence, a high misdemeanor known to the law and defined by statute.

The president had "[d]eliberately, not to say defiantly," violated a federal penal statute, Wilson asserted.[51]

A select committee appointed to draft articles after Johnson's impeachment reported back charges based entirely on events surrounding the orders for the removal of Stanton and the designation of Thomas. The House adopted nine articles.

Article 1 charged that the issuance of the order for the removal of Stanton violated the Constitution and laws of the United States and that President Johnson had issued it with intent to violate the Tenure of Office Act and with the further intent to remove Stanton from office contrary to and in violation of the act, contrary to the Constitution, and without the advice and consent of the Senate, which was then in session.

Articles 2, 3, and 8 were based on the authorization of Thomas to act as interim secretary of war. Article 2 charged that the letter of authority was issued and delivered to Thomas in violation of the Constitution, contrary to the Tenure of Office Act, without the advice and consent of the Senate, and without authority of law, there being no vacancy in the office of secretary of war. The article charged intent to violate the Constitution and the Tenure of Office Act. Article 3 charged that the appointment of Thomas as interim secretary while the Senate was in session without its advice and consent, was without authority of law, no vacancy having happened during the recess of the Senate and no vacancy existing at the time. Intent to violate the Constitution was alleged. Article 8 resembled Article 2, but charged that

51. Cong. Globe, 40th Cong., 2d Sess., 1386–7.

President Johnson issued and delivered the letter of authority to Thomas with intent unlawfully to control the disbursements of the War Department, as well as with intent to violate and disregard the Tenure of Office Act.

Articles 4–7 charged President Johnson with unlawfully conspiring with Thomas. Articles 4 and 6 were based on the federal conspiracy statute of 1861 and charged a "high crime in office."[52] Article 4 charged conspiracy with intent, by intimidation and force, unlawfully to hinder and prevent Stanton from holding the office of secretary of war, contrary to and in violation of the Constitution. Article 6 charged conspiracy by force to seize, take, and possess the property of the United States in the Department of War in Stanton's custody and control, with intent to violate and disregard the Tenure of Office Act. Articles 5 and 7 charged the common law crime of conspiracy, a misdemeanor in the District of Columbia. Article 5 charged conspiracy continuing to March 2, 1868 (the day the articles were reported to the House), to prevent and hinder the execution of the Tenure of Office Act and, in pursuance of the conspiracy, an unlawful attempt to prevent Stanton from holding his office. Article 7 charged conspiracy with intent to seize, take, and possess the property of the United States in Stanton's custody and control, with intent to violate and disregard the Tenure of Office Act.

Article 9 concerned a meeting on February 2, 1868, between President Johnson and Major General William H. Emory, commander of the military department of Washington. It charged that President Johnson had instructed Emory that a provision of the 1868 Army Appropriations Act, requiring that "all orders and instructions relating to military operations, issued by the President or Secretary of War, shall be issued through the General of the army," was unconstitutional. The act provided that "any officer who shall issue orders or instructions contrary [to the provision] shall be deemed guilty of a misdemeanor in office." The article charged intent to induce Emory to

52. The statute made it a "high crime" for two or more persons within any State or Territory to conspire by force to seize, take, or possess any property of the United States against the will or contrary to the authority of the United States (the basis for Article 6) and by force, intimidations, or threats to prevent any person from accepting or holding any office of trust or place of confidence under the United States (the basis for Article 4). Also covered were conspiracies to overthrow the government by force, to levy war against the United States, and by force to prevent, hinder, or delay the execution of any law of the United States. Act of July 31, 1861, ch. 33, 12 Stat. 284.

violate the act and to obey President Johnson's orders not issued through the general of the army and the further intent thereby to enable Johnson to prevent the execution of the Tenure of Office Act and to unlawfully prevent Stanton from holding office and discharging the duties of secretary of war.

The drafting committee had rejected an article, proposed by Benjamin Butler, that did not allege an indictable crime. Butler's suggested article charged President Johnson with making speeches in the 1866 congressional campaign attempting to bring Congress into disgrace, with the design and intent of setting aside its rightful authority and power. The speeches were alleged to have brought the office of president into contempt, ridicule, and disgrace. Butler offered the article as an amendment in committee of the whole, where it was rejected by a vote of 45 to 56.[53]

After the first nine articles were adopted, the House elected managers for the impeachment trial, including Butler. He persuaded the managers to bring his proposed article before the House again. This time it was adopted, 87 to 43, and became Article 10. In urging its adoption by the House, Butler derided the doctrine that an indictable crime was required for impeachment. He had supposed, he said, that the doctrine "was dead and buried—I knew it stunk." He ridiculed the proposition that the president could be impeached "for the lowest degree of indictable crime," but not for usurping the liberties of the people because it was not indictable:

> He may be impeached for selling liquor without a license, but he cannot be impeached if he gets into an open barouche with two abandoned women, one on each side of him, roaring drunk, and rides up and down Pennsylvania avenue, because there is no statute that I know of against that. He cannot be impeached for any violation of public decency which does not happen to be an indictable crime. He can not be impeached for debasing his high office. The statement of this proposition is its own refutation.

Butler told the House that his article was "drawn exactly within the precedent" of the eighth article of impeachment against Justice Chase, which had received more votes than any other in that trial. And he

53. Cong. Globe, 40th Cong., 2d Sess., 1616.

said, inaccurately, that Chase's counsel did not venture to argue that Article 8 did not charge an impeachable misdemeanor.[54]

In its final form Article 10 charged that, unmindful of the high duties and "the dignities and proprieties" of his office and of "the harmony and courtesies which ought to exist and be maintained between the executive and legislative branches," President Johnson, "designing and intending to set aside the rightful authority and powers of Congress," attempted to bring Congress into "disgrace, ridicule, hatred, and reproach," to "impair and destroy the regard and respect of all the good people of the United States" for Congress and its legislative powers, and "to excite [their] odium and resentment" against Congress and the laws it enacted. In pursuance of this design and intent, the article charged, Johnson made and delivered, "with a loud voice, certain intemperate, inflammatory, and scandalous harangues," uttering "loud threats and bitter menaces" against Congress and the laws duly enacted by it "amid the cries, jeers, and laughter of the multitudes then assembled and in hearing." Three specifications were included—to a speech in the Executive Mansion in August 1866, to a second speech in Cleveland in September, and to a third in St. Louis, also in September. The article concluded:

> Which said utterances, declarations, threats, and harangues, highly censurable in any, are peculiarly indecent and unbecoming in the Chief Magistrate of the United States, by means whereof . . . Andrew Johnson has brought the high office of the President of the United States into contempt, ridicule, and disgrace, to the great scandal of all good citizens.

The managers also proposed another article, sponsored originally by Thaddeus Stevens. Stevens called his proposed article "the gist and vital portion of this whole prosecution." Without it, he said, "shrewd lawyers . . . and cavilling judges" would acquit Johnson unless "they are greener than I was in any case I ever undertook before the court of quarter sessions." The article was agreed to by a vote of 108–32 and became Article 11.[55]

Article 11 stated that President Johnson had declared in substance in a speech in August 1866 that the Thirty-ninth Congress was not a

54. *Ibid.*, 1640–2.
55. *Ibid.*, 1612, 1642.

Congress authorized by the Constitution to execute legislative power, but a Congress of only part of the states, and that he thereby denied and intended to deny that its legislation was valid or obligatory upon him and that it had the power to propose amendments to the Constitution. The article charged that, in pursuance of this declaration, unlawfully and in disregard of the constitutional requirement that he take care that the laws be faithfully executed, President Johnson on February 21, 1868, attempted to prevent the execution of the Tenure of Office Act by devising and contriving (and attempting to devise and contrive) means to prevent Stanton from resuming the functions of secretary of war after the Senate refused to concur in his suspension, to prevent the execution of the Army Appropriations Act, and to prevent the execution of the Reconstruction Act. (Each of these laws was enacted just before the end of the Thirty-ninth Congress in 1867.) At the conclusion of the trial Chief Justice Salmon P. Chase construed this article narrowly, stating that "[t]he single substantive matter charged is the attempt to prevent the execution of the tenure-of-office act; and the other facts are alleged either as introductory and exhibiting this general purpose, or as showing the means contrived in furtherance of that attempt."[56]

The Issues in the Johnson Trial

As the proof and the arguments in the trial of President Johnson evolved, it was evident that the issues in the case centered on two acts—the issuance of the order for Stanton's removal and the issuance of the letter of authority to General Thomas to act as interim secretary. The key articles were 1, 2, 3, and 11.[57]

While not abandoned, the other articles were less strenuously argued. The Senate voted not to admit evidence the managers claimed was relevant to the allegation in Article 8 that Johnson issued the letter of authority to Thomas with the intent of controlling the disbursements of the War Department,[58] leaving that article on the same evidentiary footing as Article 2. The proof concerning Article 9 established that President Johnson stated his opinion to General Emory

56. 2 Johnson Trial 480–1.
57. The articles appear at 1 Johnson Trial 6–10. (Hereafter in this chapter references to the Johnson Trial will be given by volume and page numbers.)
58. I:257–68.

that the provision of the Army Appropriations Act was unconstitutional, but it provided little support for the allegation that he was seeking to induce Emory to obey his direct orders to force Stanton from office.[59] The evidence on the conspiracy articles (primarily Thomas's declarations of his intentions) failed to convince a number of senators that there was intent to use force or intimidation.[60] In addition, the defense made a number of legal arguments against these articles—among them, that the federal conspiracy law was a war statute, wholly inapplicable in the circumstances; that this law did not apply within the District of Columbia because it was not a "Territory" for purposes of that statute; and that common law conspiracy, a crime within the District of Columbia by virtue of an 1801 federal statute adopting Maryland criminal law for the district, did not apply in a federal impeachment.[61] Finally, the defense contended that the issuance of the order by Johnson to Thomas could not be characterized as a conspiratorial agreement. "[T]here can be no such thing as a conspiracy between the Commander-in-chief and a subordinate officer, arising simply from the fact, that the Commander-in-chief issues an order and his subordinate officer obeys it," former Supreme Court Justice Benjamin Curtis argued; military obedience "is not conspiracy and cannot be conspiracy."[62]

Butler devoted a considerable part of the opening argument for the managers in the trial to Article 10 and later introduced evidence on the content of the speeches and the manner of their delivery. Other managers spoke on behalf of the article in their closing arguments, but it was not pressed as vigorously as the charges involving the Stanton removal. John Bingham, who made the final argument, contended

59. I:233–9 (Emory testimony); I:701–4 (Welles testimony).

60. For testimony on this subject, see I:164–70 (Van Horn); 170–4 (Moorhead); 174–5, 209–10, 214–7, 218–20 (Burleigh); 220–3 (Wilkeson); 223–30, 231–2 (Karsner); 232–3 (Ferry); 415–50, 452–60 (Thomas).

61. II:332 (Evarts), I:406 (Curtis), II:333 (Evarts).

62. I:201. Compare John Doar's argument to the House Judiciary Committee in the Nixon inquiry: "I don't believe that it is possible to have a conspiracy involving the President of the United States. The president "is different," "supreme because of his awesome power granted to him under the Constitution." Those working for him "are more extensions of him than co-conspirators if there is a crime"; "you just don't have co-participation [or] co-equals." There is only one president, who "is in charge and directs the operation." 93d Cong., 2d Sess., House, Comm. on the Judiciary, *Summary of Information, Hearings . . . Pursuant to H. Res. 803* at 11 (hereafter Summary of Information), also appearing in Impeachment Inquiry, Book III, 1933 (July 19, 1974).

that the first specification (involving a speech delivered in the Executive Mansion) charged an indictable crime by virtue of the common law against seditious utterances. His theory of the applicable law, however, required him to abandon the portions of Article 10 involving speeches outside the District of Columbia.[63]

The defense argued that Article 10 failed to charge impeachable conduct. They did not recognize common law crimes, and in their view Johnson had violated no law. Moreover, they argued, the charge was stale; the Thirty-ninth Congress, against which the speeches were directed, had not acted upon them, and the House had not considered them sufficient for impeachment when it rejected the December resolution. To remove President Johnson for political speeches in his private capacity, they contended, would violate his constitutional right to free speech. And they suggested that the article proposed an unrealistic standard of decorum for political rhetoric, which even congressional debate did not meet, as they proceeded to demonstrate.[64]

The heart of the case, therefore, involved the orders of February 21. The defense against these charges involved a number of arguments, not entirely consistent. With respect to the order of removal, it was argued, first, that the order was not a crime under the Tenure of Office Act, which made a "removal" contrary to its provisions criminal but not an attempt to remove. Second, the Tenure of Office Act was inapplicable to Stanton. Third, the act was unconstitutional. Fourth, even if the act did apply to Stanton and was constitutional, President Johnson should not be removed for a mistaken interpretation of law, made in good faith and with the advice of his cabinet. Fifth, Johnson's intention was to test the constitutionality of the Tenure of Office Act in the Supreme Court, which as president he had a right—even a duty—to do. Sixth, even if Johnson had no such right, he should not be removed for a good faith mistake in construing his constitutional duties and powers. Finally, even if all of these arguments were unavailing, the president's conduct had resulted in no public injury; it was merely a technical crime, which was insufficient cause for his removal from office.

The arguments concerning Thomas's designation as interim secretary were closely connected with those on the removal order. The

63. II:409–10.

64. I:411–2 (Curtis); II:180–3 (Nelson); II:213–4 (Groesbeck); II:326–31 (Evarts); II:377–9 (Stanberry).

defense argued that the letter of authority was not criminal under the Tenure of Office Act, which was silent on temporary designations of officers to fill vacancies while the Senate was in session. They professed to find statutory authority for the temporary appointment in a 1795 statute, which they argued had not been repealed by a later, more limited law enacted in 1863. Even if there was no statutory authority, the president had the inherent power to provide for the continued functioning of the War Department by designating someone to perform the duties of secretary when there was a vacancy; this authority arose out of necessity, and was supported by usage and custom. And, of course, the arguments about mistake of law, lack of evil purpose, and the insubstantiality of the conduct applied to the letter of authority to Thomas, as well as the removal order.

It is not necessary to analyze each of these lines of argument in detail. Some of them, and particularly those involving statutory construction, are of merely historical interest; they are also extremely complicated, in part because it served the interests of the defense to make them complicated. As William Evarts said, in response to the contention that the meaning of the Tenure of Office Act was not ambiguous, but plain, "[W]e certainly have belied . . . the proposition of this absolute plainness, for we have spent a great many words on this subject on the one side and the other."[65] Under the defense theory of the case, the more difficult and complex the legal questions, the more favorable to President Johnson; a substantial part of their argument was devoted to creating doubt in the minds of senators about the interpretation of the law, thereby suggesting that Johnson could honestly have committed one or another legal error without fault.

Criminality, the Attempt Argument, and Article 1

Before dealing with the crux of Johnson's defense, it is necessary to consider the role of the criminality argument in the Johnson trial and its applicability, in particular, to the offense charged in Article 1—the issuance of the order of removal with intent to violate the Tenure of Office Act.

The managers made two arguments on the definition of grounds for impeachment. The first approach, advocated by the Radical Republicans—especially Butler—was that a criminal offense was not required. Butler defined an impeachable high crime or misdemeanor as

65. II:352.

> one in its nature or consequences subversive of some fundamental or essential principle of government, or highly prejudicial to the public interest, and this may consist of a violation of the Constitution, of law, of an official oath, or of duty, by an act committed or omitted, or, without violating a positive law, by the abuse of discretionary powers from improper motives, or for any improper purpose.

The proceeding was "rather more in the nature of an inquest of office" than of a trial, he contended; the Senate was "a constitutional tribunal solely, . . . bound by no law, either statute or common, which may limit [its] constitutional prerogative." "You are a law unto yourselves," he told the Senate, "bound only by the natural principles of equity and justice." In their closing arguments, other managers took a similar position. An indictable crime was not required for impeachment, John Logan asserted; impeachment is "an inquisition of office for any act of the officer or cause which the House of Representatives might present as, and the Senate adjudicate to be hurtful to the state or injurious to the common weal." George S. Boutwell repeated the contention he had made to the House in December that the President was impeachable for "any act contrary to the good morals of the office." Thaddeus Stevens argued that any "malfeasance . . . willingly perpetrated by an office-holder is a misdemeanor in office, whatever he may allege was his intention." Thomas Williams, who had written the majority report in support of the 1867 impeachment resolution, said that impeachment was not "to be tried or judged by the rigid rules and narrow interpretations of the criminal courts."[66]

Bingham, the leading conservative Republican among the managers and their chairman, acknowledged that an indictable crime was required for impeachment. The crime, however, need not be a criminal violation of a federal statute because "by the laws of the United States all crimes and misdemeanors at the common law, committed within the District of Columbia, are made indictable." At common law, he said, "an indictment lies for all misdemeanors of a public evil

66. I:88 (emphasis omitted), 89–90; II:23, 107, 223, 259. James F. Wilson was also a manager, but made no closing argument. During the trial, in support of an objection to the introduction of evidence that Johnson's cabinet advised him that the Tenure of Office Act was unconstitutional before he vetoed it, Wilson argued that the president was impeachable for any criminal failure to execute the law. "[E]very willful failure, no matter what its inducement may be, is criminal" (I:684).

example, for neglecting duties imposed by law, and for offences against common decency." The president was therefore impeachable for the "wilful violation" of acts of Congress not repealed or actually reversed by the courts. Abuse of power, as well as usurpation of power, was impeachable. "[A] refusal to do an act required by the law of an officer," an "attempt to procure another or others to violate law, on the part of such officer," and "seditious utterances by an executive officer" were all indictable at common law and therefore grounds for impeachment. Moreover, unlike a judge, who could not be held to answer for an error of law, mistakes of law by a "mere executive officer clothed with no judicial authority" could not be excused.[67]

The defense argued for a narrower interpretation of grounds for impeachment. There must be "high criminal offences against the United States, made so by some law of the United States existing when the acts complained of were done," crimes subversive of a fundamental principle of government or highly prejudicial to the public interest, "crimes against the Constitution or the laws involving turpitude or personal delinquency." Thomas A. R. Nelson took the narrowest view of all, asserting that only felonies and misdemeanors punishable by both fine and imprisonment were impeachable. And, he said, they must be crimes known to the British common law at the time the Constitution was adopted; he expressed doubt that Congress could create a crime or misdemeanor "in its nature different" from these offenses.[68]

The defense rejected Bingham's reliance on the common law of crimes in the District of Columbia. This was the essential point in their attack on the technical sufficiency of Article 1. Nelson acknowledged that there had been an attempt to remove Stanton. But, he said, the distinction between a crime and an attempt to commit a crime is "just as broad and as wide as Pennsylvania avenue"; there was no removal and therefore the penal provision of the Tenure of Office Act was inapplicable.[69]

Because the act was a penal statute, Evarts asserted, it was to be strictly construed. An indictment against Johnson would fail if Stanton had not been removed. The Senate was to try the crime as charged in the article, a removal was not charged, and so the article contained

67. II:409–10, 413, 459, 413.
68. I:409 (Curtis); II:286, 322 (Evarts); II:140, 143 (Nelson).
69. II:152.

"neither crime nor indictment." Perhaps, Evarts suggested sarcastically, it would be said that "in so small a matter as the question of the removal of a President it does not do to insist upon the usual construction of a criminal law." But if the insufficiency of the pleading would be good at law, "then it is good against impeachment, or else you must come back to the proposition that you do not need a legal crime."[70]

Henry Stanberry (who had resigned as attorney general to defend Johnson) said there had been only an unsuccessful effort to remove Stanton and "[n]o latitude of construction can torture an attempt to make a removal into an actual removal, or can turn an abortive effort to do a given thing into the accomplished fact." There was "a total failure" of the first article on this point alone, he said, and this article was "the head and front of the entire case. Strike it out, and all that remains is 'leather and prunella.' "[71]

The managers responded that the articles need not meet the technical requirements for an indictment. Moreover, it was a settled rule of criminal law—"common law as well as common sense," Bingham said—that an attempt to commit a misdemeanor is itself a misdemeanor.[72] Finally, the penal provision of the Tenure of Office Act could be construed to cover the issuance of an order of removal, especially because otherwise it would lead to an absurdity, since no removal contrary to law could legally occur.

Lest it be thought that the defense argument was merely an unimportant quibble, it should be noted that it bore some fruit, not only in its application to Article 1 (which was never voted upon by the Senate). The key votes for President Johnson's acquittal were cast by seven Republican Senators.[73] Six of these Senators filed written opinions, and four of them noted this point in discussing Article 1.[74] A fifth, P. G. Van Winkle, rested his opinion on Article 1 on an even

70. II:349.

71. II:371.

72. II:439.

73. The seven were William P. Fessenden of Maine, Joseph S. Fowler of Tennessee, James W. Grimes of Iowa, John B. Henderson of Missouri, Lyman Trumbull of Illinois, Edmund G. Ross of Kansas, and P. G. Van Winkle of West Virginia.

74. Ross, whose courage John F. Kennedy profiled, wrote no opinion. The four who indicated that the attempt argument was among the reasons they would have voted not guilty on Article 1 were Fessenden (III:22), Fowler (III:194), Henderson (III:304), and Trumbull (III:319–20).

narrower technicality. He found that the article did not charge an attempt to remove because it contained no allegation that the order had been delivered to Stanton; the order itself said that Stanton's functions would terminate upon his receipt of it, so there was not even an intention to remove until the order was delivered. "There is no clause in the act that forbids or denounces the mere issue, without some further act, of such a paper as the order in writing, and such an issue could not be even an attempt to remove from office," Van Winkle wrote. He acknowledged that Johnson had admitted delivery of the order in his answer and there was proof of it before the Senate, but this could not cure the defect in the article. The evidence could not be applicable to an article in which delivery was not mentioned, and the answer could not confess what was not charged.[75]

In explaining his vote to acquit on the eleventh article, Van Winkle acknowledged that an attempted prevention of the execution of the law was a misdemeanor. But he did not think that "merely devising and contriving means by which such prevention might be effected is an attempt to commit the act which constitutes the offense." An intention, not followed by any act, was not a misdemeanor. Another of the Republicans voting not guilty, Joseph S. Fowler of Tennessee, made a similar point. An attempt to commit a misdemeanor was itself a misdemeanor, Fowler also recognized, but "devising and contriving and attempting to devise and contrive an attempt to commit a misdemeanor can scarcely be so regarded by any tribunal other than an inquisition."[76]

The Construction of the Tenure of Office Act

Whether the Tenure of Office Act protected Stanton from removal by the president was debated at length in the trial. Stanton had been appointed by President Lincoln during his first term, to serve at the pleasure of the president, and after Lincoln's death in April 1865 he continued to serve under President Johnson. The Tenure of Office Act, passed in March 1867, provided that "every person holding any civil office to which he has been appointed by and with the advice and consent of the Senate, and every person who shall hereafter be ap-

75. III:148. Van Winkle's entire opinion, wrote Senator Charles Sumner of Massachusetts, treated the impeachment "as if it were a prosecution for sheep-stealing in the police court of Wheeling" (III:274).

76. III:152, 206.

pointed to any such office . . . , is and shall be entitled to hold" his office until a successor shall have been appointed in a like manner, "except as herein otherwise provided." There followed the proviso that cabinet officers (including the secretary of war) "shall hold their offices respectively for and during the term of the President by whom they may have been appointed, and for one month thereafter, subject to removal by and with the advice and consent of the Senate."

The proviso had been drafted in conference committee as a compromise between the Senate position that cabinet officers should be excluded entirely from the legislation and continue to serve at the pleasure of the president and the House position that they should be treated like all other officers and hold their offices until a successor was appointed. Senator John B. Henderson of Missouri wrote in his opinion supporting Johnson's acquittal that the language of the proviso was an instance of the reprehensible practice of saving important measures from defeat by having differences between the two houses "healed and covered up in conference committees with ambiguous or unmeaning phrases." Instead of clearing up doubts, Henderson wrote, "we often purposely obscure the controverted point, and devolve its solution upon the courts, or the President."[77]

Whether purposefully or not, the language in the proviso was ambiguous. What was "the term of the President" by whom Stanton was appointed? Had Lincoln's second term expired at his death and Stanton's tenure one month later, so he continued to hold office only by Johnson's sufferance? Or was Stanton protected by the proviso until April 1869, one month after the end of the term for which Lincoln had been elected? Alternatively, did the proviso have prospective application only, so that it did not affect Stanton at all? And, if he was not within the proviso, was he subject to the basic provision (applicable to "every person holding any civil office" appointed with the Senate's advice and consent) or excluded entirely from statutory protection?

The legislative history suggested that Stanton was not protected, though it was not clear-cut. Senator John Sherman of Ohio, who had been on the conference committee, had explicitly told the Senate that the compromise provision would not prevent President Johnson from removing the secretary of war or other members of the cabinet ap-

77. III:301.

pointed by Lincoln, though he had gone on to say that if one of these officers should refuse to resign when asked to do so by the president, Sherman would vote for his removal, implying that the proviso might apply. The effect of the basic provision on Stanton had not been debated at all.

The legislative history, and especially Sherman's statement, was the apparent reason that Article 1 was never brought to a vote. Senator Sherman concluded that he could not convict President Johnson for doing something that he had himself said the president could do; while he could vote guilty on other articles (including the eleventh) he could not vote guilty on articles based on the removal of Stanton.[78]

The Constitutionality of the Tenure of Office Act

The Senate had implicitly upheld the constitutionality of the Tenure of Office Act on four occasions—when it initially passed the legislation; when it passed it over President Johnson's veto, which was based on its asserted unconstitutionality; when it refused to concur in Stanton's suspension; and when it adopted the resolution of February 21 holding that the removal of Stanton and designation of Thomas was without legal authority and contrary to the Constitution. For the defense, William S. Groesbeck told the Senate, "I will not challenge its constitutionality here in your very faces; you have affirmed it."[79] Of course, he and his colleagues did argue the constitutional point, and at some length. Their purpose, however, was not so much to change the Senate's position on that issue as to buttress their argument that Johnson's opinion that the law was unconstitutional was held in good faith.

At their most extreme, the managers argued that the Senate could not even consider the constitutionality of the Act. A not guilty verdict on this basis, Butler said, would be a "conscious self-abnegation of the intelligent capacity" of Congress to legislate. The constitutionality of the law was a closed question, Bingham said; if the Senate were now

78. III:11. Senator Timothy O. Howe of Wisconsin reached a similar conclusion about the Tenure of Office Act, but indicated he would have voted guilty on Article 1 on the ground that Johnson abused his power of removal because he had no public purpose for removing Stanton (III:69). Among the Republicans who voted not guilty, five concluded that the act did not protect Stanton: Fessenden (III:21), Fowler (III:198), Grimes (III:333), Henderson (III:303), and Trumbull (III:323). Van Winkle reached the opposite conclusion (III:147).

79. II:201.

to consider it unconstitutional, it would be admitting that the members of Congress violated their oaths in passing it over President Johnson's veto. This would be making "a voluntary surrender of your good name, of your character, your conscience, in order to accommodate this accused and guilty culprit." Stevens inveighed against the idea that the Senate would reconsider the constitutionality of the law:

> And now this offspring of assassination turns upon the Senate, who have . . . rebuked him in a constitutional manner [by the resolution of February 21], and bids them defiance. How can he escape the just vengeance of the law? Wretched man, standing at bay, surrounded by a cordon of living men, each with the axe of an executioner uplifted for his just punishment. Every senator now trying him, except such as had already adopted his policy, voted for this same resolution, pronouncing his solemn doom. Will any of them vote for his acquittal on the ground of its unconstitutionality?

He warned that any who did would "suffer himself to be tortured on the gibbet of everlasting obloquy."[80]

The managers also offered a less vituperative argument, based on the constitutional responsibilities of the president. The Senate was trying the president on whether he had faithfully performed his constitutional duties, Boutwell said. It was the president's duty to see the laws executed, and this duty did not permit him to refuse to enforce laws unless they had been repealed or actually been held unconstitutional by the courts. If he could refuse to execute laws he believed unconstitutional, then his will or opinion would be substituted for the actions of the lawmaking power, and it would no longer be a government of laws, but a government of one man. And, if the Senate, trying the president upon an impeachment, could inquire into the constitutionality of a law he refused to obey, then he would be "tried for his judgment," not for his performance of his constitutional obligation. This would mean that the president, supported by one-third plus one Senators, could "set aside, disregard, and violate all the laws of the land," leaving "no security for the execution of the laws."[81]

President Johnson's vindication on the constitutional argument came not at his impeachment trial, but nearly sixty years later when

80. I:111; II:440–1, 227.
81. II:72–3.

the Supreme Court held that the president has the exclusive constitutional power to remove executive officers. Had the impeachment trial itself turned on this point, it is apparent from the written opinions that Johnson would have lost. Five of the six Republicans voting not guilty who filed written opinions acknowledged the constitutionality of the Tenure of Office Act, resting their votes for acquittal on other grounds.[82]

The President's Constitutional Duties and the Tenure of Office Act

The defense argued that President Johnson had the power to remove Stanton from office in order to obtain a Supreme Court test of the constitutionality of the Tenure of Office Act. In opening the case for the defense, Curtis said that the president was not asserting a power to refuse to enforce a law where all that was required of him was ministerial action or where the interests of third persons were affected. The occasions on which the president could take the necessary steps to have the validity of a law constitutionally decided were limited to those when

> a question arises whether a particular law has cut off a power confided to him by the people, through the Constitution, and he alone can raise that question, and he alone can cause a judicial decision to come between the two branches of the government to say which of them is right.

On these occasions, he continued, the president should carefully consider the question, determine that it necessarily arises and that the public service requires that it be decided, and obtain all competent and proper advice. If he then finds that "he cannot allow the law to operate in the particular case without abandoning a power which he believes has been confided to him by the people," Curtis said, "it is

82. Fessenden was not "convinced of its unconstitutionality" (III:19); Grimes wrote, "I shall not deny the constitutional validity" of the act, which was "not necessarily in this case" (III:331); Henderson admitted the act "to be clearly constitutional in all its parts" (III:301); Trumbull "entertain[ed] no doubt" of the power of Congress to define the tenure of offices it establishes and believed the act to be "constitutional and valid" (III:321); Van Winkle, "[c]onceding the constitutionality" of the act, went on to other issues (III:147).

The exception was Fowler, whose opinion suggests that he considered the act unconstitutional, although this was not the primary reason he gave for favoring acquittal (III:198–9).

his duty to assert the power and obtain a judicial decision thereon."[83]

The "first and paramount duty of the President" is to follow the Constitution, Groesbeck argued, and to maintain the integrity of the executive department is also a duty:

> [I]f an act of to-day is contrary to a long established interpretation of the Constitution upon a question of power, and a fit case presents itself where he is required to act, it is right and proper in a peaceable way, with a due regard to the public welfare, to test the accuracy of the new interpretation in the forum which is the highest and final interpreter of such questions.

The president's oath to preserve, protect, and defend the Constitution requires him to resist encroachments of the legislative department, Stanberry contended:

> Wherever a President is deliberately of opinion that an act of Congress calls upon him to exercise a power not given to him by the Constitution, he violates that Constitution if he follows it. Again, wherever he is called upon to execute a law which deprives him of a constitutional power, he violates the Constitution as well by executing it. A great trust is committed to his hands, sanctioned by a solemn oath, and he cannot surrender the one or violate the other.[84]

The managers argued that Johnson was asserting a power to refuse to execute any law or provision of the Constitution, that the line Curtis and other defense counsel were attempting to draw was a fictitious one, and that if the president had the power to sit judicially on the Tenure of Office Act, he could do so on every statute. "The President is not to intervene and protect the Constitution against the laws," Bingham argued. "It is a new doctrine altogether that the Constitution is exclusively in the keeping of the President."[85]

Moreover, Bingham said, Johnson's argument would give the Supreme Court control over the impeachment power. He characterized Johnson's answer to the charge that he had violated the Constitution and the laws as a claim that he was

83. I:387–8.
84. II:200, 382–3.
85. II:391, 407, 411, 415.

> vested with an unlimited prerogative to decide all these questions for himself, and to suspend even your power of impeachment in the courts of justice until some future day, which day may never come, when it will suit his convenience to test the validity of your laws and consequently the uprightness of his own conduct before the Supreme Court of the United States.

"There never was a balder piece of effrontery practiced since man was upon the face of the earth," Bingham said.[86]

The question, the managers argued, was not whether the act was unconstitutional or even whether President Johnson believed in good faith that it was unconstitutional. The laws were as obligatory upon him as upon the humblest citizen—even more so, for he was the minister of the law. The president could not controvert the constitutionality of a law, and if he did so it must be at the peril of his impeachment and removal from office. The legal presumption is in favor of the constitutionality of a law, Williams asserted:

> The President claims that this presumption shall not stand as against him. If it may not here, it cannot elsewhere. To allow this revolutionary pretension, is to dethrone the law and substitute his will. To say that he may hold his office, and disregard the law, is to proclaim either anarchy or despotism. . . . The man who can declare what is law, and what is not, is already the absolute master of the state.[87]

Intent and Seriousness

Johnson's counsel were not relying on their constitutional and statutory arguments to convince the Senate that President Johnson actually had the power to remove Secretary Stanton or even that he was necessarily within his constitutional rights in seeking a court test of the issue. Rather, they were seeking to establish that Johnson lacked criminal intent and that his conduct lacked the degree of seriousness necessary to remove a president from office.

The argument was essentially as follows: President Johnson had a good faith belief in the unconstitutionality of the Tenure of Office Act; indeed, he had been so advised by his cabinet (though the Senate

86. II:395–6, 429.
87. II:256.

rejected evidence on this point). He also had a good faith belief that Stanton was not protected by the act. He had legitimate reasons for wishing to remove Stanton as Secretary of War, related to the administration of the executive branch and the unity of his cabinet. He had attempted to avoid confrontation by suspending Stanton, hoping that the Senate would agree with his view that Stanton should be replaced. When the Senate refused to concur in the suspension, it was necessary for him to bring the issue to the courts. This he believed, again in good faith, to be within his constitutional rights and duty as president.

This elaborate argument had one additional—and critical—fillip: It did not matter whether it was right or wrong, only that it was plausible. President Johnson might be in error, the defense conceded—in error in his constitutional opinions, in his construction of the laws, in his belief that he could bring the question to court—but these were not the type of mistakes for which he should be convicted and removed from office. If he was acting in good faith, as the defense contended, then either there was no crime (because the requisite criminal intent was lacking) or there was merely a technical crime, not sufficiently serious to warrant removal. This defense dovetailed with other contentions made on Johnson's behalf, and in particular the argument that the trial was a judicial proceeding to be decided on the basis of the charges made and the proof adduced, not on rumors, speculation, and political considerations.

This argument, the heart of President Johnson's defense, interwove questions of intent and seriousness, in an effort to justify the conduct charged against him or at least mitigate his guilt.

Intent. Intent was a multifaceted issue in the defense offered for Johnson. The first contention was that the managers had to prove the allegations of their articles that the president intended to violate the law and the Constitution. Surely, Curtis argued, everyone would agree that:

> so long as the President of the United States, in good faith, is endeavoring to take care that the laws be faithfully executed, and in good faith, and to the best of his ability, is preserving, protecting, and defending the Constitution of the United States, although he may be making mistakes, he is not committing high crimes or misdemeanors.

The House had not charged honest mistakes, but wilful violations of law and the Constitution, Curtis said, and criminal intent must be proved if the articles were to be supported. If the president believed Stanton was not within the law or that the law was unconstitutional and an occasion had arisen when he must test it, then whether or not he committed an infraction of law, "he has not committed the impeachable offence with which he is charged by the House of Representatives." The question for the Senate, Groesbeck argued, was "[n]ot did the President do this or that act . . . ; but was he guilty of a high misdemeanor in the purpose with which he did the act?"[88]

There was room for mistake on both the constitutional and statutory construction issue, the defense asserted. Was the president to be impeached, Curtis asked,

> for having formed an opinion that the Constitution of the United States had lodged this power [of removal] with the President—an opinion which he shares with every President who has preceded him, with every Congress which has preceded the last; . . . an opinion . . . supported by the practice of the government from its origin down to his own day . . . ? If not, if he might honestly and properly form such an opinion under the lights which he had, and with the aid of the advice which . . . he received, then is he to be impeached for acting upon it to the extent of obtaining a judicial decision whether the executive department of the government was right in its opinion, or the legislative department was right in its opinion?

The act might be constitutional after all, but its constitutionality "is not a truth which shines with such clear and certain light that a man is guilty of a crime because he does not see it." So, too, with the applicability of the Tenure of Office Act to Secretary Stanton:

> [H]e came to the conclusion that the case of Mr. Stanton was not within this law. He came to that conclusion, not merely by an examination of the law himself, but by resorting to the advice which the Constitution and laws of the country enable him to call for to assist him in coming to a correct conclusion. Having done so, are the Senate prepared to say that the conclusion he reached must have been a wilful misconstruction—so wilful, so

88. I:386, 411, 691; II:193.

> wrong, that it can justly and properly, and for the purpose of this prosecution, effectively be termed a high misdemeanor? . . . How is it possible for this body to convict the President of the United States of a high misdemeanor for construing a law as those who made it construed it at the time when it was made?[89]

The managers argued that intent need not be separately proved but could be inferred from the illegal act under normal doctrines of criminal law. There was no need for direct proof of criminal intent, Butler said, for if President Johnson violated the law in removing Stanton, "the law supplies the intent, and says that no man can do wrong intending right." When the act is unlawful in itself, said Bingham, the law "declares that the intent was criminal, and it is for the accused to show justification." The allegations of intent in the articles, while not surplusage, were not necessary; error in judgment was no excuse for an executive officer who had no judicial authority.[90] Wicked or unlawful intention need not be proved, said Stevens, and it was unwise to aver it in an impeachment. Motive did not matter:

> Mere mistake in intention, if so persevered in after proper warning as to bring mischief upon the community, is quite sufficient to warrant the removal of the officer from the place where he is working mischief by his continuance in office.
>
> The only question to be considered is: is the respondent violating the law? His perseverance in such a violation, although it shows a perverseness, is not absolutely necessary to his conviction. The great object is the removal from office and the arrest of the public injuries which he is inflicting upon those with whose interests he is intrusted.

When the president was charged with infringing the Constitution or disobeying or violating the commands of a statute, Williams argued,

> he cannot plead either that he did it ignorantly or by mistake, because ignorance of the law excuses nobody, or that he did it only from the best of motives, and for the purpose of bringing the question of its efficacy, or his obligation to conform to it, to a legal test. . . . The motives of men, which are hidden away in

89. I:393, 392, 384.
90. I:502, 506; II:416, 415.

> their own breasts, cannot generally be scrutinized, or taken into the account, where there is a violation of the law.[91]

The point that the defense was making, however, was not so much that a violation of criminal law had not been established but that this violation was insufficient for removal from office. Criminal intent might be presumed upon an indictment for a violation of the penal provision of the Tenure of Office Act, but that was not the subject of the impeachment. This "mere technical statutory offence" might be punished "by a fine of six cents and no more," Evarts argued. The only subject that gave gravity to the trial was the imputation by the House that Johnson's purpose was injury to the public interest and the public safety. If the House had produced an article charging President Johnson with the intent and purpose of raising a case for the Supreme Court between the Constitution and the act, "it would have been a laughing stock of the whole country." Johnson's intent, Evarts said, was "no violence, no interruption of the public service, no seizure of the military appropriations, nothing but the purpose . . . either to procure Mr. Stanton's retirement, as was desired, or to have the necessary footing for judicial proceedings."[92]

In his closing argument Evarts argued strenuously against "this dry, dead interpretation of law and duty by which act, act, act, unqualified, unscrutinized, unweighed, unmeasured, is to form the basis of necessary action of the guillotine of impeachment." Johnson's "whole criminality, in act, in purpose, and in consequence," he said, "is a formal contravention of a statute"—"a violation of a law, if it shall be so held, in support of and in obedience to the higher obligation of the Constitution." That was not a crime, "[i]n sentence and measure of punishment, at least, if not in formal decision and judgment":

> Surely we have not forgotten our rights and our liberties, and upon what they rest, that we should bring a President of the United States under a formal apparatus of iron operation, that by necessity, if you set it agoing, shall, without crime, without fault, without turpitude, without moral fault even of violating a statute that he believed to be a statute binding upon him, bring about this monstrous conclusion . . . of depriving him of his office and the people of the country of an executive head.

91. II:223, 220, 259.
92. I:475, 603.

"[U]nless there be some measure of guilt, some purpose, or some act of force, of violence, of fraud, of corruption, of injury, of evil," he said, there was no foundation for impeachment in "mistaken, erroneous, careless, or even indifferent excesses of authority making no impression upon the fabric of government, and giving neither menace nor injury to the public service."[93]

President Johnson acted under a claim of right, and nothing was done except to put the case in the attitude that would raise the point for judicial determination. "[T]he moment you put the coercion of punishment upon the assertion of a right, a claimed right, in a manner not violating the peace and not touching the public safety, you infringe one of the necessary liberties of every citizen." Only where there was an "intervention of force" did an offender act at his peril in violating what he claimed to be an unconstitutional law.

The "great exculpatory fact [that] must shield him" even if everything else were ruled against the president, Stanberry asserted, was that the intention of testing the constitutionality of the Tenure of Office Act accompanied every act touching the suspension and removal of Stanton. No unlawful intent could be predicated on the president's act, Nelson argued. It "beggars all belief to say that the President intended anything wrong. It outrages our ideas of common justice and of common sense." If the president believed that the law was unconstitutional, then until the question was adjudicated by the Supreme Court, he "had the right to exercise his judgment, and you cannot hold that he was guilty of any criminal intention."[94]

The president's purpose was to "change the War Department," "to get rid of the poisoned conditon of his cabinet," and "have unity and peace restored to it," said Groesbeck. He considered it "one of the strongest facts in this case" that the president executed the Tenure of Office Act in other respects:

> He did not take up this law and tear it to pieces. . . . He did not trample it under his feet. That is lawlessness. He took it up to have it interpreted in the case that pressed upon him individually, and in all other respects he executed it without the surrender of his own convictions.

93. II:297, 292, 294–5, 338.
94. II:294, 353, 387, 170.

The suspension of Stanton under the act was "an overture from the President . . . to get out of this difficulty, and to conciliate you in the hope that you would relieve and let him have a cabinet such as any of you would demand if you were in his place." President Johnson did his best to get to the courts; he "ran after a case by which he could have carried it there. Where is his criminality?" Groesbeck asked. "Is he criminal because he did not surrender the convictions of his mind on the constitutionality of the act?" Groesbeck acknowledged that it was the president's duty to execute the laws, but argued that his failure to do so in order to test the Tenure of Office Act in the Supreme Court did not justify his removal:

> He shall execute your laws; he shall execute even the doubtful laws; but when you bring to him a question like this, when he has all this precedent behind him and around him, all these voices sounding in his ears, as to what is the right interpretation of the Constitution, and only one [the Tenure of Office Act] the other way, I say you are going too far to undertake to brand him with criminality because he proposed to go to the Supreme Court and ascertain how it is. To go there is peaceable, is constitutional, is lawful. What is that tribunal there for? For this very purpose.[95]

The managers made two arguments in response to these contentions. The first was factual: President Johnson's defense was a subterfuge, an afterthought, unsupported by the evidence. Boutwell conceded that if a law passed by Congress was "equivocal or ambiguous in its terms," the executive could apply his own best judgment or seek counsel from his advisors, and "acting thereupon, without evil intent or purpose, he would be fully justified, and upon no principle of right could he be held to answer as for a misdeameanor in office." But, said Boutwell, "that is not this case." President Johnson understood the intention of Congress. His offense was not that he misunderstood the statute's meaning and acted upon a misinterpretation, but that, "understanding its meaning . . . , he, upon his own opinion that the same was unconstitutional, deliberately, wilfully and intentionally disregarded it."[96] Especially significant in this regard, the managers

95. II:209, 210, 206–7.
96. II:97.

argued, were the president's veto message, indicating that he believed the law covered every officer he appointed, the initial suspension of Stanton, and a letter from Johnson to General Grant before the Senate refused to concur in the suspension, which suggested that his purpose was to prevent Stanton from resuming office. They asserted that intent had been fully proved.

The managers' second argument was that, as a matter of law, a good purpose would not justify an illegal act. Said Butler:

> [T]he question is, is it best to break the law of the land by the chief executive officer in order to get [Stanton] out? Is it best to strain the Constitution and the laws in order to get him out? However much he may desire to do it, the fact that the Secretary is a bad officer does not give the President a right to do an illegal thing to get him out.

If that was a justification, Butler said, then the president or any executive officer could "break the law of the land if he can show that he did what he thought was a good thing by doing it." This was not merely a question of intention, Wilson asserted, but the main question in the case: the validity of President Johnson's claim "that he may determine for himself what laws he will obey and execute, and what laws he will disregard and refuse to enforce." The constitutionality of the Tenure of Office Act was not at issue; the president is required to execute all laws until they are repealed or adjudged unconstitutional by the courts. His opinion as to their unconstitutionality or the necessity of disobeying them, therefore, is immaterial. Said Wilson:

> The judgment of the individual intrusted, for the time being, with the executive power of the republic may reject as utterly erroneous the conclusions arrived at by those invested with the legislative power; but the officer must submit and execute the law. He has no discretion in the premises except such as the particular statute confers on him; and even this he must exercise in obedience to the rules which the act provides.[97]

The defense attacked the managers' argument that the president had to execute all laws. The "sum and substance" of this argument, said Groesbeck, was that "the President of the United States is but the constable of Congress; no more; that he is put into his place merely to ex-

97. I:502, 682, 687.

ecute the laws of Congress." The managers were contending, said Nelson, that the president "is a mere man in buckram; that he has no power or authority to decide anything; that he can do nothing on the face of the earth unless it is nominated in the bond; that he must be the passive instrument of Congress; and that he must be subjected to the government and control" of the legislative branch.[98]

Gravity. In addition to asserting that President Johnson's intentions were good, the meaning of the Tenure of Office Act uncertain, and the constitutional question debatable, the defense argued that there had been no public injury from Johnson's actions. Groesbeck said:

> It almost shocks me to think that the President of the United States is to be dragged out of his office on these miserable little questions, whether he could make an *ad interim* appointment, for a single day, or whether in anything he did there was so great a crime that you should break the even flow of the administration of the country, disturb the quiet of the people, and impair their confidence in a great degree in the stability of their government.

Evarts contended that the entire case, except for Articles 9 and 10, rested on what President Johnson did between noon and one o'clock on February 21. And, he said, "What he did was all in writing. What he did was all public and official. What he did was communicated to all the authorities of the government having relation to the subject." The fault charged by the House was "not of personal delinquency, not of immorality or turpitude, not one that disparages in the judgment of mankind, not one that degrades or affects the position of the malefactor," but merely an offense of a political character. It was a crime because Congress passed a law, for the first time in the nation's history, making it a crime. The secretary was not removed; force was not used; violence was not meditated, prepared, attempted, or applied. "No; it was all on paper, and all went no further than making the official attitude out of which a judgment of the Supreme Court could be got."[99]

The articles involving the designation of Thomas as interim secretary rested on an even less substantial offense, Evarts argued:

> Truly, indeed, we are getting very nice in our measure and criticism of the absolute obligations and of the absolute acuteness and

98. II:199, 166.
99. II:215, 291, 274.

> thoroughness of executive functions when we seek to apply the process of impeachment and removal to a question whether an act of Congress required him to name a head of a department to take the vacant place *ad interim* or an act of Congress not repealed permitted him to take a suitable person. You certainly do not, in the ordinary affairs of life, rig up a trip-hammer to crack a walnut.[100]

Stanberry made a similar argument, stressing that the president did not succeed in getting Stanton out of office or putting General Thomas in. There was no public mischief, he contended:

> The lawful officer has not been disturbed; the lawful custody of the public property and public money of the department has not been changed. No injury has been done either to the public service or to the public officer. . . . Where, now, is the mischief; where now is the injury to any individual or to any officer of the government brought about by the action of the President? Whether actuated by good motives or bad, no injury has followed; no public interest has suffered; no officer has been changed, either rightfully or wrongfully; not an item of public property or public money has passed out of the custody of law, or has been appropriated to improper uses.

The offenses were "all founded upon mere forms of executive administration—for the violation . . . of the rules laid down by the legislative department to regulate the conduct of the executive department in the manner of the administration of executive functions belonging to that department."[101] How could it be deemed necessary to remove the president "for making an order of removal on one day, advising the Senate of it the same day, and sending the nomination of a successor the next day?" Stanberry asked. "Was ever a matter more purely formal than this?" How could it be considered, "not in merely *technical* language, 'but in reality, in substance, and effect,' a high crime and misdemeanor within the meaning of the Constitution?"[102]

The managers asserted that the charges did involve grave issues. In his opening argument, Butler characterized the issue in the first eight articles:

100. II:336.
101. II:363–4, 380, 364.
102. II:365–6. Stanberry was quoting from Burke's argument in the Hastings trial.

> Has the President, under the Constitution, the more than kingly prerogative at will to remove from office and suspend from office indefinitely, all executive officers of the United States, either civil, military, or naval, at any and all times, and fill the vacancies with creatures of his own appointment, for his own purposes, without any restraint whatever, or possibility of restraint by the Senate or by Congress through laws duly enacted? . . . [T]he momentous question, here and now, is raised whether the *presidential office itself* (*if it has the prerogatives and power claimed for it*) *ought, in fact, to exist as a part of the constitutional government of a free people.*

Williams described the issue as "but a renewal on American soil of the old battle between the royal prerogative and the privileges of the Commons"—"a struggle for the mastery between a temporary executive and the legislative power of a free state over the most momentous question that has ever challenged the attention of a people." Williams replied to the defense argument that the removal of a department head "is an affair of state too small to be worthy of such an avenger as this which we propose." That might be, Williams acknowledged, if it were "[s]tanding alone, stripped of all the attendant circumstances that explain the act and show the deadly *animus* by which it was inspired." But the House had "but singled out from many others of equal weight the facts now charged, as facts for the most part of recent occurrence, of great notoriety, and of easy proof, by way of testing a much greater question without loss of time." The history of President Johnson's administration was "one long and unseemly struggle by the Executive against the legislative power" to accomplish the object of forcing the rebel states into the Union on his terms, contrary to the will of Congress. The specific offenses charged in the impeachment were "but the culminating facts, and only the last of a long series of usurpations."[103]

Boutwell reiterated the argument he had made to the House in December in support of the Judiciary Committee's resolution of impeachment. "[H]is crime is one—the subversion of the government. From the nature of the case we are compelled to deal with minor acts of criminality by which he hoped to consummate this greatest of crimes." Manager Logan said that the House had presented "not his most flagrant offences, but only his last offendings. Should he com-

103. I:96; II:231, 232, 234.

plain that they denounce for the lesser, when he is equally guilty of the greater crimes?"[104]

Logan reminded the Senate that the allegation came "from the people in their sovereignty—in their supreme capacity as the rulers of us all." It could not be said that charges coming from a whole people "are frivolous and vain," that what the community in its aggregate capacity asserts "is insufficient and of no avail. . . . The fiat of a people when solemnly pronounced against one to whom they have delegated official favors, and whom they have charged with derelictions of official duty, can never be treated as an empty sound, nor their inquiry regarded as an idle ceremony." The only insufficiency in the charges that could inure to the benefit of the president "must be such an entire want of substance as takes all soul and body from the charge and leaves it nothing but a shadow."[105]

Johnson's counsel responded that the president had to be tried on the articles, not on other matters. Said Evarts:

> I am not to be told that it was competent for the managers to prove that there were *coup d'etats*, hidden purposes of evil to the state, threatened in this innocent and formal act apparently. Let them prove it, and then let us disprove it, and then judge us within the compass of the testimony and according to the law governing these considerations.

The act under inquiry, charged and proved, "must be of itself such as, within its terms and regular and natural consequence, . . . touches vital interests or fundamental principles," Evarts asserted. "You may [not] accuse of a definite and formal crime, and then have outside of your indictment, not covered by charge or admitted for proof or countervailing proof, large accusations that touch these general subjects."[106] The Senate must make its judgment on the charges within each article independently, on the evidence adduced and not on political opinions. It must judge impartially:

104. II:105, 16.
105. II:18.
106. II:355, 286. Evarts described the arguments of the managers as the "method of forensic controversy which may be called the method of concussion"—the making of "a violent, noisy, and explosive demonstration in the vicinity of the object of attack." He compared it to the Chinese method of warfare, which he said "consists of a great braying of trumpets, sounding of gongs, shouts, and shrieks in the neighborhood of the opposing force, which rolled away and the air clear and calm again, the effect is to be watched for" (II:285).

> You are not to reach over from one article to another; you are to say guilty or not guilty of each as it comes along; and you are to take the first one as it appears; you are to treat it as within the premises charged and proved; you are to treat the President of the United States, for the purpose of that determination, as if he were innocent of everything else, of good politics and good conduct; you are to deal with him under your oath to administer impartial justice within the premises of accusation and proof as if President Lincoln were charged with the same thing, or General Grant . . . ; you are to treat it as if the respondent were innocent, as if he were your friend, as if you agreed in public sentiment, in public policy; and nevertheless the crime charged and proved is such as that you will remove General Washington or President Lincoln for the same offence.[107]

The Outcome

The defense arguments on behalf of President Johnson, once past the purely legal issues of statutory construction and constitutionality, had the great strength of turning every doubt in favor of the president, if not in proof of his innocence of wrongdoing then in mitigation of the offense. Their weakness, however, was that they were factual arguments—an elaborate contrivance that did not necessarily comport with reality. On analysis, there are serious inconsistencies in the defense explanation of Johnson's motives. For example, if Johnson really believed that the act did not apply to Stanton, then he could not have believed that he could test its constitutionality by removing Stanton. The Supreme Court would never reach the constitutional issue, and Stanton was the wrong officer to choose for a test case. Similarly, if Stanton was not actually removed and Johnson did not intend to force

107. II:355. Evarts also argued that the impeachment involved a contest between the omnicompetence of Congress and the supremacy of the Constitution, all the worse because the president pro tempore of the Senate would succeed to the presidency if Johnson were convicted and removed. Furthermore, the Senate had already passed on the issue in the trial in its political capacity, Evarts said; it was inadmissible for the Senate to judge a case to which it was a party. "The Constitution never brings a Senate into an inculpation and a condemnation of a President upon matters in which and of which the two departments of the government in their political capacities have formed and expressed political opinions. It is of other matter and of other fault, in which there are no parties and no discriminations of opinion. It is of offence, of crime, in which the common rules held by all of duty, of obligation, of excess, or of sin, are not determinable upon political opinions formed and expressed in debate" (II:323).

him out of office, then there was no logical explanation for designating Thomas as interim secretary. Johnson could replace Stanton by having a successor confirmed by the Senate, under any interpretation of the Tenure of Office Act. Unless he believed that no successor could be confirmed, then he was saddling himself with Stanton in order to challenge the constitutionality of the act—a result contrary to the public necessity of removing Stanton that the defense said was one of the prerequisites to the President's authority to test the law in court. Moreover, Johnson could have initiated litigation at the time he suspended Stanton rather than waiting more than six months until the Senate had rejected the suspension. And there was evidence in the case suggesting that Johnson did not intend to go to court at all or even believe that it was possible to initiate court proceedings.

Nevertheless, the defense was successful—though just barely so—in obtaining an acquittal. The key votes, as previously noted, were those of seven Republicans for acquittal. The three articles that were voted on—11, 2, and 3, in that order—each failed by a single vote, with 35 Senators (all Republicans) voting guilty and 19 Senators (12 Democrats and the 7 Republicans) voting not guilty. The six opinions filed by Republicans voting for acquittal indicate that the defense arguments had an impact.[108] While other considerations undoubtedly influenced the outcome of the trial, these Republicans explained their votes largely on the basis of the approach to the case the defense had taken. In addition to issues of statutory construction, they considered Johnson's intent, the gravity of the offense, and the justification for his conduct that the defense had offered.

The Johnson impeachment trial does not provide much ammunition on either side of the debate on whether an indictable crime is required for impeachment of a president. The defense, not the managers, put the most stress on going beyond the narrow confines of criminal law, while simultaneously arguing that a criminal offense was required and taking full advantage of technical points of criminal law. Their basic argument was that a mere crime was not sufficient to impeach the president; the nature and duties of the presidential office, the magnitude and consequences of presidential actions had to be considered, at least in mitigation of his crime. They all but turned the

108. The vote and related parliamentary maneuvering appears at II:486–98. The opinions appear at III:16 (Fessenden), III:193 (Fowler), III:328 (Grimes), III:295 (Henderson), III:319 (Trumbull), and III:147 (Van Winkle).

noncriminal definition of grounds for impeachement upside down: the president cannot be impeached except for a statutory crime, but that crime is not sufficient cause for his removal unless it involves conduct subversive of constitutional government and highly prejudicial to the public interest.

If anything, the managers lost ground by focusing their case on criminal offenses related to the Stanton removal order. They had what they thought was an easily proved crime; the problem was that the Tenure of Office Act simply could not bear the intense scrutiny to which it was put during the trial. There were too many circumstances, too many legal questions, which, if they did not provide the legal basis for a conclusion that Johnson had committed no crime, at least supported the conclusion that it was a niggling offense. In effect, the House had agreed to the proposition that indictability could be equated with seriousness, that the existence of a crime—especially one labelled a "high misdemeanor" by statute—made the case "perfect," as James F. Wilson told the House. What the House had really done, however, was to accept a pretextual charge as a basis for impeaching President Johnson. As a consequence, Johnson's counsel were able to stress the triviality of the offense, while at the same time limiting the case to only that offense. The criminal charge could be used as a shield for President Johnson. Having alleged a specific crime the House could not be permitted to prove a great constitutional fault; it was restricted to what it had pleaded. Charged as a criminal President Johnson could defend himself as chief magistrate; he could benefit not only from the strictness of the criminal law, but also could invoke the responsibilities, powers, and duties of his office.

3. *GROUNDS FOR IMPEACHMENT: THE NIXON INQUIRY*

In the Nixon inquiry constitutional grounds for impeachment and removal of the president were first considered in the abstract, with emphasis on the criminality issue. By the time the Judiciary Committee began its deliberations on specific articles of impeachment, that issue had all but evaporated. The federal criminal code simply did not seem very germane to the decisions the committee had to make, at least as the majority of its members saw the situation. As for other elements of the constitutional standard for impeachment of the president—and notably the requirement that the wrongdoing charged against him be serious—the key questions in the Nixon inquiry were factual. Despite some arguments in opposition to impeachment designed to suggest factors in mitigation or justification of conduct charged against President Nixon, there was little question that if the evidence supported the allegations they were sufficiently serious to warrant his impeachment. There was no doubt, for example, that if the evidence showed that President Nixon had engaged in a plan to obstruct investigations of the Watergate break-in and related unlawful activities, especially if his involvement began before March 21, 1973 (when he claimed to have learned about the Watergate cover-up for the first time), this would warrant his impeachment. And on this charge, the crux of the case, a majority of the committee found the evidence against President Nixon to be clear and convincing.

At the periphery of the Nixon case and in some of the academic commentary during it, however, allegations were considered that raised the question of how the charges in an impeachment proceeding are to be evaluated. Must each charge, taken independently, be serious enough to warrant impeachment and removal from office, or are the charges to be considered as a whole in making this determination? This was not a new question; like the criminality issue, it had first been raised in the Chase trial and had appeared again in the Johnson impeachment (both during the initial, unsuccessful effort at impeachment and in the trial). It was not a crucial question in the Nixon proceeding, again because of the acknowledged independent gravity of the Watergate charge. In other circumstances, however, it could very well be the most critical issue in deciding whether a president should be impeached and removed.

The Issues in the Nixon Inquiry

When the House Judiciary Committee began its investigation of President Nixon, one of the first tasks the committee assigned to its staff was the preparation of a legal analysis of grounds for presidential impeachment, including the question of whether an indictable crime was required. In the century since the Johnson impeachment, there had been no serious consideration of impeaching a president, much less a House investigation, and it was not surprising that the remedy was an unfamiliar one. Impeachment had been discredited by its "political" use against President Johnson; and, insofar as it was mentioned at all, it was thought to be reserved for horrendous crimes. A typical description of the Johnson case—and the status of presidential impeachment—was provided by Clinton L. Rossiter in his book on the American presidency written in the late 1950s. The power of impeachment, Rossiter wrote,

> is the "extreme medicine" of the Constitution, so extreme—and so brutally administered in the one instance in which it was prescribed for a President—that most observers now agree with Jefferson that it is a "mere scarecrow" and with Henry Jones Ford that it is a "rusted blunderbuss, that will probably never be taken in hand again."

The Johnson impeachment was "vengefully political in motivation and purpose," and his acquittal "made clear for all time that impeachment is not an 'inquest of office,' a political process for turning out a President whom a majority of the House and two-thirds of the Senate simply cannot abide." Although rusted, however, the blunderbuss "still endures, stacked away defiantly in the Constitution." It could yet be used, Rossiter wrote, but he predicted "confidently" that the next president to be impeached "will have asked for the firing squad by committing a low personal rather than a high political crime—by shooting a Senator, for example." Later in the book, Rossiter said that this comment was "in jest"; he did not think such a trial was ever again likely to occur. In any case, he asserted, "impeachment is not a *political* process, an inquest of office by the House and Senate acting as legislative bodies, but a *judicial* process, a trial of the President for crimes known to law."[1]

This, in the view of historians and political scientists, was the teaching of the Johnson impeachment. If it had not totally destroyed presidential impeachment, it had at least made its use improbable and imposed strict limitations on the circumstances in which it might be pursued. Presidential accountability was to be enforced not by the impeachment mechanism but rather through the political constraints of our democratic system.

Impeachment was applied to a comparatively unimportant problem after the Johnson trial. It was invoked, almost exclusively, against judges suspected of corruption, drunkenness, or other misdeeds. The House Judiciary Committee investigated a number of judges, some more than once. Several resigned before the House could vote on their impeachment, but six were impeached, of whom two resigned before trial, two were tried and acquitted by the Senate, and two were convicted. The last trial, and the last conviction, occurred in 1936. Judge Halsted L. Ritter was found guilty by a single vote of misbehavior bringing his court into disrepute. This charge, incorporated in the seventh article of impeachment against Judge Ritter, was supported by specifications to the charges in the preceding six articles (on each of which Ritter had been acquitted) and one additional indiscretion.[2]

The Ritter impeachment and the previous cases established conclusively that judges could be impeached and removed for noncriminal misbehavior. For both practical and legal reasons, however, these cases did not necessarily affect the grounds for impeachment of a president. The practical reason was that it seemed inappropriate to determine the fate of an elected chief executive on the basis of law devel-

1. Clinton Rossiter, *The American Presidency* 52, 53, 208 (emphasis in original) (2d ed. 1960).

2. The investigations and trials before 1936 are discussed in 3 Hinds' §§2444–85, 2504–20, and 6 Cannon's §§489–552. Later precedents of the House have not been published. The Ritter trial is described in Impeachment Inquiry Staff Grounds Memo 55–7.

oped in proceedings directed at petty misconduct by obscure judges. The legal reason was that the Constitution provides that judges shall serve during good behavior. This clause could be interpreted as a separate standard for the impeachment of judges or it could be interpreted as an aid in applying the term "high crimes and misdemeanors" to judges. Whichever interpretation was adopted, it was clear that the clause made a difference in judicial impeachments, confounding the application of these cases to presidential impeachment.

The judicial impeachments also established that impeachment was a clumsy method of policing the conduct of federal judges. After the Ritter trial, the pace of impeachment investigations by the House Judiciary Committee slowed appreciably. No impeachments were recommended to the House at all, and after 1945 only one official, Justice William O. Douglas, was the subject of an impeachment investigation. The Douglas investigation was conducted by a Special Subcommittee of the Judiciary Committee in 1970. Counsel for Justice Douglas invoked the familiar arguments in support of the proposition that "actual criminal conduct" was required to impeach a judge. Rep. Gerald R. Ford, then minority leader of the House, contended on behalf of the proponents of the charges against Douglas that "an impeachable offense is whatever a majority of the House of Representatives considers it to be at a given moment in history; conviction results from whatever offense or offenses the other body considers to be sufficiently serious to require removal of the accused from office." Ford relied expressly on the good behavior clause; unlike judges, he said, the president and vice president could be removed only for "crimes of the magnitude of treason and bribery." The subcommittee investigating the allegations against Justice Douglas concluded there was no creditable evidence that would warrant his impeachment on any theory, though it suggested that the House could impeach a judge for serious misconduct even if it were not criminal.[3]

The Douglas investigation, as well as the inadequacy of impeachment as a method for removing unfit judges, rekindled academic in-

3. 93d Cong., 2d Sess., House, Comm. on the Judiciary, Impeachment Inquiry Staff, "Memorandum: Presentation Procedures for the Impeachment Inquiry," Appendix at 9 (April 3, 1974) (unpublished) (hereafter Impeachment Inquiry Staff Procedures Memo); 91st Cong., 2d Sess., House, Comm. on the Judiciary, Special Subcomm. on H. Res. 920, *Legal Materials on Impeachment* 24 (1970); 116 Cong. Rec. 11912–3 (1970); 91st Cong., 2d Sess., House, Comm. on the Judiciary, *Assoc. Justice William O. Douglas, Final Report by the Special Subcommittee on H. Res.* 920 (1970).

terest in impeachment. A number of scholars—most notably Raoul Berger—published analyses of the remedy, with particular reference to its application to the judiciary. Many, though not all, of these studies concluded (as did Berger) that "high crimes and misdemeanors" need not be indictable crimes and that the framers intended that a president be removable from office for the commission of great offenses against the Constitution. As the Nixon inquiry got under way, other scholars and legal groups echoed this conclusion.[4]

Nevertheless, President Nixon and his lawyers argued that a criminal offense was required to impeach a president. In an analysis submitted to the Judiciary Committee at the end of February 1974, the president's lawyers examined English history, the intention of the framers of the Constitution, case law, and rules of constitutional and statutory construction and asserted that "high crimes and misdemeanors" means "great crimes against the state." They found that the framers adopted "the general criminal meaning and language" of the English impeachment process, while "rejecting the 17th century aberration where impeachment was used as a weapon by Parliament to gain political supremacy at the expense of the rule of law." The American impeachment precedents did suggest that judges may be impeached for something less than indictable crimes, but "all the evidence points to the fact that a President may not. He may be impeached only for indictable crimes clearly set forth in the Constitution." A broad construction of the impeachment power, President Nixon's counsel contended, can be reached

> only by reading constitutional authorities selectively, by lifting specific historical precedents out of their precise historical context, by disregarding the plain meaning and accepted definition of technical, legal terms—in short, by placing a subjective gloss on the history of impeachment that results in permitting the Congress to do whatever it deems most politic.

A broad impeachment power would be "destructive of our system of government, and to the fundamental principle of separation of powers inherent in the very structure of the Constitution." The framers, they

4. Berger, *Impeachment* 298; see Committee on Federal Legislation, Bar Association of the City of New York, *The Law of Presidential Impeachment* 8–9 (Jan. 1974).

concluded, "never intended that the impeachment clause serve to dominate or destroy the executive branch of government."[5]

The analysis by the president's counsel was submitted a week after the impeachment inquiry staff had provided the Judiciary Committee with a memorandum on the constitutional grounds for presidential impeachment. The staff memorandum reviewed English impeachment history, the intention of the framers, and past American impeachment cases and reached a quite different conclusion. The "central aspect of impeachment" in England, known to the framers, was that it was a "parliamentary effort to reach grave abuses of governmental power." Impeachment was adopted in the Constitution as the "ultimate check on the conduct of the executive," intended to deal with his excesses while maintaining balance between the executive and legislative branches. Criminality was not central in past impeachments; in some cases the issue was not raised at all. "The emphasis has been on the significant effects of the conduct—undermining the integrity of office, disregard of constitutional duties and oath of office, arrogation of power, abuse of the governmental process, adverse impact on the system of government." A restriction of grounds for impeachment to conduct that was criminal would be incompatible with its constitutional purpose: "where the issue is presidential compliance with the constitutional requirements and limitations on the presidency, the crucial factor is not the intrinsic quality of behavior"—whether or not it would be criminal, as private conduct—"but the significance of its effect upon our constitutional system or the functioning of our government." Not all presidential misconduct is sufficient grounds for impeachment, the staff concluded. There is a further requirement—substantiality—to be considered in terms of the facts as a whole in the context of the office:

> Because impeachment of a President is a grave step for the nation, it is to be predicated only upon conduct seriously incompatible with either the constitutional form and principles of our government or the proper performance of constitutional duties of the presidential office.[6]

5. James D. St. Clair et al., "An Analysis of the Constitutional Standard for Presidential Impeachment," printed in 10 Weekly Comp. of Pres. Doc. 270–83 (Feb. 28, 1974).

6. Impeachment Inquiry Staff Grounds Memo, 26–7.

Two other contemporaneous analyses deserve mention. One was prepared by the Office of Legal Counsel of the Department of Justice as part of a series of memoranda on impeachment "designed to serve as resource material" without reaching conclusions or proposing solutions. Its analysis of grounds for impeachment was indeed agnostic: "There are persuasive grounds for arguing both the narrow view that a violation of criminal law is required and the broader view that certain non-criminal 'political offenses' may justify impeachment." The "one lesson to be learned" from the historical material "is that nothing can be considered resolved concerning the concept of impeachable offenses. The same basic arguments are repeated in each succeeding proceeding."[7]

The other analysis was a memorandum prepared by members of the minority staff of the impeachment inquiry in response to a request by Republicans on the Judiciary Committee for arguments in favor of the criminality limitation.[8] The most interesting aspect of this memorandum is that, unlike the White House brief, it explicitly defined "crimes" to include indictable offenses under federal or state statute or at common law. (While the White House brief did not address the question, it apparently limited impeachable crimes to violations of federal criminal statutes.) The memorandum asserted, "The notion that criminal law will not reach wilful misconduct in office by public men is demonstrably untrue." Most such conduct would violate a statute, and new laws could be passed to fill the interstices. Beyond that, breaches of public trust and misconduct in public office were indictable offenses at common law, as the memorandum established with extensive citation of authority.[9]

7. Department of Justice, Office of Legal Counsel, "The Law of Impeachment, Appendix I: The Concept of Impeachable Offense," prefatory page (Feb. 21, 1974); "Legal Aspects of Impeachment: An Overview" 33 (Feb. 1974); "The Law of Impeachment, Appendix I: The Concept of Impeachable Offense" 9.

8. [Samuel Garrison III et al.], "The Argument for Criminality as a Necessary Element of Impeachable Conduct" (March 1974) (unpublished).

9. The memorandum went on to argue that the indictability of misconduct in office at common law "does not render meaningless the question whether crime is an essential element of impeachable conduct." While much conduct constituting a willful violation of the president's oath of office or other constitutional duties would be indictable as misconduct in office at common law, there are types of misconduct (such as ineptitude or "technical" violations of rules or statutes) that would not be indictable and could not be made indictable because, for example, *mens rea* or criminal intent would be lacking.

This approach to the criminality requirement, reminiscent of the definition Bingham

As the Nixon inquiry evolved from the stage of abstract consideration of the law of impeachment to examination of the specific allegations against the president, the criminality argument all but evaporated. One reason was that President Nixon conceded that obstruction of justice—the offense central to the Watergate charges, viewed in criminal terms—was a serious crime that would be an impeachable offense.[10] Additional allegations, too, could have been cast in criminal terms, a few rather straightforwardly, others by applying some of the more expansive language of federal criminal statutes. In fact, part of the problem of applying a criminality test to the charges against President Nixon was that it was too mechanical; it obscured the heart of the case in a literalistic application of criminal statutes. It was also too easy. As Philip B. Kurland wrote in the spring of 1974, "in this day and age it is not at all difficult to find behavior that constitutes a colorable crime, even behavior of the most highly placed."[11] The criminality requirement, by itself, would not have provided a more stringent standard of impeachment in the Nixon case; on the contrary, it probably would have proved a more elastic one.

The president's counsel argued in favor of the criminality limitation from the proposition that impeachment was not intended to destroy the separation of powers or permit Congress to dominate the executive. But this specter was simply inapplicable to the Nixon case. The charges themselves (with the exception of noncompliance with the

---

used in the Johnson trial, did in fact leave very little to argue about. Indeed, it served as the basis for a portion of the minority views in opposition to the articles of impeachment recommended by the Judiciary Committee—but with one significant alteration. The minority report made no mention of the common law crime of misconduct in office, or of common law crimes at all. Instead, it abridged the argument, abandoning a requirement of indictable common law crimes in favor of a requirement of criminal intent. Willful misconduct by the president was impeachable, the minority argued, not because it was indictable at common law, but because it was misconduct and was willful. 93d Cong., 2d Sess., H. Rept. No. 93–1305, *Impeachment of Richard M. Nixon, President of the United States*, "Minority Views of Messrs. Hutchinson, Smith, Sandman, Wiggins, Dennis, Mayne, Lott, Moorhead, Mariziti and Latta" 371 (hereafter the report will be cited as Nixon Impeachment Report and the views of these members as Minority Views).

10. 93d Cong., 2d Sess., House, Comm. on the Judiciary, *Statement of Information, Hearings . . . Pursuant to H. Res. 803, Appendix I: Presidential Statements on the Watergate Break-in and its Investigation* 73 (1974) ("President's News Conference of March 6, 1974") (hereafter statements of information from the Nixon impeachment inquiry will be cited as Statement of Information).

11. "Watergate, Impeachment, and the Constitution," 45 *Miss. L.J.* 531, 558 (1974).

committee's own subpoenas) did not involve a confrontation between president and Congress. The committee, it is safe to say, saw no parallel between its task and the Andrew Johnson impeachment. The motivation for the impeachment inquiry was not political; the inquiry was conducted with great emphasis on fairness, as a fact-finding proceeding; and the relative strength of Congress and president, as government had developed over the preceding century, made it inconceivable that the removal of Richard Nixon would lead to congressional supremacy.

The president's counsel, like its own inquiry staff, pointed the committee toward the intention of the framers in adopting the impeachment remedy. But the debates in the Constitutional Convention, the state ratifying conventions, and the First Congress indicated that criminality was not at all what Madison, Mason, Randolph, Wilson, and the rest had been discussing. The function they envisioned for impeachment and the limitations they placed upon the process to prevent its misuse related to the structure of the government they were creating. Impeachment is a constitutional remedy, not a substitute for criminal indictment of the president. From that premise, it is an easy step to conclude that impeachment is directed at constitutional wrongs, not statutory offenses. The gravity of the proceeding and the awesomeness of the remedy combined to make criminality unimportant, even immaterial.

Furthermore it would have been incongruous for members of the committee to confront their critical task by debating such questions as the meaning of "endeavor" under 18 U.S.C. §1503, especially on national television.[12] Apart from every other consideration, it seems unlikely that perceptive politicians would have wanted their recommendation for or against impeachment of the president to appear to rest on technical questions of criminal law. A standard for impeachment derived from the president's constitutional obligations, by contrast, was both easily expressed and sacrosanct in its origins.

Whatever the reasons, the decisions by the committee on proposed articles of impeachment left no doubt that a majority believed that the relevant standards were constitutional, not criminal. The touchstones for judging a president's conduct were recognized to be his oath faith-

12. 18 U.S.C. §1503 is the basic obstruction of justice provision in the federal criminal law. An "endeavor" to obstruct justice—a felony under that section—has been defined expansively by the courts; it is, essentially, any step to achieve the illegal objective, including a step that does not meet the technical requirements for an attempt.

fully to execute the office and to preserve, protect, and defend the Constitution to the best of his ability and his duty to take care that the laws be faithfully executed. Article 1, adopted by the committee by a vote of 27 to 11, charged President Nixon with engaging in the Watergate cover-up, wrongdoing for which he had been named a coconspirator by a federal grand jury. The article could have been drafted in criminal law terms; instead, the committee expressly tailored it to the constitutional duties of the president. The committee report explained that President Nixon's actions, as charged in the article, "were contrary to his trust as President and unmindful of the solemn duties of his high office. It [is] this serious violation of Richard M. Nixon's constitutional obligations as President, and not the fact that violations of Federal criminal statutes occurred, that lies at the heart of Article I."[13] Article 2, on President Nixon's abuse of power, was even more explicitly noncriminal. The question it raised, according to its sponsor, William L. Hungate of Missouri, was "whether we shall say that you can be President as long as you are not subject to a criminal charge, whether that is the level of conduct we require, or whether we shall set a somewhat higher standard."[14] Article 2 was adopted by a vote of 28 to 10; the committee report summarized the charge as follows:

> Richard M. Nixon, in violation of his constitutional duty to take care that the laws be faithfully executed and his oath of office as President, seriously abused powers that only a President possesses. He engaged in conduct that violated the constitutional rights of citizens, that interfered with investigations by federal authorities and congressional committees, and that contravened the laws governing agencies of the executive branch of the federal government. This conduct, undertaken for his own personal political advantage and not in furtherance of any valid national policy objective, is seriously incompatible with our system of constitutional government.[15]

Ten Republican members of the committee voted against all three articles of impeachment adopted by the committee, though they

13. Nixon Impeachment Report 136.

14. 93d Cong., 2d Sess., House, Comm. on the Judiciary, *Debate on Articles of Impeachment, Hearings . . . Pursuant to H. Res. 803* at 339 (July 29, 1974) (hereafter Debate on Articles of Impeachment).

15. Nixon Impeachment Report 139.

unanimously changed their minds on the first article after the revelation of the June 23, 1972, transcripts,[16] and one indicated that he would favor Article 2 as well. These members did not argue that an indictable crime is necessary for impeachment. In their minority views on the articles, they acknowledged that it was "beyond argument" that a violation of the president's oath or duty to take care that the laws be faithfully executed must be impeachable or there would be no means of enforcing the Constitution. "[S]erious misconduct dangerous to the system of government established by the Constitution" was grounds for impeachment, they agreed, but there must be "extrinsic and objective standards" for separating impeachable misconduct from "errors in the administration of his office," for which the president could not be impeached. The standard they advocated was criminal intent—"an intent to do wrong," as one legal commentator they quoted had expressed it.[17]

The near-unanimity in rejecting the criminality limitation in the Nixon inquiry did not, of course, mean that there was positive agreement on a definition of grounds for impeachment. Clearing away the underbrush of the criminality dispute merely changes the terms of the debate: if, as in the Johnson trial, a president accused of crime can defend himself as chief magistrate, so can a president accused of violating constitutional duties and breaching constitutional obligations point to conflicting duties and other interpretations of his responsibilities. Above all—and this was a significant thread of the arguments offered on Nixon's behalf—he can argue that the allegations against him, even if true, are not sufficiently serious to warrant the extreme step of his removal from office.

16. On August 5, 1974, six days after the Judiciary Committee completed its deliberations, President Nixon released partial transcripts of his conversations with H. R. Haldeman, his chief staff assistant, on June 23, 1972. That same day the recordings of these conversations, subpoenaed for the Watergate cover-up criminal trial of Haldeman and five other former Nixon subordinates and associates, had been provided to the special prosecutor by the district court, in accordance with the Supreme Court's mandate in *United States v. Nixon*. The transcripts revealed that, contrary to claims made on his behalf during the impeachment inquiry, President Nixon knew of the involvement of his reelection committee in the Watergate break-in at least as early as six days after its occurrence and that he directed Haldeman to have the Central Intelligence Agency block an investigation of the break-in by the Federal Bureau of Investigation in order to avoid revelation of this involvement.

17. Nixon Impeachment Report, Minority Views 371, 365. The quotation is from Alexander Simpson, A *Treatise on Federal Impeachments* 29 (1916), also published as "Federal Impeachments," 64 *U. Pa. L. Rev.* 651, 675 (1916).

The Nixon inquiry was primarily, almost exclusively focused on factual questions involving the actions, knowledge, and intentions of the president. The facts were complex, all the more so with tape recordings and edited transcripts of presidential conversations available to the committee. With such an abundance of evidentiary material—much of it very raw, some of it ambiguous—it is hardly surprising that the arguments for and against impeachment, especially for the Watergate cover-up, were largely factual and that legal doctrine played a less significant role.

Nevertheless, there were a few attempts to fashion a legal defense—that is, a defense aimed at suggesting that President Nixon's misconduct, even if proved, did not constitute grounds for impeachment. The argument on Nixon's behalf most comparable to defense arguments in the Chase and Johnson trials was perhaps James St. Clair's "proof of the pudding" defense. In defending Nixon against impeachment on Watergate charges, St. Clair made three factual assertions: that there was no evidence that President Nixon had knowledge of the cover-up plot before March 21, 1973; that he did not join the cover-up conspiracy on that date by authorizing a payment to Howard Hunt (one of those involved in the break-in and other illegal covert activities), who was demanding (and received) "hush money" payments; and that after March 21, when the existence of the conspiracy was disclosed to him by his counsel, John Dean, President Nixon conducted a personal investigation and, in coordination with the Justice Department, took action by removing key White House staff members. This action, St. Clair's brief to the committee noted, "was a function of his constitutionally-directed power to see that the laws are 'faithfully executed' and was well within the wide discretion afforded him under the executive power doctrine."[18]

St. Clair told the committee in his oral presentation that on March 21 Dean gave the president information about the scope of the cover-up conspiracy for the first time, including the involvement of various members of the White House staff. St. Clair suggested that it was "hard to be critical of a President who would stand by his what he thought were faithful aides until such time as there was evidence developed that they should be released." The president had used judg-

18. See 93d Cong., 2d Sess., House, Comm. on the Judiciary, *Brief on Behalf of the President of the United States, Hearings . . . Pursuant to H. Res. 803* at 35–68 (July 18, 1974); the quotation is from 68 (hereafter Nixon Brief).

ment in wanting to know "a little more about the evidentiary support for these charges before acting on them." St. Clair asked whether it could be said that President Nixon's conduct "perverted the administration of criminal justice, prevented it from functioning, distorted the end results that can be expected by [its] proper functioning."

"The proof of that pudding is in its eating," St. Clair asserted. Indictments against the participants in the cover-up were pending, indictments that were the ultimate result of President Nixon's "cooperation and contribution . . . in conjunction with" the Justice Department. "If there was a delay in term of days," St. Clair asked, "was there any real prejudice developed for the people of the United States by reason of that delay?"[19]

St. Clair's argument on allegations of attempted misuse of the Internal Revenue Service to harass and obtain information about political opponents, including members of the staff and contributors to the campaign of President Nixon's Democratic opponent in the 1972 election, Senator George McGovern, was similar to the "proof of the pudding" argument on Watergate. The critical point of this defense was that the attempts to misuse the IRS were unsuccessful. While presidential aides may have communicated improper intentions about the use of the IRS to their colleagues or some individuals there, "no abuse of the IRS ever occurred resulting from Presidential action. No action by the IRS resulted." Moreover, St. Clair argued, the reason that no action was taken by the IRS was to President Nixon's credit. The president's most important duty with respect to the IRS is to appoint the commissioner; President Nixon had appointed commissioners (and secretaries of the treasury) who resisted attempts by White House staff members to misuse the IRS. The president "in no way prevented" independent commissioners of internal revenue "from resisting any improper political pressure"; "the ultimate fact is that the President's appointees did . . . resist any improper suggestions for the use or misuse of the agency."[20]

A different version of this argument about the IRS—somewhat more elegant, but also more sweeping in its implications about presidential control of the executive branch—appeared in the minority report on the paragraph of Article 2 relating to endeavors to misuse the IRS. The minority wrote:

19. Nixon Brief 23, 24; Impeachment Inquiry, Book III, 1905, 1906.
20. Nixon Brief 100, 13, 98.

> Because such efforts were unsuccessful, certainly the conclusion that the President was seriously intent on, or interested in the misuse of the IRS is negated. Given the plenary powers of a President to manage, direct and control the operations of the executive branch of government, if he had desired an illegitimate goal to be accomplished, it would have been accomplished.

There was, the minority asserted, a "serious question as to the degree of the President's true interest" in misusing the IRS to audit McGovern staff and contributors or for other improper purposes. And the "depth of the President's personal commitment to the achievement of some specific improper objective" was relevant to the impeachability of his conduct.[21]

The response of the majority of the committee to these arguments was primarily to point out that the evidence established something quite different about President Nixon's intentions and actions. There was, the majority found, a convincing case that Nixon engaged in a course of conduct or plan to cover up the Watergate break-in from shortly after its occurrence. On the IRS allegations, there was convincing evidence that Nixon knew of, encouraged, and approved efforts by his subordinates to misuse the IRS for his political advantage. The majority of the committee also disagreed with the contention that an unsuccessful endeavor was less culpable than a successful undertaking. St. Clair's "proof of the pudding" argument, Paul Sarbanes (D., Md.) said during the committee's deliberations, was nothing but a variant on the argument that the ends justify the means; in our democratic system, Sarbanes contended, we are concerned not only with the result attained but with the process employed to attempt to achieve

21. Nixon Impeachment Report, Minority Views 435. This argument echoed the Watergate defense that Samuel Garrison III had suggested to the committee on behalf of the minority staff of the impeachment inquiry. Like St. Clair, Garrison argued that the evidence failed to establish that Nixon had joined the cover-up conspiracy before, on, or after March 21. If, nevertheless, the committee did conclude that the president joined the conspiracy, Garrison argued that the time when he entered it and the degree of his activity as part of it should be taken into consideration. If Nixon had merely acted to "buy time" after March 21, Garrison suggested, the lesser degree of his culpability would "warrant the House, in the exercise of its political judgment in this case, to conclude that the only sanction available in the impeachment process—removal—should not be imposed." 93d Cong., 2d Sess., House, Comm. on the Judiciary, *Minority Memorandum on Facts and Law, Hearings . . . Pursuant to H. Res. 803* at 23–4 and 51–2. Garrison's argument also appears in Impeachment Inquiry, Book III, 2087–8 (July 22, 1974).

it.[22] The committee report on Article 2 quoted Justice William Johnson of the Supreme Court, who had considered a similar argument in 1808:

> If an officer attempt an act inconsistent with the duties of his station, it is presumed that the failure of the attempt would not exempt him from liability to impeachment. Should a president head a conspiracy for the usurpation of absolute power, it is hoped that no one will contend that defeating his machinations would restore him to innocence.[23]

Two other arguments on President Nixon's behalf were also aimed at reducing the seriousness of alleged wrongdoing, if not at disproving the existence of wrongdoing entirely. The first was really not at issue, though there was repeated discussion of it. It involved the question of the president's responsibility for wrongdoing by his subordinates, not undertaken at his command or with his approval or ratification. The idea of imposing vicarious liability upon a president—putting him at peril of impeachment for the conduct of his subordinates—was much criticized. "[I]t serves no purpose," the minority ultimately wrote in its report in opposition to Article 2, "to impose sanctions on a person for that of which he has no knowledge." The president "should not be removed from office for the act of a subordinate, unless he took some step to make that act his own—by knowingly assisting or approving it, or knowingly failing to exercise his control over a subordinate to prevent the commission of the act."

These comments by the minority were directed at Paragraph 4 of Article 2, as adopted by the committee, which alleged that President Nixon had failed to take care that the laws be faithfully executed by "failing to act when he knew or had reason to know that his close subordinates endeavored to impede and frustrate lawful inquiries." The minority had no disagreement, on principle, that the president was responsible for failing to act when he had actual knowledge of illegal conduct by subordinates. Their argument was with the imposition of liability on the president when he did not actually know, but only had reason to know of past or threatened unlawful action by subordinates.

22. Debate on Articles of Impeachment 74 (July 25, 1974).
23. Gilchrist v. Collector of Charleston, 10 F. Cas. 355, 365 (No. 5,420) (C.C.D.S.C. 1808), quoted in Nixon Impeachment Report 139, n. 1. (The case is discussed in chapter 4 below.)

"[M]ere negligence in failing to discover official misconduct" is not sufficient to justify a president's removal unless it is so habitual and egregious that it "assumes the character of a willful abdication of responsibility," the minority wrote.[24]

The standard that the committee majority was endorsing by adopting this paragraph of Article 2, however, had little to do with the president's accountability through impeachment for the acts of his subordinates. Instead, it involved the president's own constitutional obligation to take care that the laws were faithfully executed. This duty, the committee report stated, "imposes an affirmative obligation upon him to take reasonable steps to insure that his close subordinates, who serve at his pleasure and rely on his authority in the conduct of their positions, do not interfere with the proper functioning of government." The report quoted Robert McClory (R., Ill.), who had said in debate that there was "a clear violation of the President's responsibility when he permits multiple acts of wrongdoing by large numbers" of his close subordinates in the White House. It was not a question of vicarious liability, but of violation of the president's own constitutional duty.

The committee, in fact, specifically said in its report that it had relied upon "evidence of acts directly attributable to Richard M. Nixon himself" in considering Article 2 and found it "unnecessary in this case to take any position on whether the President should be held accountable, through exercise of the power of impeachment, for the actions of his immediate subordinates, undertaken on his behalf, when his personal authorization and knowledge of them cannot be proved." (The committee noted, however, that President Nixon had "governed behind closed doors, directing the operations of the executive branch through close subordinates, and sought to conceal his knowledge of what they did illegally on his behalf" and called attention to "the dangers inherent in the performance of the highest public office in the land in an air of secrecy and concealment.")[25]

The statement in the majority report involved what had come to be called the "Madison superintendency theory." James Madison, arguing in the First Congress in favor of the president's exclusive power to remove subordinates within the executive branch, had said that this power made the president responsible for their conduct, for it would "subject him to impeachment himself, if he suffers them to perpetrate

24. Nixon Impeachment Report, Minority Views 464.
25. Nixon Impeachment Report 171, 182.

with impunity high crimes or misdemeanors against the United States, or neglects to superintend their conduct, so as to check their excesses." The committee, Sarbanes explained, was not relying upon the full scope of this theory under Article 1, which made the president responsible for acts of subordinates only if they were undertaken in pursuance of his cover-up policy (or, as the article was later amended, his course of conduct or plan to cover up).[26] Nor was Article 2 based on this theory; acts of subordinates (as in the endeavors to misuse the IRS) were imputed to the president only if they had been undertaken pursuant to his authorization or with his knowledge, or he had ratified them after they occurred.

The problem with the Madison dictum—and, indeed, many of Madison's remarks about grounds for impeaching a president—is that it contains no modifiers. It suggests that the president is to be held accountable for neglecting to check "excesses" of any subordinate, no matter how inconsequential the excesses or how distant the subordinate. A literal application of the Madison theory would have meant the abandonment of any semblance of a gravity test in presidential impeachment. Instead, the Judiciary Committee added requirements to Madison's theory that made it a more stringent standard. The difference between the standard advocated by the minority (in opposition to Paragraph 4 of Article 2) and the standard that the majority was implicitly adopting was minimal. The crucial distinction was that the majority and minority reached different conclusions about the evidence before the committee.

The other argument on President Nixon's behalf was directed at charges of illegal wiretaps and the operations of the Plumbers, which eventually were incorporated in Paragraphs 2 and 3 of Article 2. The majority of the committee, it should be stressed, found clear and convincing evidence that these activities were not undertaken for any legitimate national security purpose.

The president's counsel, as well as the minority of the committee opposed to Article 2, argued that there was a national security justification. St. Clair contended before the committee:

> [T]he administration thought it was faced with a crisis in the conduct of the affairs of this country by extensive leaks in newspapers

26. Annals 1st Cong., 1st Sess., 372–3; Debate on Articles of Impeachment 268–9 (July 27, 1974).

> relating not only to the Pentagon papers but to the India-Pakistan relationship, the Okinawa decisions and negotiations with Japan, the SALT negotiations, and perhaps others. . . . [I]t would seem to me the information would suggest that if the President stood idly by and did nothing about the circumstance of this situation, and if these conditions continued, that in turn might well have been justification for an article of impeachment.

The minority report developed this theme in more general terms. "[N]o President who attempts to make full use of the lawful powers of his office is likely to complete his term without having committed, even in good faith, a constitutional violation," the minority asserted. His duties and responsibilities "frequently expose him to conflicting constitutional demands," when he must choose whether to act, knowing that his action may prove to violate the Constitution, or to refrain from acting, knowing that inaction while technically not a violation of his oath of office may be the worst policy of all. The critical question, the minority contended, "is whether the President's action was undertaken in good faith: whether he acted under color of law and in furtherance of his constitutional duties as he honestly saw them."[27]

The arguments made by those opposed to the impeachment of President Nixon, while tailored to the allegations before the Judiciary Committee, bore some resemblance to those made on behalf of Chase and Johnson. Criminality might not have been considered controlling by the end of the Nixon inquiry, but motive, intent, mistake, justification, consequences—all of which had figured in the earlier impeachments—were mentioned by opponents of Nixon's impeachment. They contended that the proof did not establish that President Nixon had engaged in intentional wrongdoing serious enough to warrant his removal from office; that any improprieties the evidence did establish were too paltry, too attenuated, committed in good faith or through honest error. The President should not be impeached unless there is proof of a great offense, a smoking pistol; the case cannot rest on charges outside the articles or inferences from the evidence; wrongful intent must be proved; there must be a violation of positive law; the impeachment process cannot be used to create a new standard of conduct.

27. Nixon Brief 13; Impeachment Inquiry, Book III, 1895; Nixon Impeachment Report, Minority Views 434.

Making the Crime Fit the Punishment

Two propositions about the constitutional grounds for impeachment of a president seem to be established: there must be wrongdoing by the president, and it must be serious. The definition of presidential wrongdoing is a question of law—constitutional law under the standard endorsed by the Judiciary Committee in the Nixon impeachment inquiry, criminal law under the indictability standard the Judiciary Committee rejected. It is apparent that the constitutional duties and responsibilities of the president are broadly defined. Faithful execution of the office and taking care that the laws be faithfully executed are duties stated in general terms. They gain content from the circumstances to which they are applied and from the expectations of the people and their representatives about the presidential office and the proper behavior of its occupant. The impossibility of spelling out in detail each and every way in which a president may fail to execute his office faithfully does not make the consitutional duty any less a standard for judging his conduct or make its application any less a question of law. Determining if the president has violated his constitutional obligations is not a political decision by the House or Senate. Removal of a president from office must be based on proof of past misconduct, established in an adjudicative proceeding, not on disagreement with his policies or his loss of popular support. Impeachment and trial in our system of government are not a substitute for a vote of no-confidence in a parliamentary system.

One source of difficulty in determining if a president has violated his constitutional duties is that little guidance is available from court-made law. Allegations of executive abuse of power or dereliction of duty are not ordinarily ruled upon by the courts. At least since *Marbury v. Madison*, the courts have refused to intervene to control the president's exercise of discretionary powers derived from the Constitution. Chief Justice John Marshall wrote in that case:

> By the constitution of the United States, the president is invested with certain important political powers, in the exercise of which he is to use his own discretion, and is accountable only to his country in his political character and to his own conscience.

Where executive discretion is used by the president or officers acting by his authority or in conformity with his orders, "there exists, and can exist, no power to control that discretion"; the acts "are only politically examinable."[28] Chief Justice Marshall did not mention impeachment as one mode of holding a president accountable "in his political character," but later cases did. In *Kendall v. United States* the Court noted that insofar as the president's powers are derived from the Constitution, "he is beyond the reach of any other department, except in the mode prescribed by the constitution through the impeaching power."[29] In *Mississippi v. Johnson* Attorney General Henry Stanberry (later to defend President Johnson in his impeachment trial) argued to the Supreme Court that the president could not be called upon "to answer for any dereliction of duty, for doing anything that is contrary to law or failing to do anything which is according to law" in the ordinary courts. "[O]nly one court or *quasi* court" has jurisdiction, Stanberry asserted, and "that is not this tribunal but one that sits in another chamber of this Capitol." In his opinion for the Court, Chief Justice Salmon P. Chase (later to preside at the Johnson impeachment trial) endorsed the view that the president could be impeached for refusing to execute the laws and suggested that this was one reason that the Court could not enjoin him from enforcing the laws or compel him to enforce them.[30]

Thus, among the considerations that put the exercise of discretionary powers by the president outside the province of the courts is his accountability to Congress through impeachment for abuse of these powers. But because these are nonjusticiable political questions, there is little case law to guide the House or Senate in determining if there has been an abuse of presidential power or if the abuse is serious enough to warrant impeachment and removal from office. Court review of presidential actions is generally limited to determining whether or not he has the power to engage in particular conduct; impeachment involves a further question: if the power exists, has it been exercised properly? Presidential wrongdoing can include the misuse of a power that a president unquestionably has, as well as the attempt to usurp a power that is not constitutionally granted.

28. 5 U.S. (1 Cr.) 137, 165–6 (1803).
29. Kendall v. United States *ex rel.* Stokes, 37 U.S. (12 Pet.) 524, 610 (1838).
30. 71 U.S. (4 Wall.) 475, 484, 500–1 (1867).

It is sometimes suggested that holding a president accountable for abuse of his powers involves a subjective decision, dependent only on the opinions of Congress. Charles E. Wiggins (R., Calif.), for example, argued during the deliberations on the second article proposed against President Nixon that abuse of power is "an empty phrase, having meaning only in terms of what we pour into it." To impeach the president when he has violated no law, Wiggins contended, would be to ratify Gerald Ford's statement that impeachment means whatever Congress says it means at a given moment; it would be imposing "an impossible standard" on future presidents, who would be required to anticipate "what Congress may declare to be abusive in the future"; and it would make it the legal duty of the president to comply with congressional "notions of morality and propriety."[31]

The impeachment process, however, offers a commonsense answer to this criticism, embodied in the requirement that impeachable wrongdoing be serious. If there is little law on what constitutes a violation of presidential duties because the impeachment of presidents has been so rarely considered, and if the standard is necessarily broad and somewhat amorphous, it is nonetheless exceedingly unlikely that a president will be impeached and removed unless he goes substantially beyond the line between excusable error and culpable wrongdoing. The remedy of removal is now considered too drastic (in part because it has never actually been applied) to be used in doubtful instances. In the nature of the case, the critical question is probably not whether a president's conduct is wrongful, but whether wrongdoing convincingly established by the evidence is so egregious that his continuation in office is intolerable.

The defense strategy in the Johnson impeachment trial and the arguments offered in opposition to President Nixon's impeachment were directed largely at establishing that whatever wrongdoing there was did not warrant the drastic sanction of removal of the chief executive. The procedures followed by the House in impeachment proceedings and by the Senate in impeachment trials may facilitate this approach, for they focus attention on the seriousness of each separate charge rather than the seriousness of the wrongdoing considered cumulatively or in its entirety.

From the first American impeachment in 1797, the House and

31. Debate on Articles of Impeachment 336 (July 29, 1974).

Senate have looked to English impeachment cases as a procedural model. At the time of the first impeachment, the leading English precedent was the most recent—the impeachment of Warren Hastings, undertaken in 1786 and ended, nine years later, with a judgment of acquittal. In impeaching Senator William Blount the House of Representatives copied the procedures of the House of Commons in the Hastings case. After Blount was impeached, a select committee was appointed to conduct a further investigation and to prepare articles of impeachment for prosecution in the Senate. The charge against Blount was that he had violated his public trust and duty as a senator by engaging in a plot to induce the Creek and Cherokee Indian nations to undertake a military expedition to seize the Spanish possessions of Louisiana and Florida and turn them over to Great Britain. There was only one plot—indeed, the crucial evidence against Blount was a single letter he had written—but five separate articles were prepared, comparable to five counts in a criminal indictment, each focusing on a different offense encompassed within the plot.[32]

Articles of impeachment in English cases resembled criminal indictments for a very simple reason: in England impeachment was a criminal proceeding, with criminal sanctions (including capital punishment) upon conviction. Though there was a separate parliamentary law of crimes and some procedural latitude not found in ordinary criminal cases, impeachment was a criminal prosecution. After trial the House of Lords not only judged whether the accused was guilty of the offenses charged against him but also passed sentence. Like the court in an ordinary case, it had discretion in determining the sentence to be imposed. Guilt on more than one article presumably affected the sentencing decision, as did the seriousness of the offenses. While it is unlikely that the House of Commons would prosecute trivial offenses, impeachment could theoretically reach any offense

32. Annals 5th Cong., 1st Sess., 41–3, 448–50 (1797), 951 (1798). Each of the articles was probably sufficient to charge the common law crimes of conspiracy and, perhaps, sedition. The Sedition Act of 1798, Act of July 14, 1798, ch. 73, 1 Stat. 596, became law after the articles against Blount were prepared and adopted by the House, but before the case reached the Senate. Had the act applied to Blount's conduct, the articles apparently would have been sufficient to charge five counts of violating the statute, which declared a violation to be a "high misdemeanor."

The Senate dismissed the impeachment of Blount, whom it had already expelled from the Senate for the same conduct. Among the arguments in favor of dismissal of the impeachment were that a senator is not a "civil officer" subject to impeachment and that Blount was no longer a senator.

against parliamentary law. The gravity and number of offenses influenced the punishment, not the definition of impeachable wrongdoing.

Under the American Constitution there is no comparable latitude in imposing a sanction. Judgment on impeachment is constitutionally limited to removal from office and disqualification from holding future office. Upon conviction of treason, bribery, or other high crimes and misdemeanors, the president (or any other civil officer) must be removed from office. Although the issues were unsettled at the time of the Blount impeachment, these provisions of the Constitution have since been interpreted to mean that impeachment lies only for the stated offenses and only against civil officers and that removal is mandatory upon conviction, while disqualification is discretionary and requires only a majority vote of the Senate after conviction. The Senate may not impose sanctions other than removal and disqualification; its discretion is limited, if it convicts, to deciding simply to remove or both to remove and to disqualify. Accordingly, the ultimate issue in a presidential impeachment proceeding is whether the president should be removed from office, nothing less and very little more. (How little more is suggested by the lack of serious consideration of proceeding with the Nixon impeachment after his resignation for the purpose of insuring his disqualification from future federal office.)

In the American system of impeachment, the Senate cannot tailor the sanction to the wrongdoing, but instead must decide if the only available sanction—removal from office—is warranted. It must decide, in short, whether the crime fits the punishment.

Because the sanction is fixed, it would seem that the offenses a president (or other officer) has committed should be considered together in deciding whether it should be imposed. Taken separately, the offenses may not seem serious enough to justify the removal of an elected chief executive; viewed cumulatively, they may establish a pattern of wrongdoing sufficiently serious to demonstrate his unfitness to continue in office.

The procedure followed by the Senate in the first impeachment trial to go to judgment—the Pickering case, in 1804—seemed to recognize this distinction. As in the Blount impeachment, the House had prepared separate articles, in this case four articles all concerning Judge Pickering's conduct of a single admiralty proceeding. The Senate in the Pickering case first voted on whether Judge Pickering was guilty as charged in each article, then (after conviction) on whether to impose judgment of removal from office. Gradually, however, the distinction between guilt and innocence on an article and the ultimate question of removal from office was lost. In the Chase trial, perhaps in reaction to the criticism of the form of question used in the Pickering case, the Senate passed judgment on whether Justice Chase was guilty of the high crime or misdemeanor alleged in each article. The House had described the charges against Justice Chase as high crimes and misdemeanors, but it did not use the term in each article, just as it had not in the Blount and Pickering articles. The form of the question propounded to the Senate in the Chase trial, derived from English impeachment practice, suggested that each article was to be considered in terms of its adequacy as an independent basis for Chase's removal. A judgment of acquittal was entered by unanimous consent after none of the articles attained a two-thirds guilty vote.

Not until the Andrew Johnson impeachment did the House explicitly label the charge in each article as a high crime or a high misdemeanor; it probably did so then because some of the articles charged statutory "high misdemeanors" and others "high crimes." After the Johnson case it became customary in articles of impeachment to denominate each charge separately as a high misdemeanor. And, by the Ritter trial, the Senate considered removal to follow upon conviction on a single article as a matter of course.[33] Articles of impeachment had evolved, for whatever reasons, into independent allegations of impeachable offenses, and the ultimate issue of removal from office came to depend on guilt or innocence on the articles considered independently of one another, without any intervening consideration of the seriousness of the offenses taken together.

This probably had little or no impact on the outcome of impeachment trials in the Senate. It seems highly unlikely that any impeachment failed because senators thought that the charges, as divided into articles, were not independently serious enough to warrant removal from office. The Senate customarily deliberated on the articles in closed session before voting and presumably could have adopted a different voting method if conviction actually turned on the question of which article or articles were sufficient to warrant removal. And by this century the House had developed its own response to the prob-

33. Annals 8th Cong., 1st Sess., 366–7 (1804) (Pickering); *ibid.*, 665–9 (1805); 2 Chase Trial 484–94; 93d Cong., 2d Sess., Senate, *Procedure and Guidelines for Impeachment Trials in the United States Senate* 81–2 (Aug. 8, 1974).

lem—a final "catchall" article, which cumulated the charges contained in the other articles. Such an article, in one form or another, was included in each of the three most recent judicial impeachments; it charged that the judge's course of conduct undermined the integrity of his court or brought it into disrepute. These articles, of course, were partly based on the "good behavior" clause, so it may be contended that they are weak precedent in executive impeachments. The seriousness of the wrongdoing charged against a judge, moreover, may be less critical to the outcome of an impeachment against him than the gravity of the charges potentially is in a presidential impeachment.

The separation of charges into independent articles of impeachment, each alleging a high crime or misdemeanor, did affect the proceedings in the House, primarily because of another procedural change, which occurred contemporaneously with the introduction of the catchall article of impeachment. From the Blount impeachment, it had been customary to consider the general question of impeachment without reference to particular articles. Only after the House had voted to impeach was a committee assigned the task of preparing articles of impeachment. The committee was usually composed of members of the House who had favored impeachment; when the House considered the proposed articles, it was already committed to prosecuting the case in the Senate and there was generally little substantive debate on the proposed articles.

Beginning with the Archbald impeachment in 1912, the Judiciary Committee included proposed articles as part of its recommended resolution of impeachment.[34] Both the committee and the House considered how to frame the pleading at the same time they were deciding whether to impeach. As a matter of parliamentary procedure, an impeachment resolution containing articles is a divisible question, so the House debated and voted on each article separately before adopting

34. 62d Cong., 2d Sess., H. Rept. No. 946 (1912). There were earlier instances in which a committee recommending impeachment included draft articles, or detailed specifications resembling articles, in its report. In no instance before the Archbald impeachment, however, did the House adopt an impeachment resolution containing articles. The change in procedure seems to have resulted from the difficulty the House had in reaching agreement on articles of impeachment against Judge Charles Swayne in 1905. After voting to impeach Swayne by a substantial margin (against the recommendation of a majority of the Judiciary Committee), the House was closely divided on the adoption of specific articles drafted by a select committee appointed in the traditional fashion. See 39 Cong. Rec. 810–3 (1905), discussed in Nixon Impeachment Report, Minority Views 430.

the resolution of impeachment. Opponents of impeachment could stress the insufficiency or weakness of each article, one at a time, in making their case against impeachment. In order to impeach, the House had to agree both on the merits of impeachment and on the form in which the case should be presented to the Senate. This procedure potentially raised the question, really for the first time in the House, whether each individual article alleged an "impeachable offense"—that is, an independent ground for impeachment and removal.

Two procedural innovations in the Nixon impeachment inquiry increased the emphasis on the form of each article and its independent sufficiency as a reason for the removal of the president. First, the Judiciary Committee's debate on recommended articles of impeachment was conducted in public and broadcast over national television. Second, the articles were technically all the committee was debating. Its procedures provided that the committee would not vote on the general question of impeaching President Nixon or even on reporting the resolution containing the articles it recommended to the House.[35] Instead, the resolution of impeachment was considered adopted once the committee agreed to one article of impeachment. The provision of the resolution impeaching President Nixon for high crimes and misdemeanors was deemed to be merely formal, prefatory language, like the enacting clause of a bill. The members of the committee were not required to vote for or against the general proposition that a case for President Nixon's removal from office should be prosecuted in the Senate. Their deliberations centered on the contents of the pleading that would be carried to the Senate.

It is common legislative practice to avoid controversy by using language that compromises or even obscures a potentially divisive point. This occurred in the framing of articles of impeachment by the Judiciary Committee. One of the objectives of those supporting impeachment was to gain as broad a consensus as possible in favor of the proposed articles. Compromise, even ambiguity, in the language of the articles was one of the necessary means of reconciling diverse views. Similarly, it is a common opposition tactic to offer amendments to a pending measure in order to dilute its effect or point up its weaknesses. During the Judiciary Committee's deliberations, a

35. See Impeachment Inquiry, Book III, 2105–28 (July 23, 1974); Nixon Impeachment Report 10.

number of amendments were offered by opponents of impeachment to highlight what they considered to be weak points in the case or unclear language (some of it purposeful) in the articles. Most of these amendments failed, but a few resulted in changes, not all of them necessarily helpful to those who might have had to prosecute the impeachment in the Senate.

But articles of impeachment are not ordinary legislation. They are an accusatory pleading for an adjudicative proceeding, intended to distill judgments about what the evidence will establish at trial and to articulate a legal theory by which this evidence will support conviction and removal from office. It is difficult for any relatively large group of lawyers to agree upon a legal theory for structuring a complex case, especially when they are not in complete agreement on what the evidence establishes or what the applicable law is. It is all the more difficult when the theory must be publicly defended in a political forum at the same time it is being developed, and defended not only against those who would structure the case differently or put more stress on other evidence, but also against those who believe there is no case at all. One of the minor miracles of the Judiciary Committee's deliberations—and a tribute to its chairman, special counsel, and members who supported impeachment—was that agreement was reached and maintained during the public debate. The reason it could be, was the overriding necessity, as these members saw it, of obtaining the broadest possible support for impeachment.

The achievement of this objective, even at the risk of diluting or limiting the charges against President Nixon, was undoubtedly critical to the impeachment proceeding. Nevertheless, the procedure adopted by the Judiciary Committee may not be the appropriate method for making impeachment decisions. The older House procedure, by which impeachment was first considered as a general proposition and then articles drafted from a prosecutorial perspective, has its advantages. It permits the committee and the House to focus initially on the whole case, rather than its details. Impeachment investigations rarely involve only one allegation, and it is unlikely (short of some truly outrageous conduct) that a president will ever again be impeached for what he wrote between noon and one o'clock on a Friday afternoon, to recall one of Evarts's points in belittling the charges against Andrew Johnson. Unquestionably, members of the Judiciary Committee reached their individual decisions on whether to support articles of impeachment against President Nixon partly on the basis of the totality of the wrongdoing established by the evidence. Representative Sarbanes made the point in an interview with a reporter shortly before the committee began its public deliberations. The case established by the evidence, he said, reminded him of going to a vegetable store, where you "go over to the tomatoes and the first one is rotten and the next one is rotten and you go over to the other side of the bin and it's rotten, and then you try some other vegetables and they're the same way. After you've been through that for a while and it keeps happening, you say 'What kind of a store is this?' "[36] It was partly the cumulative impact of the evidence that led to the determination that President Nixon should be impeached, but the procedure of the committee provided no mechanism for expressing this conclusion.

The procedure followed by the Judiciary Committee placed more stress on the form of the articles than it probably deserved.[37] Since the last impeachment trial in 1936, there have been extensive changes in the procedural rules in federal courts. Especially in civil proceedings, the rules for pleading a case have been substantially simplified and modernized. Most of the old technical requirements (reflected in past articles of impeachment) no longer apply; notice pleading—a clear, concise, and straightforward statement of the allegations, intended

36. Elizabeth Drew, *Washington Journal: The Events of 1973–1974* at 329 (1975).

37. The Judiciary Committee did accomplish some long-overdue pleading reforms in its Nixon articles. One, about which the committee wrangled in its public deliberations, was the omission of detailed specifics from the articles. Another, which went totally unnoticed, was the abandonment of the antiquated, boiler-plate sentence with which every earlier set of articles had closed. This sentence, among other things, included a "protestation" reserving to the House the right to reply to the answer filed by the impeached official, offer proof, and bring further charges or an additional impeachment. A protestation was a pleading formality reflecting strict pleading rules, which required a party to join issue on only one contention in each plea of his opponent. Under those rules, the practice arose of protesting other contentions in order to avoid an implied admission of what it was impermissible to deny. By 1798, when the House first included a protestation in the Blount articles, the practice was obsolete. The inclusion of a protestation in every set of articles in American impeachments shows a close attention to precedent, but served no purpose.

A modernized version of the traditional concluding language (omitting the term "protestation") was prepared by the impeachment inquiry staff for the Nixon articles (see New York Times, July 20, 1974, at 17, second set of articles). It was not included in the Donohue resolution, which served as the basis for the Judiciary Committee's deliberations, however, and it was not proposed as an amendment both because it was unnecessary and because it might have appeared to raise the ultimate question, on which the committee was not voting, of whether Nixon should be impeached.

merely to notify the opponent of what is involved—is now the rule. The role of pleadings in framing the issues in a case has also been diminished, with liberal allowance for amendment. The change is not as complete in criminal proceedings, but there is also a trend away from technical pleading rules in criminal procedure. In any event, it has traditionally been said that impeachment is not governed by usual pleading rules. "[T]he nature of the proceeding," Alexander Hamilton wrote in *The Federalist* No. 65, "can never be tied down by such strict rules . . . in the delineation of the offence by the prosecutors . . . as in common cases serve to limit the discretion of courts in favor of personal security."[38] Justice Joseph Story wrote some forty years later, in his *Commentaries on the Constitution:*

> [I]t is obvious, that the strictness of the forms of the proceeding in cases of offences of common law are ill adapted to impeachments. . . . [T]he adherence to technical principles, which, perhaps, distinguishes this branch of the law, more than any other, are all ill adapted to the trial of political offences in the broad course of impeachments. . . . There is little technical in the mode of proceeding; the charges are sufficiently clear, and yet in a general form; there are few exceptions which arise in the application of the evidence, which grow out of mere technical rules and quibbles.[39]

Even apart from modern procedural trends, it may be questioned whether the form of the articles warrants the attention it received during the deliberations of the Judiciary Committee in the Nixon inquiry. This is particularly true when the pleadings are being perfected not with the objective of strengthening the case at trial, but rather for the purpose of gaining broad support in the House in favor of taking the case to trial. It might be preferable to use another vehicle for this purpose, such as a resolution instructing the managers on the range of allegations to be included in the prosecution.[40]

38. At 425–6.

39. 3 Story §763.

40. One reason for including articles in the initial resolution of impeachment is that it compresses what historically proved to be a time-consuming process involving three separate committees (the investigating committee, the committee to draft articles, and the managers). In several impeachments the managers, who were responsible for prosecuting the case in the Senate, proposed changes in the articles. The Johnson impeachment is an example of an instance where this occurred after articles were drafted by a select committee composed of proponents of impeachment. Most recently, it occurred

Focusing the initial deliberations of the Judiciary Committee and the House on the general question of impeachment, coupled perhaps with a nontechnical specification of the grounds for impeachment, would have several advantages. First, it would permit these deliberations to highlight matters of substance rather than form. Second, it would permit the committee and the House to maintain the adjudicative rather than accusatory posture that seems to be required in the modern political climate. Third, it would give those who ultimately have to prosecute the case the latitude they need to make tactical decisions about how best to frame the accusation, decisions that cannot necessarily be articulated or defended on the basis of constitutional principles. It would, in short, divide the question of impeachment into its two, quite different component parts: the high constitutional issue of whether to impeach and the strategic, litigative question of how best to win the case once it has been undertaken.

The Concept of an "Impeachable Offense"

Procedural cavils apart, the House Judiciary Committee produced a reasonably sensible set of allegations against President Nixon. The articles were tailored to the charges that a majority of the committee found to be convincingly established by the evidence; more than that, they focused on conduct considered by the committee—and, as events showed, by the nation—to be sufficiently serious, if proved, to warrant President Nixon's removal from office. Whatever else might have happened, the Nixon impeachment would not have failed in the Senate for want of a sufficiently serious allegation of wrongdoing.

Nor, despite the division of the case into separate articles, would it have been easily fractionated, for there was an underlying theme in the proposed articles that served to unify them. All the charges involved conduct in violation of President Nixon's constitutional duties, wrongdoing intended to further his personal political interests rather than any national policy objective. Not only the Watergate article, but also the article on abuse of power and even that on noncompliance

---

in the Ritter impeachment, where the articles were initially drafted by the Judiciary Committee as part of its impeachment resolution.

The process could be similarly accelerated by giving the managers the task of proposing articles in the first instance, under instructions from the House. This would also insure that the articles were drafted primarily with a view to litigation strategy in the Senate.

with the subpoenas of the Judiciary Committee, emphasized a single pattern of conduct: unlawful activities intended primarily to obtain political intelligence for the benefit of the president, followed by efforts to conceal and impede investigation of these activities. "[C]oncealment, duplicity, dissembling" were the essence of the wrongdoing charged against President Nixon, John Doar told the Judiciary Committee in advocating impeachment,[41] and each of the proposed articles built, in one way or another, on this common pattern. While there were loose ends (particularly in some of the paragraphs of Article 2), by and large it was a coherent case. And the element of seriousness was reinforced by this pattern, for concealment implied knowledge of wrongfulness and the political purpose of the conduct precluded an attempt to justify it on the basis of inherent presidential powers or prerogatives under even the most expansive theory of executive power.

The pattern was not a construct of the committee or its inquiry staff; it arose naturally from the central allegations under investigation, and especially from those concerning the Watergate cover-up. The existence of this pattern not only provided a basis for framing the charges against President Nixon, but it also created its own standard for judging the seriousness of other allegations against President Nixon. In this respect, to add a substantive quibble to the procedural cavil, it may have created a false impression about what are and are not grounds for impeachment of another president at another time. As a matter of common sense and (one would hope) constitutional law, it simply cannot be true that presidents can be removed from office only for what they do in secret and thereafter try to conceal from the people and investigating authorities. Nor, despite the fact that impeachment is a legal proceeding in which lawyers and legal values play a crucial role, can it be said that the primary governmental function impeachment is designed to protect is the administration of justice. It would be misreading the Nixon case to give it this limited interpretation.

Nevertheless, there may be a tendency to misinterpret the decisions of the Judiciary Committee—and particularly its negative decisions to reject or ignore certain allegations—in just this way. One reason involves a concept that unavoidably came up during the Nixon inquiry, partly because it was in the air, partly because it gained respectable scholarly endorsement, and partly because it was a convenient way to

41. Summary of Information 11; Impeachment Inquiry, Book III, 1933 (July 19, 1974).

avoid an inordinate amount of circumlocution. It is the concept of an "impeachable offense."

As a matter of logic, an impeachable offense undoubtedly exists—a single act of wrongdoing so serious, so subversive of constitutional government that it alone warrants impeachment and removal from office. A single act of treason, under the constitutional definition, undoubtedly meets this test, as might one instance of bribery (though that may be more questionable, since bribery can range from a rather trivial wrong to an extremely egregious one). Apart from these offenses, one can conceive in the abstract of a high crime so shocking that by itself it would be an impeachable offense.[42]

Most of the allegations against President Nixon did not constitute separate impeachable offenses in this sense. It was necessary to combine distinct actions into a pattern or course of conduct to establish grounds for removal from office. Except semantically, it could not be said that each of the articles proposed by the Judiciary Committee (with the possible exception of Article 3, on noncompliance with its subpoenas) charged a single impeachable offense. What they did charge was a continuing course of conduct, or a repeated type of wrongdoing, that provided a reason for President Nixon's removal.

Some involved in the Nixon inquiry seemed preoccupied at times with a search for the "impeachable offense." The origins of this search may be traceable to a pastime engaged in by prominent constitutional scholars in late 1973 and early 1974—the making of *ex cathedra* pronouncements about whether this or that type of presidential conduct was an impeachable offense. Charles L. Black, Jr., of the Yale Law School, for example, wrote that impeachable offenses must meet a threefold test: they must be extremely serious, they must in some way corrupt or subvert the political and governmental process, and they must be plainly wrong.[43] Black proceeded to apply this test to particular problems suggested by the allegations against President Nixon

42. Grammatical arguments concerning that overscrutinized phrase, "treason, bribery, or other high crimes and misdemeanors," should not be taken too seriously. Nevertheless, it is interesting to note that the catchall term is plural, suggesting that the framers did not consider a single "impeachable offense" to be required. The term could just as readily, and almost as sparely, have been stated in the singular as "or any other high crime or misdemeanor." Moreover, "maladministration," for which the term was a substitute, surely would have encompassed a pattern of misconduct as well as a single act.

43. Charles L. Black, Jr., *Impeachment: A Handbook* 37 (1974) (hereafter Black).

(though not necessarily reflecting the actual evidence in the case). He concluded that serious tax fraud is an impeachable offense, as is misuse of the tax system to harass opponents; impoundment is not; presidential warlike activity would be only in "a very extreme and not now visible case"; and so on.[44] Similarly, Arthur M. Schlesinger, Jr., wrote that the Nixon doctrines of unlimited impoundment and unreviewable executive privilege "do not . . . seem to me to constitute impeachable offenses."

The reasoning of Schlesinger and Black on impoundment illustrates their approach. Schlesinger wrote that impoundment was not an impeachable offense because President Nixon was "perfectly open in his claims" of an unlimited power to impound funds. Nixon avowed the doctrine publicly and "gave Congress and the people fair warning." Moreover, the doctrine had "a vaguely arguable, if to my mind entirely factitious, constitutional basis," Schlesinger wrote, and the Johnson case taught that impeachment "is not a good way to resolve constitutional disputes." Black's rationale on impoundment was somewhat more complicated. He wrote that, in his opinion, the president violated his constitutional duty to take care that the laws be faithfully executed by using his discretionary power over expenditures for the improper purpose of dismantling or severely crippling programs regularly enacted in lawful form, if he disingenuously invoked the motive of economy when his real motive was dislike for the programs. But, Black went on, this was only his opinion, and in this gray area opinions could differ. Black suggested that the president has statutory responsibility to operate within debt and expenditure ceilings and perhaps even "some residual responsibility not to see the country descend into financial ruin." The president "might think (though others would disagree) that these responsibilities were to be served best by cuts where his judgment advised they might least hurtfully be made, rather than by cuts across the board." In addition, many appropriation statutes authorize, but do not mandate spending. Finally, in many cases there are judicial remedies for those who have a clear legal right to impounded funds, and the president may think that by impounding he is merely referring a doubtful question to the courts. "On the whole, and for all these reasons, I incline to think 'impoundment' not an impeachable offense," Black concluded, adding that he hesitated to an-

44. *Ibid.*, 41–6.

ticipate what his judgment would be if a flagrant instance came to light.[45]

Both Schlesinger and Black apparently recognized that their conclusion that impoundment is not an impeachable offense was a matter of opinion. Other scholars, including Henry Steele Commager, disagreed with it.[46] The question is now purely academic; under legislation enacted in 1974 the Nixonian form of impoundment cannot recur, at least without a much more clear-cut challenge to congressional control of the spending power.

But the important point is that the question was hypothetical even in late 1973 and early 1974 when Schlesinger and Black were writing. To the extent impoundment was at issue in the Nixon inquiry (and it was not proposed for inclusion in the committee's recommended articles), it was in the context of the whole case against President Nixon. Whether or not, in the abstract, it was a separate impeachable offense was not pertinent to the committee's deliberations. If impoundment had been included in the articles, it undoubtedly would have been pleaded in a manner that did not suggest that it was a self-sufficient reason for President Nixon's removal—for example, as an instance of abuse of presidential power in an article charging that as a ground for his impeachment. That impoundment was neither included nor seriously considered for inclusion by the Judiciary Committee says less about the definition of grounds for impeachment than it does about the case against Richard Nixon.

Two other allegations, however, were considered and specifically rejected by the committee. Each shared some, but not all of the elements of the pattern of conduct charged in the articles the committee did agree to. The first was a suggested article charging President Nixon with concealment from Congress of the facts concerning American bombing in Cambodia and the submission of false and misleading statements to Congress on this subject, in derogation of the power of Congress to declare war, make appropriations, and raise and support armies. The other charged President Nixon, first, with receiving emoluments from the United States in the form of government expenditures on his San Clemente and Key Biscayne properties in violation of

45. Arthur M. Schlesinger, Jr., *The Imperial Presidency* 469 n. 15 (Popular Library ed. 1974); Black 42–3.

46. Henry Steele Commager, *The Defeat of America: Presidential Power and the National Character* 146–7 (1974).

Article II, section 1 of the Constitution (which provides that the president shall receive no emoluments from the United States other than compensation that shall not be increased or decreased during his term) and, second, with willfully attempting to evade income taxes by knowingly failing to report income and claiming deductions not authorized by law, including a substantial deduction for a gift of papers to the United States.

Opponents of these articles made a number of arguments against them. On the concealment of the Cambodia bombing, it was contended that there was congressional acquiescence in the bombing (and complicity by members who were informed in concealing it from Congress as a whole), that it was a valid exercise of the president's power as commander in chief in acting to end the war in Southeast Asia and protect American lives,[47] and that the issue had been resolved by the subsequent adoption of the War Powers Resolution of 1973, which would prevent future occurrences of this type.[48] On the article involving personal finances, it was contended that the expenditures on President Nixon's property were made pursuant to Secret Service requests (and that the Secret Service must be accorded great latitude in deciding what is necessary to provide protection for the president) and there was no direct evidence that he knew that the improvements and services involved were paid for out of public rather than personal funds. On the tax charge included in this article, it was argued that the evidence before the committee was insufficient to establish a clear and convincing case of tax fraud, that the conduct was not sufficiently related to the president's official duties to be a proper subject of impeachment, and that it could be handled by the ordinary courts.[49]

In the circumstances, the decision to reject these articles was probably sound. The most compelling reason for doing so, however, was not that the wrongdoing they charged had no place in an impeachment proceeding or was too trivial to warrant impeachment, but rather that these charges would have complicated the case enormously with-

47. Unknowingly echoing the "errand boy" arguments in the Johnson trial, Rep. Delbert L. Latta (R., Ohio) warned against reducing the office of president "to merely a choir boy for the Congress of the United States." Debate on Articles of Impeachment 493 (July 30, 1974).

48. *Ibid.*, 489–517. See Nixon Impeachment Report 217–9.

49. Debate on Articles of Impeachment 517–59 (July 30, 1974). See Nixon Impeachment Report 220–3.

out adding much weight to the allegations against President Nixon. The Cambodia article, though tailored exclusively to the deception of Congress and not the actual bombing, would have introduced the divisive issue of the Indochina War into the impeachment proceedings. The tax and emoluments article—in addition to being based on evidence that might be considered inconclusive—raised complex legal and factual questions that were far different in character from those in the articles that had been adopted. Some members of the committee recognized that these articles could properly be rejected as a matter of litigation strategy. M. Caldwell Butler (R., Va.), who supported the first two articles of impeachment, had argued against the third article partly on this basis:

> [A]fter adoption of articles I and II by the House of Representatives, we will have placed the issue of Presidential conduct sufficiently before the Senate of the United States for a determination of whether the President should be continued in office or not. And any additional articles would extend the proceeding unnecessarily.

In opposition to the personal finances article, Butler pointed out that impeachment is discretionary. "Sound judgment would indicate that we not add this article to the trial burden we already have." Similarly, Ray Thornton (D., Ark.), who voted for the first three articles, suggested in opposition to the article on personal finances, "Our charge is serious and full enough."[50]

Still, there were some committee members who felt impelled to state reasons of principle for rejecting these articles, reasons for concluding that the conduct they charged did not constitute impeachable offenses. Indeed, some of the arguments suggested that the committee was drafting a constitutional amendment concerning the duties of the president rather than framing an impeachment case against Richard Nixon. Jerome R. Waldie (D., Calif.), a staunch advocate of every other article of impeachment considered by the committee, opposed the personal finances articles, although he characterized President Nixon's conduct as "shabby," "unacceptable," "disgraceful even." Impeachment, Waldie contended, is a process "designed to redefine Presidential powers in cases where there has been enormous abuse of those powers and then to limit the powers as a concluding result of the im-

50. Debate on Articles of Impeachment 477, 550, 549 (July 30, 1974).

peachment process"; in this instance, no presidential power had been "so grossly abused that it deserves redefinition and limiting."[51]

Such a lofty view of the impeachment process was understandable, especially given the substantial commendation the committee had received for the statesmanlike fashion in which it had conducted its earlier deliberations on articles of impeachment. Rejecting some articles of impeachment, moreover, served to underscore the judiciousness of the committee in evaluating the allegations against President Nixon. All this notwithstanding, it is questionable that the framers of the Constitution in fact considered impeachment to have the function Waldie ascribed to it. And, even if impeachment is in part a standard-setting process, it is still debatable whether each and every allegation in an impeachment case must involve constitutional issues of the first magnitude. No matter how appropriate the rejection of these articles in the context of the case against Richard Nixon, the reason that some members articulated for their decision—the elusive search for the "impeachable offense," measured against some immutable standard, all by itself—was unfortunate.

Concluding Observations on Grounds for Impeachment

The Nixon impeachment inquiry should have put an end to one of the longest-running, if sporadic, sideshows in American constitutional law—the effort to define "high crimes and misdemeanors." Analysis of the historical meaning of the term in English impeachments between the late fourteenth and late eighteenth centuries, commentary by eighteenth-century English legal writers, the cryptic record of its adoption by the Constitutional Convention in 1787, later dicta by the framers and their colleagues, the charges in past American impeachments—analysis that has been repeated almost every time impeachment has been undertaken or considered—ultimately leads to a very simple conclusion: the text of the Constitution poses no obstacle to behaving sensibly. The term the framers used, now so enigmatic, does not mean what it seems to connote—criminality—but neither does it make a president (or any other official) removable for whatever reason strikes the congressional fancy.

51. *Ibid.*, 548.

An attempt to articulate an all-purpose definition of grounds for impeachment is an unedifying enterprise. The elements of any such definition are judgmental and overlapping. Consider, for example, Black's threefold test. It is not a bad definition, and it reflects general legal opinion on the subject. Black later restated it as follows:

> "[H]igh Crimes and Misdemeanors," in the constitutional sense ought to be held to be those offenses which are rather obviously wrong, whether or not "criminal," and which so seriously threaten the order of political society as to make pestilent and dangerous the continuance in power of their perpetrator.

Black recognized that this definition was only an approximation and observed that the further question of substantiality had to be addressed in terms of a particular case. "The answer, when answer must be given, must probably be to some extent political; law can lead us to the point where 'substantiality' becomes the issue, but law cannot tell us what is 'substantial' for the purpose of decision."[52] Black's point, however, applies not just to some additional requirement of substantiality, but to the very essence of his definition—what is "rather obviously" wrong, what "seriously threaten[s]" the political order, what makes continuance in office "pestilent and dangerous." Degree, seriousness, substantiality are at the center of the definition and link together each of its parts. And, when an actual case arises, factual particulars overwhelm the general theory. The arguments for and against impeachment or removal have less to do with some abstract standard than with the conduct under scrutiny and the circumstances surrounding it. There are common themes, even repeated use of the same stratagems, in past impeachment cases. But these themes and stratagems do not establish principles of impeachment law.

Wrongful intent is an example. If it means, as was argued at length in the Chase and Johnson trials, that mere mistakes—"errors of the head and not of the heart," to use the expression popular with the framers and their contemporaries—are not grounds for impeachment, then it is probably correct. But a requirement of proving wrongful intent would place a difficult burden on the proponents of removal, for it is rarely possible to adduce direct evidence of an intent to do wrong. (Tape recordings of a president's deliberations are a recent, and

52. Black 39–40, 48–9.

one-shot, exception.) Ordinarily, wrongful intent is inferred from the circumstances and nature of conduct, not separately proved. The difficulty in impeachment is that the nature of the wrongdoing may not lead automatically to the inference that it was undertaken with an intent to do wrong or in bad faith. As the Johnson trial suggests, it is possible to spin out elaborate explanations of how a president can violate a law with a pure heart and for a good purpose. Mistake of law (as in the Johnson defense) or mistake of fact (as in the argument that Nixon thought that considerations of national security impelled the wiretapping of reporters and White House aides) can be postulated for virtually any action by a president and buttressed by reference to his awesome duties and sometimes conflicting responsibilities. And, again as the Johnson trial suggests, even if the arguments are not sufficient to undercut an inference of wrongful intent, they may aid in achieving the objective (perhaps more important in a presidential impeachment defense) of diminishing the apparent seriousness of the wrongdoing.

The all-encompassing definitions of grounds for impeachment, like Black's, Benjamin Butler's in the Johnson trial, and others, have limited usefulness, and that mostly for testing hypothetical—and improbable—cases. It is impossible to guess how many times wife-murdering presidents were hypothesized in lawyers' discussions in early 1974, but the figure must be staggering. There were also an inordinate number of imagined presidents who retired to the French Riviera or some other pleasure spot without bothering to resign from office. The purported reason for contriving these absurdities was to test the principle that impeachable wrongdoing must be office-related and to dispose of any supposed distinction between acts of commission and neglect of duty. Enjoyable as these discussions could sometimes be, it is unlikely that they advanced anyone's understanding of presidential impeachment or helped very much in the Nixon inquiry.

"When sorrows come, they come not single spies / But in battalions," Shakespeare wrote.[53] The same is likely to be true of allegations against a president whose removal from office is being contemplated. Evaluating these allegations, winnowing them down, fashioning them into a case for his removal from office (if they warrant removal) is the purpose of an impeachment investigation by a House committee. There have been only three such investigations in our history, and the

53. *Hamlet*, act IV, scene 5.

first two (involving President Johnson) failed in the sense that the result desired by the committee majority was not achieved.

Political excesses apart, the two attempts to impeach President Johnson in some respects are more instructive on the practical meaning of grounds for presidential impeachment than the Nixon inquiry. Unlike the Nixon case, where the critical questions were evidentiary and the committee considered its task to be more adjudicative than prosecutorial, the Johnson impeachment was directed more to the tactical issue of how to impeach successfully. From beginning to end, there was little question that a majority of the House thought that Johnson was a wretched president and wanted him out of office. The impeachment investigations were, in essence, a search for the perfect "impeachable offense" that would lead to his removal. No single great crime existed on which to construct a case for removal until Johnson seemed to provide one by attempting to oust Secretary Stanton. Whether Johnson intentionally forced the issue or not, it turned out that his action provided an abundance of ammunition for his defense—a defense designed to miss the obvious point, and even to insist that it was immaterial and inadmissible in the trial. That point was that the House had seized upon the removal of Stanton as a symbol, the latest and most specific instance of its general complaint against President Johnson. But, having selected its "impeachable offense" and pleaded various permutations of it, the House was stuck with only that offense. When it was found wanting (though by the slimmest of margins), the case for removal failed.

The Johnson impeachment underscores the critical importance of the seriousness criterion in a presidential impeachment and suggests why it should not be considered in terms of disconnected impeachable offenses. It is not that Johnson should have been removed or that the House and its managers performed commendably. To the contrary, the political overtones of the impeachment and especially the invective of the Radical managers (most notably Butler and Stevens) seem outrageous in an age used to more polite, if far less colorful and much less polished, legal and political discourse. But the case should be considered not only as a lesson in the politics of hatred and the fruits of vituperation but also as a legal proceeding. From that perspective, it points up the reasons why a search for an impeachable offense is misguided.

The concept of an impeachable offense guts an impeachment case of the very factors—repetition, pattern, coherence—that tend to establish the requisite degree of seriousness warranting the removal of a president from office. Just as a recidivist deserves a more stringent sentence than a first offender, so presumably a repeated offender is more likely to deserve removal from an office of public trust, and especially the highest trust in the land. Rules against duplicity and prejudicial joinder apply in criminal cases to prevent a jury from taking guilt on one charge to establish guilt on another. Something comparable should apply in impeachment proceedings, in terms of judging whether wrongdoing has been proved. But, beyond that, it is necessary to take a less divided view of the charges. Because the remedy is not additive, the offenses must be considered cumulatively in deciding whether or not it should be imposed. The House must decide whether or not to prosecute an impeachment on the basis of the charges taken as a whole. And, unless the Senate is to accept the determination of the House without question, it too must judge the combined seriousness of the wrongdoing that is proved.

It is sometimes suggested that without the concept of an impeachable offense, proponents of impeachment of a president (or another official) will seek to make a case on the basis of an accumulation of trivia—to make many nothings into a something, many legal naughts into a unit, many innocent acts into a crime, as Robert Goodloe Harper put it in the Chase trial. That seems to be an exaggerated fear. To begin with, impeachment must be based on wrongdoing, not innocent acts. The question is not whether a string of zeroes will sum to one, but whether a number of fractions will. Each allegation in an impeachment must involve wrongdoing, meeting whatever criteria are applicable with respect to relationship to the office or effect on the system of government. The argument goes only to the substantiality of each act of wrongdoing, again in terms of its effect on government, on ability to conduct the office, the obviousness of its wrongfulness, or whatever.

Another point is probably implicit in the first. Unlike offenses do not add as readily as those that fall within a common pattern. To use Sarbanes's metaphor, it is when vegetable after vegetable is rotten that one wonders about the store. If some of the tomatoes are rotten, the lettuce overpriced, and the cashier surly, one is more likely to write it off as a typical day at the market. Allegations that reinforce the pattern of wrongdoing, rather than distract attention from it, are more likely to belong in an impeachment case—as a matter of prosecution strategy, if not necessarily of law—even if, taken by themselves, they are less serious. Framing and adjudicating the case in this manner hardly seems unfair to a president whose fitness to continue in office is under scrutiny.

The most pertinent precedent in this nation's history for framing a case for the removal of a chief executive may well be the earliest—the Declaration of Independence. In expressing reasons for throwing off the government of George III, the Continental Congress did not claim that there had been a single offense justifying revolution. Instead, it pointed to a course of conduct—"a long train of abuses and usurpations," "a history of repeated injuries"—which was described in eighteen separate specifications of monarchical wrongdoing. And the Declaration alleged that there was a pattern in this conduct; it "pursu[ed] invariably the same Object" and evinced a common design; it "all [had] in direct object the establishment of absolute Tyranny over these States." It was this pattern of wrongdoing taken together, not each specification considered alone, that showed the unfitness of George III to be the ruler of the American people. Impeachment, to be sure, is hardly revolution, and a president is not a king. But the unfitness of a president to continue in office is to be judged in much the same way: with reference to the totality of his conduct and the common patterns that emerge, not in terms of whether this or that act of wrongdoing, viewed in isolation, is an impeachable offense.

4. *THE PRESIDENT AND EXECUTIVE OFFICERS*

The wrongdoing for which a president may be impeached is defined primarily by reference to the constitutional powers and duties of the presidential office. This proposition finds support not only in the actions of the House Judiciary Committee in the Nixon inquiry, but also in the views of the framers of the Constitution on impeachment and presidential accountability, the historical meaning of "high crimes and misdemeanors" in English parliamentary law, and the charges in past American impeachment cases. In this respect, the impeachments of judges do provide guidance, for (like the other cases) they suggest that an officer's conduct is to be assessed in terms of the nature and functions of his office. "Good behavior" by a judge, like faithful execution of the office by a president, is a constitutional criterion for determining what conduct is wrongful.

The law of presidential powers and duties is not well defined. Justice Robert H. Jackson wrote in 1952 that there is a "poverty of really useful and unambiguous authority applicable to concrete problems of executive power as they actually present themselves,"[1] a situation that remains substantially unchanged. Most opinions on presidential powers, Justice Jackson also wrote, "suffer the infirmity of confusing the issue of a power's validity with the cause it is intended to promote, of confounding the permanent executive office with its temporary occupant," an infirmity apt to be more pronounced than ever in the aftermath of the Indochina War and the Nixon presidency. The courts provide occasional guidance concerning the extent of the constitutional and statutory powers of the president, usually through review of the legality of actions of subordinates who are carrying out his orders.

1. Youngstown Sheet & Tube Co. v. Sawyer, 343 U.S. 579, 634 (1952) (concurring opinion) (hereafter Steel Seizure Case).

For constitutional and prudential reasons involving the scope of judicial power and the doctrine of separation of powers, however, the courts will not ordinarily consider whether the president has misused powers that he does possess. As a result, significant areas of presidential conduct remain outside the province of the courts, including most allegations that a president has breached his constitutional duties.

Nor are the president's constitutional duties apt to be defined by the impeachment process. Impeachment is invoked far too rarely to serve a standard-setting function; it would require a calamitous succession of wrongdoing presidents to establish a useful body of precedent through impeachment proceedings. And impeachment is directed only at serious wrongdoing; the constitutional standards presumably forbid less egregious forms of misconduct as well. Despite the emphasis the Judiciary Committee placed on the constitutional aspects of President Nixon's wrongdoing, its inquiry and the articles of impeachment it adopted primarily focused on the most fundamental violation of his constitutional obligations—his direct involvement in or ratification of conduct that was clearly illegal. The evidence potentially available to the committee—and particularly the tape recordings of his conversations—made it at least theoretically possible to determine (as Senator Howard Baker repeatedly formulated the issue during the summer of 1973) what the president knew and when he knew it; the existence of this evidence put a premium on just such a determination. Because the evidence ultimately showed that President Nixon had been directly involved in unlawful conduct and had violated the obligation, which he shared with every citizen, not to disobey the law, it was less necessary to determine whether he should also be held accountable for other types of constitutional violations. In particular, it was not necessary to assess the full extent of his culpability for failing "to take care that the laws be faithfully executed."

The responsibility for seeing the laws faithfully executed has been called "the central idea of the office" and "the embracing function" of the president outside the realm of foreign affairs.[2] Yet the take-care clause is one of the least-analyzed constitutional provisions. It originated with the Committee on Detail, which prepared the first draft of the Constitution, and appears to have been derived from a similar

2. Benjamin Harrison, *This Country of Ours* 98 (1897); Steel Seizure Case, 343 U.S. at 610 (Frankfurter, J., concurring).

provision in the New York Constitution.[3] It was never debated in the Constitutional Convention and was little discussed in most commentaries on the Constitution.[4] The clause, however, has important implications concerning the president's relationship to the executive branch of government; it both imposes limits on his authority to control the actions of officers of the executive branch who are directly engaged in executing the laws and makes him accountable for at least some of what they do.

In this chapter the meaning of the president's duty to "take care that the laws be faithfully executed" is discussed, not with an eye to defining what violations are impeachable, but rather with the objective of ascertaining the scope of the clause and its application to the president's relationship to the executive branch of government. Serious and repeated violations of the president's take-care duty may lead to an impeachment, but for the most part obedience to this duty, like other legal standards applicable to the president, must be achieved through the political process.

The President's Relationship to Executive Officers

The framers of the Constitution provided for a single executive in order to assure energy, dispatch, and responsibility in the administration of government, but they recognized that the president could not perform executive duties unaided. Gouverneur Morris pointed out to the convention that "[t]here must be certain great officers of State; a minister of finance, of war, of foreign affairs &c." These officers would "exercise their functions in subordination to the Executive"; without them, "the Executive can do nothing of consequence." In particular, Morris argued that the executive could "do no criminal act without Coadjutors who may be punished" and that their amenability to impeachment made it unnecessary to provide for his. He later changed his mind on this point, recognizing that the chief executive

3. 2 Farrand 171, 185; Edward S. Corwin, *The President: Office and Powers, 1787–1957* at 7 (1957) (hereafter Corwin).

4. In *The Federalist* No. 70 at 501, Hamilton included "faithfully executing the laws" among the "class of authorities" of the president to which "no objection has been made" and that could not "possibly admit of any." Story wrote of the take-care duty merely that it "follows out of the strong injunction of [the president's] oath of office, that he will 'preserve, protect, and defend the constitution,' " the accomplishment of which "is the great object of the executive department" (3 Story §1558).

was "not the King but the prime-Minister" and must be held personally accountable. The convention affirmed the direct accountability of the president by making him removable upon impeachment and conviction (and punishable under the criminal law), as well as by rejecting proposals for a council to advise him in the performance of his duties. The executive power was to have "no screen," James Wilson explained to the Pennsylvania ratifying convention; the president "cannot act improperly, and hide either his negligence or inattention; he cannot roll upon any other person the weight of his criminality." Power was granted to the president, Wilson later wrote, and "[t]o him the provident or improvident use of it is to be ascribed." Similarly, James Iredell told the North Carolina ratifying convention:

> No man has an authority to injure another with impunity. No man is better than his fellow-citizens, nor can pretend to any superiority over the meanest man in the country. If the President does a single act by which the people are prejudiced, he is punishable himself, and no other man merely to screen him.[5]

Holding the president accountable for his own actions, of course, does not clarify the extent to which he is to be held responsible for or empowered to control the actions of inferior executive officers. The "executive power" is vested in the president; "he shall take care that the laws be faithfully executed." These constitutional provisions imply that his superintendence of the executive branch is both a right and an obligation. But the Constitution says little about how his supervision is to be carried out. Article II, section 2, provides that "he may require the opinion, in writing, of the principal officer in each of the executive departments, upon any subject relating to the duties of their respective offices"—a provision that Hamilton described as "a mere redundancy in the plan" and that has been so considered ever since.[6] Hamilton explained that "the right for which it provides would result of itself from the office."[7] The administration of government—"[t]he actual conduct of foreign negotiations, the preparatory plans of finance, the application and disbursement of the public moneys in con-

5. 2 Farrand 53–4, 64, 69; 2 Elliot 480, 1 Wilson 319; 4 Elliot 109.
6. *The Federalist* No. 74 at 482. See Steel Seizure Case, 343 U.S. at 641, n. 9 (Jackson, J., concurring) ("inherent in the Executive if anything is"). The relationship of this provision to executive privilege is discussed in chapter 6 below.
7. *The Federalist* No. 74 at 482.

formity to the general appropriations of the legislature, the arrangement of the army and navy, the direction of the operations of war, . . . and other matters of a like nature"—involves "executive details and falls peculiarly within the province of the executive department."

> The persons, therefore, to whose immediate management these different matters are committed, ought to be considered as the assistants or deputies of the chief magistrate . . . and ought to be subject to his superintendence.[8]

The extent of the president's authority to superintend executive officers was extensively debated in 1789 by the First Congress when it enacted the legislation creating the first executive departments. The issue was whether the president has the ultimate supervisory authority over executive officers he appoints with the advice and consent of the Senate—the power to discharge them. Through parliamentary maneuvering in the House and the tie-breaking vote of Vice President John Adams in the Senate, the First Congress decided that the removal power was conferred on the president by the Constitution. This "decision of 1789" was criticized during the Jackson administration, when large numbers of officeholders were replaced under the spoils system and a secretary of the treasury who would not carry out President Jackson's wishes was ousted. It was legislatively reversed by the Tenure of Office Act of 1867, whose meaning and constitutionality were extensively argued in the Johnson impeachment, and by subsequent legislation. But it received Supreme Court sanction in 1926, when the Court held that legislation restricting the president's power to remove a postmaster was unconstitutional.

One of the major arguments made by proponents of the president's removal power in the 1789 debate in the House (the Senate debate was not recorded) was that the president needed the removal power in order to carry out his responsibility for the execution of the laws. James Madison, the principal advocate of the president's power of removal, contended that it was implied by the constitutional requirement of "the highest possible degree of responsibility in all Executive officers," which was "a principle that pervades the whole system." If the president alone could remove an executive officer, Madison said,

8. *Ibid.*, No. 72 at 468–9.

> we have in him security for the good behaviour of the officer. If [the officer] does not conform to the judgment of the President in doing the executive duties of his office, he can be displaced. This makes him responsible to the great Executive power, and makes the President responsible to the public for the conduct of the person he has nominated and appointed to aid him in the administration of his department.

If, on the other hand, the removal power were shared by the president and the Senate, Madison asserted, executive officers and the Senate might "mutually support each other, and for want of efficacy reduce the power of the President to a mere vapor; in which case, his responsibility would be annihilated, and the expectation of it unjust." The duty to see the laws faithfully executed implied a constitutional intent that the president "should have that species of power which is necessary to accomplish that end," including the removal power:

> If the President should possess alone the power of removal from office, those who are employed in the execution of the law will be in their proper situation, and the chain of dependence be preserved; the lowest officers, the middle grade, and the highest, will depend, as they ought, on the President, and the President on the community. The chain of dependence therefore terminates in the supreme body, namely, in the people, who will possess, besides, in aid of their original power, the decisive engine of impeachment.

Other proponents of the president's removal power echoed this argument. The president should be made "as responsible as possible for the conduct of the officers who were to execute the duties of his own branch of the Government," Benjamin Goodhue of Massachusetts said. It was his "peculiar duty to watch over the executive officers," and for his inspection to be of any avail he must have the "power to correct the abuses he might discover" through removal from office. Fisher Ames of Massachusetts contended that the Constitution vested the executive power in the president "with a view to have a responsible officer to superintend, control, inspect, and check the officers necessarily employed in administering the laws." Without "control over officers appointed to aid him in the performance of his duty," the president could not see the laws faithfully executed. Take the removal power from the president, Ames asserted, "and you virtually strip him of his authority; you virtually destroy his responsibility—the great security which this Constitution holds out to the people of America."

George Clymer of Pennsylvania, like Madison a delegate to the Constitutional Convention, made a similar argument: "If the President is divested of his power, his responsibility is destroyed; you prevent his efficiency, and disable him from affording that security to the people which the Constitution contemplates." If the president did not have the removal power, Clymer said, he "ought to resign the power of superintending and directing the Executive parts of Government into the hands of the Senate at once"—a step, he added, that would make the government "a dangerous aristocracy" or "more destitute of energy than any Government on earth." Richard Lee of Virginia argued that the removal power "adds to the responsibility of the most responsible branch of the Government," without which "we should have little security against the depredations and gigantic strides of arbitrary power." With the power of removal, Lee said, "it will be [the president's] fault if any wicked or mischievous action is committed; and he will hardly expose himself to the resentment of three millions of people, of whom he holds his power, and to whom he is accountable every four years." It was also suggested that removal might often be the only effective supervisory tool the president had. The president had "the superintendence, the control, and the inspection" of the conduct of department heads, John Lawrence of New York argued:

> Shall the person having these superior powers to govern, with such advantages of discovering and defeating the base intentions of his officers, their delinquencies, their defective abilities, or their negligence, be restrained from applying these advantages to the most useful, nay, in some cases, the only useful purpose which can be answered by them?

Thus, the proponents of the president's removal power contended that his responsibility for the conduct of executive officers was a basic constitutional principle and that he had a duty to superintend their actions. The removal power was implied by his constitutional responsibility and was necessary to enable him to perform his duty. They further argued that the president could be held accountable if he abused the removal power. If he "displace from office a man whose merits require that he should be continued in it," Madison said,

> he will be impeachable by this House, before the Senate for such an act of mal-administration; for I contend that the wanton removal of meritorious officers would subject him to impeachment and removal from his own high trust.

Opponents of the president's removal power denied that he was responsible for the conduct of executive officers. "Why shall we make the President responsible for what goes through other hands?" Alexander White of Virginia asked. The president was not solely responsible for the conduct of executive officers; "why then talk of obtaining a greater degree of responsibility than is known to the Constitution?" Department heads were creatures of the law, not of the president, Elbridge Gerry of Massachusetts (also a delegate to the convention) contended. The Constitution provided through the impeachment clause that they were to bear their own responsibility. Giving the President the removal power would not increase his responsibility, but diminish it. Said John Page of Virginia:

> I hold it an incontrovertible maxim, that the more power you give him, the more his responsibility is lessened. By making the heads of all the departments dependent upon the President, you enable him to swallow up all the powers of Government; you increase his influence, and every one will be studious to please him alone.

Rather than increasing his responsibility, William Smith of South Carolina contended, the removal power would increase the President's authority by making executive officers his "abject slave[s]" to do his bidding. According to Page,

> [t]he heaped-up powers on the Chief Magistrate . . . [do] not render him more responsible; but, on the contrary, by increasing his importance, and multiplying his dependants, directly [tend] to diminish his responsibility, and secure him, if not against suspicion, at least against charges of delinquency.

He could not be impeached for abusing the removal power, said Smith:

> He will tell you he thought it incumbent on him to displace the officer, because he apprehended the public tranquillity was in danger; and if he erred, it was the error of the head, not of the heart. And will any House of Representatives ever be found to impeach the Chief Magistrate of the United States for an error in opinion?

Gerry asserted that Madison's argument that the president would be subject to impeachment for dismissing a good man involved "an absurdity. How can the House impeach the President for doing an act which the Legislature has submitted to his discretion?" He later elaborated on this argument:

> Suppose an officer discharges his duty as the law directs, yet the President will remove him; he will be guided by some other criterion; perhaps the officer is not good-natured enough; he makes an ungraceful bow, or does it left leg foremost; this is unbecoming in a great officer at the President's levee. Now, because he is so unfortunate as not to be so good a dancer as he is a worthy officer, he must be removed. The Senate, and this House, may think it necessary to inquire, why a good officer is dismissed. The President will say, it is my pleasure; I am authorized by law to exercise this prerogative; I have my reasons for it, but you have no right to require them of me.

"This language may be proper in a monarchy," Gerry observed, "but in a republic every action ought to be accounted for." "[S]uch unbounded power," he concluded, would make the officers of the government "the mere puppets of the President, to be employed or thrown aside as useless lumber, according to his prevailing fancy."

The removal power would also secure the president against impeachment for other causes, White argued, because it would "fence him round with a set of dependent officers, through whom alone it is probable you could come at the evidence of the President's guilt." The way to increase responsibility in the executive branch, the opponents argued, was not to increase the president's power but to provide checks upon it, including independent department heads responsible for their own actions. With the removal power, the president could "dragoon your officer into a compliance with his designs," said Smith, but if the officer were established on a better tenure

> he would dare to be honest; he would know himself invulnerable in his integrity, and defy the shafts of malevolence, though aimed with Machiavellian policy. He would be a barrier to your Executive officer, and save the State from ruin.[9]

The "decision of 1789" was reversed by Congress in the Tenure of Office Act of 1867 and subsequent legislation, whose constitutionality finally came before the Supreme Court in 1926. In holding the legislation unconstitutional,[10] the Court, in an opinion by Chief Justice (and former president) William Howard Taft, relied heavily upon the president's constitutional duties as the source of his removal power:

> Made responsible under the Constitution for the effective enforcement of the law, the President needs as an indispensable aid to meet it the disciplinary influence upon those who act under him of a reserve power of removal.

Replying to the argument that "executive officers appointed by the President with the consent of the Senate are bound by the statutory law and are not his servants to do his will," the chief justice acknowledged that different types of duties were performed by executive officers and that "[t]he degree of guidance in the discharge of their duties that the President may exercise over executive officers varies with the character of their service as prescribed in the law under which they act." But, he wrote, the president needed and had the removal power in all cases.

"The highest and most important duties" the president's subordinates perform are those where they act for him, "exercising not their own but his discretion," the chief justice wrote. In this "very large" field, "sometimes described as political,"

> the discretion to be exercised is that of the President in determining the national public interest and in directing the action to be taken by his executive subordinates to protect it.

9. Annals 1st Cong., 1st Sess., 379, 462, 496, 499 (Madison), 378 (Goodhue), 474, 539–40 (Ames), 489–90 (Clymer), 525 (Lee), 485 (Lawrence), 498 (Madison), 382–3 (White), 535–6 (Gerry), 519 (Page), 458 (Smith), 549 (Page), 508 (Smith), 502, 574, 575 (Gerry), 519 (White), 472 (Smith).

10. Myers v. United States, 272 U.S. 52. The quoted portions of the opinion appear at 132–5.

Each department head "is and must be the President's *alter ego* in the matters of that department where the President is required by law to exercise authority" and "must do his will." Because the president must place "implicit faith" in these subordinates, he must have the power to remove them "[t]he moment that he loses confidence in [their] intelligence, ability, judgment or loyalty."

The "ordinary duties of officers prescribed by statute come under the general administrative control of the President by virtue of the general grant to him of the executive power," Chief Justice Taft wrote,

> and he may properly supervise and guide their construction of the statutes under which they act in order to secure that unitary and uniform execution of the laws which Article II of the Constitution evidently contemplated in vesting general executive power in the President alone.

Where a law specifically empowers a department or bureau head to adopt regulations to make the law workable and effective, the president "must consider and supervise in his administrative control" both the "ability and judgment manifested by the official thus empowered" and the official's "energy and stimulation of his subordinates. . . . Finding such officers to be negligent and inefficient, the President should have the power to remove them."

Chief Justice Taft also recognized that "there may be duties so peculiarly and specifically committed to the discretion of a particular officer as to raise a question whether the President may overrule or revise the officer's interpretation of his statutory duty in a particular instance" and "duties of a quasi-judicial character" where "decisions after hearing affect interests of individuals," the discharge of which the president "can not in a particular case properly influence or control." Nevertheless, Taft contended that the president

> may consider the decision after its rendition as a reason for removing the officer, on the ground that the discretion regularly entrusted to that officer by statute has not been on the whole intelligently or wisely exercised.

The Court acknowledged that the president's removal power did not imply absolute presidential control over the performance of the duties of executive officers. The result, Edward S. Corwin wrote, was a paradox: the Constitution permitted Congress to impose quasi-judicial duties on executive officers and require that they exercise their own independent judgment, but it also permitted the president "to guillotine such officers for exercising the very discretion that Congress had the right to require!"[11] Nine years later the Supreme Court attempted to resolve the paradox by confining the holding in the earlier case to executive officers "restricted to the performance of executive functions" and "charged with no duty at all related to either the legislative or judicial power." The 1926 case, the Court said, involved an officer (a local postmaster) who was "merely one of the units in the executive department and, hence, inherently subject to the exclusive and illimitable power of removal by the Chief Executive, whose subordinate and aid he is." The decision reached "all purely executive officers," but "putting aside *dicta*" in Chief Justice Taft's opinion, it went no further. The Court now held that Congress has undoubted authority to create quasi-legislative and quasi-judicial agencies and to "require them to act in discharge of their duties independently of executive control." Such an agency "occupies no place in the executive department and . . . exercises no part of the executive power vested by the Constitution in the President"; it "cannot in any proper sense be characterized as an arm or an eye of the executive." As an appropriate incident of its authority to create such an agency, Congress could restrict the president's power to remove its members, "[f]or it is quite evident that one who holds office only during the pleasure of another, cannot be depended upon to maintain an attitude of independence against the latter's will."[12] The Court's decision limiting the scope of the president's removal power involved the Federal Trade Commission; it established the independence of regulatory agencies "outside" the executive branch. The Court later applied the same doctrine to the War Claims Commission, whose function, it said, had an "intrinsic judicial character" that made it one of those agencies "whose tasks require absolute freedom from Executive interference." The act establishing the commission required that war claims be "adjudicated according to law"—that is, the Court said, "on the merits of each claim, supported by evidence and governing legal considerations, by a body that was 'entirely free from the control or coercive influence, direct or indirect,' . . . of either the Executive or the Congress." "[O]ne must take for granted" that the act "precluded the President from influencing the

11. Corwin 89–90.
12. Humphrey's Executor v. United States, 295 U.S. 602, 627–9 (1935).

Commission in passing on a particular claim," Justice Frankfurter wrote for the Court. A *fortiori*, it has to be inferred that "the Damocles' sword of removal by the President for no reason other than that he preferred to have on that Commission men of his own choosing" did not hang over the commission.[13]

The Court's decisions leave unanswered the constitutional question of legislative power to control the tenure of officers whose duties are mixed.[14] Depending on what definition one adopts of "executive" duties or duties involving the exercise of the president's power, this might be a substantial class of executive officers, including virtually all department and agency heads. The question would appear to be academic, since Congress has not attempted to limit the president's power to remove these officers, and (if a case were ever to arise, which is itself unlikely) the Court would probably be reluctant to imply any limitations where an officer is even partly the president's "*alter ego*," who "must do his will" in performing some of his duties.

In any event, Chief Justice Taft's opinion was not quite as paradoxical as Corwin suggested. In differentiating among the types of duties executive officers perform and the extent of the president's supervisory power over them, Taft also proposed standards for the exercise of his removal power. Those who were exercising the president's discretion and were to do his will could be removed when he lost confidence in their "intelligence, ability, judgment or loyalty." Those performing "ordinary duties" prescribed by statute under the president's "general administrative control" could be removed if he found them to be "negligent and inefficient." Those performing duties "peculiarly and specially committed to [their] discretion," such as quasi-judicial duties, could be removed if the president found that their discretion had "not been on the whole intelligently or wisely exercised."[15]

It is sometimes suggested that whatever legal limitations theoretically apply to the president's power to control the actions of executive officers are overwhelmed by his removal power. "Whom the President may remove he may dominate," Corwin wrote,[16] and the Supreme Court decisions limiting the removal power reflect similar reasoning.

13. Wiener v. United States, 357 U.S. 349, 353–6 (1958). The quotation is from Humphrey's Executor v. United States, 295 U.S. at 629.

14. Compare Corwin 92.

15. 272 U.S. at 134–5.

16. Corwin 69.

As a practical matter, this may be true most of the time—but then most of the time presidents are not overstepping the limits of their supervisory power. If, on the other hand, an executive officer is willing to resist presidential pressure, he may have a degree of independence that is not contemplated by law. The removal of an executive officer is itself an extreme step, with potential political consequences for a president. The president's sword of Damocles, like Congress' blunderbuss of impeachment, may prove an unwieldy weapon in many situations.

Limits on the President's Supervisory Power

The "decision of 1789" involved an officer—the secretary of foreign affairs—who was expected to carry out the will of the president. The bill creating the Department of Foreign Affairs provided that the secretary was to perform such duties relative to foreign affairs as were "from time to time enjoined on, or intrusted to him by the President" and to conduct the business of the department "in such manner as the President . . . shall from time to time order or instruct." It was clearly intended that the secretary be under the complete control of the president, whether simply by legislative enactment or (as seems to have been the more common opinion) because the conduct of foreign affairs is inherently a presidential responsibility for which he needed an assistant, not a potential rival within the executive branch. One of the arguments for the president's removal power was that the secretary's authority was derived from the President, whose "mere instrument" he was to be—"as much an instrument in the hands of the President," Theodore Sedgwick of Massachusetts suggested, "as the pen is the instrument of the Secretary in corresponding with foreign Courts." He was to be "an arm or an eye" for the president, over whom the president "ought to have a complete command," John Vining of Delaware said.[17]

The "decision of 1789," however, was also carried over to legislation establishing the departments of war and treasury. The duties of the principal officers of the Treasury Department, unlike those of the officers of the two other departments, were prescribed directly by statute and were not so obviously the president's direct responsibility as was the conduct of foreign affairs or the management of the armed

17. Act of July 27, 1789, 1 Stat. 28; Annals 1st Cong., 1st Sess., 522 (Sedgwick), 511 (Vining)—see also 479–80 (Thomas Hartley of Pennsylvania).

forces. The distinction was explicitly recognized by James Madison when the office of comptroller of the treasury was under consideration. Madison proposed that the comptroller serve for a fixed term subject to removal by the president rather than simply at the president's pleasure. Madison observed that, among the arguments adduced to show that the president had a constitutional right to remove subordinate officers,

> it was urged, with some force, that these officers were merely to assist him in the performance of duties, which, from the nature of man, he could not execute without them, although he had an unquestionable right to do them if he were able.

But, Madison said, "I question very much whether [the president] can or ought to have any interference in the settling and adjusting the legal claims of individuals against the United States," the principal duty of the comptroller. "The necessary examination and decision in such cases partake too much of the Judicial capacity to be blended with the Executive." The office of comptroller, he suggested, was neither executive nor judicial, but "rather distinct from both, though it partakes of each." And, he asserted,

> [w]hatever . . . may be my opinion with respect to the tenure by which an Executive officer may hold his office according to the meaning of the Constitution, I am very well satisfied, that a modification by the Legislature may take place in such as partake of the judicial qualities, and that the legislative power is sufficient to establish this office on such a footing as to answer the purposes for which it is prescribed.

Madison's proposal failed to gain support, and he ultimately withdrew it.[18] Having established the principle that officers of executive departments charged with executive functions assigned by the president were removable by him, the House proceeded to apply its determination to officers whose duties were of a different character and were prescribed directly by statute.

And Congress also began to assign statutory duties to officers who were removable by the president alone. After it had created the three original departments, the First Congress passed legislation changing

18. Annals 1st Cong., 1st Sess., 611–5.

the name of the Department of Foreign Affairs to the Department of State and assigning duties outside the realm of foreign affairs to the secretary.[19]

Whether the secretary of state was subject to the exclusive control of the president or could also be controlled by the courts, and specifically by the Supreme Court, was the issue in that most famous of all constitutional law cases, *Marbury v. Madison,* decided in 1803.[20] Chief Justice John Marshall's opinion for the Court is better known for its assertion of judicial power to pass upon the constitutionality of legislation than for its analysis of presidential power. But before reaching the conclusion that the Court lacked original jurisdiction to issue a writ of mandamus to the secretary and that the provision of the Judiciary Act of 1789 purporting to confer this jurisdiction was unconstitutional, Chief Justice Marshall considered the nature of the secretary's duties and the president's power to control their performance. At issue was the secretary's duty to affix the seal of the United States to the commission of officers, one of the additional responsibilities assigned to him by the 1789 legislation renaming the department. The question was whether the secretary could be compelled to seal and deliver a commission to Marbury, who had been appointed as a justice of the peace for the District of Columbia.

In deciding this question, Chief Justice Marshall distinguished between the duties assigned to the secretary of state by the president under the original act and the duties (such as affixing the seal) assigned to him by the later act. In performing the duties prescribed by the original act, Marshall wrote, the secretary "is to conform precisely to the will of the president. He is the mere organ by whom that will is communicated." The president's responsibility for foreign affairs was one of the "political powers" vested in him by the Constitution,

> in the exercise of which he is to use his own discretion, and is accountable only to his country in his political character and to his own conscience. To aid him in the performance of these duties, he is authorized to appoint certain officers, who act by his authority, and in conformity with his orders.

19. Act of Sept. 15, 1789, 1 Stat. 68.
20. 5 U.S. (1 Cr.) 137. The quoted portions of the opinion appear at 165–6, 158, 164, 166, and 171.

"In such cases, their acts are his acts," and department heads "are the political or confidential agents of the executive, merely to execute the will of the president, or rather to act in cases in which the executive possesses a constitutional or legal discretion."

But the duty of the secretary to deliver Marbury's commission after the president had signed it, completing Marbury's appointment, "is prescribed by law, and not to be guided by the will of the president," Marshall declared.

> It is the duty of the secretary of state to conform to the law, and in this he is an officer of the United States, bound to obey the laws. He acts, in this respect, . . . under the authority of law, and not by the instructions of the president.

The delivery of the commission was not "a mere political act, belonging to the executive department alone, for the performance of which entire confidence is placed by our constitution in the supreme executive." When Congress directs an officer "peremptorily to perform certain acts" and the rights of individuals depend on their performance, "he is so far the officer of the law; is amenable to the laws for his conduct; and cannot at his discretion sport away the vested rights of others." In the performance of these acts, "he is not placed under the particular direction of the president." The president "cannot lawfully forbid" their performance, and "therefore is never presumed to have forbidden."

Five years later the federal circuit court for South Carolina considered the limitations on presidential control of subordinates.[21] The Embargo Act of 1808 authorized collectors of customs

> to detain any vessel ostensibly bound with a cargo to some other port of the United States, whenever, in their opinions, the intention is to violate or evade any provisions of the acts laying an embargo, until the decision of the president of the United States be had thereupon.

The secretary of the treasury had written the collectors, informing them that the president "considered unusual shipments, particularly of flour and other provisions . . . , as sufficient causes for the detention of [a] vessel" and recommended that "every shipment of the above ar-

21. Gilchrist v. Collector of Charleston, 10 F. Cas. 355 (No. 5,420) (C.C.D.S.C. 1808). The Embargo Act is 2 Stat. 501.

ticles, for a place where they cannot be wanted for consumption, should be detained." The owners of ships berthed in the Charleston harbor sought to avoid having their ships detained there during the embargo because of the risk of damage by worms, which were "peculiarly destructive" to vessels' bottoms in Charleston during the summer. Among them were the owners of the *Resource*, who obtained a cargo of cotton and rice and requested a clearance to sail to Baltimore. The collector acknowledged that in his opinion there was no intention to evade or violate any of the provisions of the acts laying an embargo, but denied the clearance on the basis of the instructions he had received from the secretary, "which as a public officer he thinks he is bound to obey."

The circuit court granted a writ compelling the issuance of the clearance. In a later explanation of the court's decision, Supreme Court Justice William Johnson, who had presided, wrote that the writ would have been refused had the collector contended that he caused the detention in pursuance of the Embargo Act, for "he would then have claimed that exercise of discretion which the law vested in him." Instead, the collector deliberately sought "a legal sanction" for his acquiescence in the instructions or "a legal exemption" from them.

The court relied on three grounds for its decision. First, as it construed the instructions, they did not apply to the *Resource* because Baltimore, unlike Charleston, had no internal supplies of rice. Second, the instructions were only a recommendation, not a command; "at the utmost the collector could only plead the influence of advice, and not the authority of the treasury department in his justification." Third, and most basic, "without the sanction of law, the collector is not justified by the instructions of the executive, in increasing restraints upon commerce, even if this case had been contemplated by the letter." Justice Johnson wrote for the court: "The granting of clearances is left absolutely to the discretion of the collector; the right of detaining in cases which excite suspicion is given him, with a reference to the will of the executive." Because Congress had vested this discretion in the collector, "the right of granting clearances remains in him unimpaired and unrestricted."

Attorney General C. A. Rodney wrote a letter to President Jefferson criticizing this decision, which found its way to the newspapers and prompted Justice Johnson to write a rebuttal, also for publication in the press. Rodney's letter ignored the court's first two grounds, implying that the secretary's instructions were intended to reach the *Resource* and to be mandatory upon the collector. The issue that the attorney general raised was, as Justice Johnson put it, whether "every power, given to an officer removable at the will of the executive, is given to the executive."

Justice Johnson reiterated that under the law the collector had the discretion to grant clearances in the first instance; he was obliged "to act according to the dictates of his own judgment, to which the law of congress had committed the interests of his fellow citizens, and not surrender a right of judging, which must ever be entirely personal." The president had no controlling power, according to Justice Johnson; he could act when the collector had ordered detention but was not authorized "to prescribe to the collector in what cases he should detain." Congress could easily have declared that the president "should dictate generally to the collector upon this subject, if such had been their intention," giving the president and the secretary of the treasury "that latitude of power which was necessary to justify their instructions to the collector." But the authority could not "be extorted from the law under which they acted." The collector's duties were "immediately assigned him by law" and were to be performed according to law. The president could not, "on the ground of [his] appellate jurisdiction" in cases of detention, "[swallow] up the power of the court of the first resort."

Justice Johnson strongly criticized the argument that all officers who hold their offices at the will of the president are his agents, that power given to them is to be exercised in subordination to his will, and that they cannot be restrained by the courts because he cannot be restrained. This argument, Johnson asserted,

> might be urged to show that the whole executive department, in all its ramifications, civil, military, and naval, should be left absolutely at large, in their conduct to individuals. . . . But such is not the genius of our constitution. The law assigns everyone his duty and his rights; and for enforcing the one and maintaining the other, courts of justice are instituted.

James Madison, Chief Justice Marshall, and Justice Johnson did not consider that the president's removal power implied (or was implied by) a constitutional power to control the conduct of executive officers in every particular. That position was asserted, however, during the administration of President Andrew Jackson. In 1831 Attorney General Roger B. Taney advised that the president had the power to compel a United States attorney to exercise discretionary authority vested in him to drop a pending suit because, if the attorney did not follow the president's order, the president could remove him and appoint someone who would.[22] Three years later, President Jackson invoked a similar argument to defend his removal of the secretary of the treasury and his appointment of Taney as a temporary successor.

The incident arose out of Jackson's battle against the Bank of the United States. He had ordered Secretary of the Treasury William Duane to exercise his statutory authority to withdraw all government deposits from the bank. (The 1816 act establishing the bank directed that all government funds be deposited in it "unless the Secretary of the Treasury shall otherwise order and direct," notifying congress of his reasons.) Duane refused to follow Jackson's order and also refused to resign; Jackson removed him and made a recess appointment of Taney, who withdrew the deposits. After Congress reconvened, the Senate passed a resolution declaring that Jackson had "assumed upon himself authority and power not conferred by the Constitution and laws, but in derogation of both." Jackson responded with a letter of protest denying that he had usurped or abused power.[23] He argued that it was "settled by the Constitution, the laws, and the whole practice of the Government that the entire executive power is vested in the President" and that the right of appointing and removing officers "who are to aid him in the execution of the laws" was also vested in him "as incident to that power," subject only to constitutional limitations on the appointment power. Jackson wrote:

> Being thus made responsible for the entire action of the executive department, it was but reasonable that the power of appointing, overseeing, and controlling those who execute the laws—a power in its nature executive—should remain in his hands.

The secretary of the treasury, appointed by the president and constitutionally removable by him, was "an executive officer, the mere in-

22. 2 Op. Atty. Gen. 482 (1831).

23. 3 James Richardson, *Compilation of the Messages and Papers of the Presidents, 1787–1897*, at 69, 85, 79, 81, 85, 90 (1897) (hereafter Richardson). Jackson also argued at length that the Senate had no authority to censure the president. The Senate refused to print his protest in its journal, but ultimately expunged its resolution. For a description of the incident, see Corwin 83–4.

strument of the Chief Magistrate in the execution of the laws, subject, like all other heads of Departments, to his supervision and control." The custody of public money was an executive function that had always been exercised by the secretary and his subordinates under the president's control, and in all important measures the secretary consulted the president and received his approval and sanction. Jackson asserted:

> [T]he law establishing the bank did not, as it could not, change the relation between the President and the Secretary—did not release the former from his obligations to see the law faithfully executed nor the latter from the President's supervision and control.

The doctrine denying the president the power of supervising, directing, and controlling the secretary had a "dangerous tendency," Jackson wrote:

> The President is the direct representative of the American people, but the Secretaries are not. If the Secretary of the Treasury be independent of the President in the execution of the laws, then is there no direct responsibility to the people in that important branch of this Government to which is committed the care of the national finances. And it is in the power of the Bank of the United States, or any other corporation, body of men, or individuals, if a Secretary shall be found to accord with them in opinion or can be induced in practice to promote their views to control through him the whole action of the Government (so far as it is exercised by his Department) in defiance of the Chief Magistrate elected by the people and responsible to them.

A similar claim of unlimited presidential supervisory authority reached the Supreme Court four years later. Congress had enacted a statute directing the postmaster general to pay a contractual claim for the carriage of mail. Postmaster General Amos Kendall refused to pay the full claim, President Jackson refused to order him to do so, and the contractors sued in the District of Columbia for a writ to compel payment. The lower court granted the writ, observing that the president was bound to see that the postmaster general faithfully discharged the duties assigned to him by law, but was not authorized to direct him how to discharge them or to control their exercise.[24] On appeal to the Supreme Court, the attorney general argued that, if the president is satisfied as to the meaning of a law, "it is his bounden duty to see that the subordinate officers of his department conform with fidelity to that meaning; for no other execution, however pure the motive from which it springs, is a faithful execution of the law." Kendall's attorney argued that, because the president was liable through impeachment for malexecution of the laws, the courts could not assume the direction of their execution.[25]

In its opinion affirming the issuance of the writ, the Supreme Court rejected the argument that "the postmaster–general was alone subject to the direction and control of the president, with respect to the execution of the duty imposed upon him by this law" by virtue of the president's take-care duty. That doctrine, the Court said, "would be vesting in the president a dispensing power, which has no countenance for its support in any part of the constitution." If carried out fully, the principle would

> cloth[e] the president with a power entirely to control the legislation of congress, and paralyze the administration of justice. . . . To contend, that the obligation imposed on the president to see the laws faithfully executed, implies a power to forbid their execution, is a novel construction of the constitution, and entirely inadmissible.

The Court recognized that so far as the president's powers are derived from the Constitution, he is "beyond the reach of any other department," except through impeachment, and that "certain political duties [are] imposed upon many officers in the executive department, the discharge of which is under the direction of the president." But, the Court said, "it by no means follows, that every officer in every branch of that department is under the exclusive direction of the president":

> [I]t would be an alarming doctrine, that congress cannot impose upon any executive officer any duty they may think proper,

24. United States *ex rel.* Stokes v. Kendall, 26 F. Cas. 702, 752–4 (No. 15,517) (1837).

25. Kendall v. United States *ex rel.* Stokes, 37 U.S. (12 Pet.) 524, 600, 552 (1838).

> which is not repugnant to any rights secured and protected by the constitution; and in such cases, the duty and responsibility grow out of and are subject to the control of the law, and not to the direction of the president.[26]

The *Kendall* case, and especially its language about the president's lack of power to forbid the execution of the laws, was relied upon in the Nixon years to dispose of claims of an inherent presidential power to require executive officers to impound funds appropriated by Congress; after more than a century and a quarter of neglect, the case was rediscovered. The opinion, however, is as interesting for what it does not say as for what it does. It does not assert that the president lacks authority to construe the laws and seek to make executive officers conform to his construction, but only that his construction must comport with the law. Duties that are "subject to the control of the law, and not to the direction of the president" are not necessarily completely outside his supervisory power; they are simply not under his "exclusive direction." In short, *Kendall* says no more than *Gilchrist*, or for that matter *Marbury v. Madison:* the president cannot forbid what the law requires or require what the law forbids. It leaves open, as *Gilchrist* left open, the question of presidential "advice" about how a duty is to be performed.

For the reason Justice Johnson suggested, it would be highly unusual for the courts to be faced with the question of the legality of the president's "guidance" or "advice" to an executive officer about how to perform his duty. A presidential order cannot make legal what is otherwise illegal;[27] as a corollary, it does not matter whether an executive officer acts illegally at the request of the president or on his own initiative, and the courts will not normally inquire into the reasons for an executive officer's action. As a result, there are no cases—and probably will be none—settling the extent of the president's supervisory power. That issue, as it involves the president's duty, is reserved to the impeachment process and the political arena. The port collector case is as close as the courts are likely to come to a determination that

26. *Ibid.* at 612–3, 610. Taney, by now chief justice, dissented on other grounds, but wrote, "[W]herever congress creates . . . an office . . . , by law, it may, unquestionably, by law, limit its powers and regulate its proceedings; and may subject it to any supervision or control, executive or judicial, which the wisdom of the legislature may deem right" (at 626).

27. Little v. Barreme, 6 U.S. (2 Cr.) 170 (1804).

presidential interference with the performance of a duty assigned to an executive officer is a violation of the president's own constitutional duty. And that case, as Justice Johnson observed, was something of a fluke; the president's supervisory authority came before the court because the port collector permitted the issue to be framed for judicial review by acknowledging that his refusal to grant the clearance was the result of a directive invoking the president's authority.

The Applicable Rules

The courts have recognized two sets of distinctions between duties imposed on executive officers by statute. The first involves "executive" duties, on the one hand, and "quasi-legislative" and "quasi-judicial" duties, on the other. In terms of the president's authority to control the actions of an executive officer—in contrast to an "independent" agency—on whom such duties are imposed, there would seem to be no meaningful difference between "quasi-legislative" and "executive" duties. "Quasi-judicial" duties are a more important category. The president has no authority to interfere with or attempt to influence the performance of these duties, at least when they involve adjudicative proceedings affecting the rights of private persons. Where an official is required to make an adjudicative decision, it is to be made on the merits and based on the evidence adduced in the proceeding and applicable rules of law. Endeavors to influence the decision, whether by the president or anyone else, may violate the procedural rights of the parties and are improper for that reason.

The other distinction the courts make—between "ministerial" and "discretionary" duties—is more relevant to whether courts will settle disputes than it is to the limits on the president's supervisory power. As the law has developed, "ministerial" duties mean clear duties, the performance of which the courts may mandate,[28] including the duty to exercise discretionary authority. That says very little about the president's authority to control their performance. He presumably has the power to direct that a duty be done, that an officer obey the law; and his order to do what the law compels is, at worst, supernumerary. Just as obviously, he cannot even suggest or advise that the duty not be performed, for to do so would be to endeavor to forbid what the law requires rather than to see it faithfully carried out.

28. Mississippi v. Johnson, 71 U.S. (4 Wall.) 475, 498 (1867); National Treasury Employees Union v. Nixon, 492 F. 2d 587 (D.C. Cir. 1974).

This elementary proposition has an important implication: the president cannot impose his judgment on an officer required by law to reach his own decision. He cannot, as Henry Clay said in 1835, "enter the offices of administration, and where duties are specially confided to officers, . . . substitute his will to their judgment."[29] When a duty is assigned by law to a particular official, the president cannot arrogate it to himself. If he did, Attorney General William A. Wirt advised President James Monroe in 1823, "he would not only be not taking care that the laws be faithfully executed, but he would be violating them himself."[30]

A law conferring discretionary authority on an officer requires that he exercise his own discretion. "[I]f the word 'discretion' means anything in a statutory or administrative grant of power," the Supreme Court has said, "it means that the recipient must exercise his authority according to his own understanding and conscience."[31] Because authority conferred on executive officers by law is not authority conferred on the president, he cannot control their exercise of it without, in effect, forbidding them from performing their duty to use their own judgment and understanding.

If a president may not order, however, he may seek to provide guidance to executive officers in their exercise of discretionary authority. Again to quote Henry Clay, his "parental eye is presumed to survey the whole extent of the system in all its movements"; his station "is one of observation and superintendence."[32] The president's overall responsibility for the executive branch—whatever its practical limits—does imply some general power of supervision even where he lacks specific power to control. The propriety of presidential guidance to executive officers ultimately depends not so much on whether he describes his advice as a recommendation or a command as on its content and purpose. The issue is whether the president is attempting to have an executive officer violate the law by abusing his discretionary authority.

Abuse of discretion may occur in a number of ways, but the prin-

29. Quoted in 2 Johnson Trial 42.

30. 1 Op. Atty. Gen. 624, 625 (1823).

31. Accardi v. Shaughnessy, 347 U.S. 260, 266–7 (1954). "Whenever a statute gives a discretionary power to any person, to be exercised by him, upon his own opinion of certain facts, it is a sound rule of construction, that the statute constitutes him the sole and exclusive judge of the existence of those facts." Martin v. Mott, 25 U.S. (12 Wheat.) 19, 31–2 (1827).

32. Quoted in 2 Johnson Trial 42.

cipal rule is that where a law conferring authority prescribes standards for its exercise, the officer's actions must conform to those standards. He cannot make decisions "on the basis of considerations Congress could not have intended to make relevant" in granting the decision-making authority.[33] The standards imposed or implied by the legislation determine the extent of the officer's discretion and the factors he may take into account in exercising it. The president's preferences and the officer's desire to be loyal to the administration are not relevant factors.

There are grants of discretionary authority for which there are no applicable statutory standards, among them prosecutorial discretion. "[T]he Executive Branch has exclusive authority and absolute discretion to decide whether to prosecute a case," the Supreme Court reaffirmed in *United States v. Nixon*.[34] This means that the courts cannot compel the executive branch to prosecute cases it prefers not to. It does not mean, however, that no standards whatever exist for the exercise of prosecutorial discretion, for there is an implicit requirement that it be exercised in good faith and in the public interest. The attorney general cannot lawfully exercise his prosecutorial discretion to violate the constitutional rights of individuals. In particular, discriminatory enforcement of the laws on the basis of factors (such as political affiliation) that are not relevant to the public interest is improper. Prosecutorial discretion is not a license to enforce the laws "with an evil eye and an unequal hand."[35] Whether a president "orders" discriminatory enforcement of the laws or merely "guides" administrative discretion by recommending an impermissible use of it surely makes no difference in assessing his culpability.

It has been suggested that limitations on the president's supervisory power over the executive branch are incompatible with present-day governmental requirements. In his book on presidential accountability in the post-Watergate period, for example, Theodore Sorensen writes,

> I do not join with those who criticize any presidential "interference" in the executive branch, or who deny that this collection of agencies created by Congress is his to direct. The modern President could not meet his responsibilities if foreclosed from welding

33. Kalodnis v. Shaughnessy, 180 F. 2d 489, 491 (2d Cir. 1950) (L. Hand, J.); Wong Wing Hang v. I & NS, 360 F. 2d 715, 719 (2d Cir. 1966) (Friendly, J.).

34. 418 U.S. 683, 693 (1974).

35. Yick Wo v. Hopkins, 118 U.S. 356, 373–4 (1886).

> a coherent and consistent approach to national problems among the executive departments.[36]

There certainly is a risk that Congress, by parcelling out executive functions in a manner that creates or permits the development of independent fiefdoms, will prevent the president from performing the policy-making and coordinating function that is expected and demanded of a modern chief executive. Attorney General Caleb Cushing made this point in an opinion written in 1855 for a distinctly unmodern president, Franklin Pierce. Cushing argued that the president's will must govern the performance of all executive duties.

> If it were not thus, Congress might by statute so divide and transfer the executive power as utterly to subvert the Government, and to change it into a parliamentary despotism, like that of Venice or Great Britain, with a nominal executive chief utterly powerless,—whether under the name of Doge, or King, or President, would then be of little account, so far as regards the question of the maintenance of the Constitution.[37]

On the other hand, it is not the sole responsibility of even the most modern of presidents to weld "a coherent and consistent approach to national problems among the executive departments," whatever political expectations may be. That responsibility is one he constitutionally shares with Congress; it involves his role in the law-making process—especially in recommending legislation—much more than his administrative control over the execution of laws. Dissenting from the decision that the Constitution vests the power to remove executive officers solely in the president, Justice Oliver Wendell Holmes, Jr., wrote, "The duty of the President to see that the laws be executed is a duty that does not go beyond the laws or require him to achieve more than Congress sees fit to leave within his power."[38] Justice Frankfurter endorsed Holmes's statement as a comprehensive description of the president's take-care duty, and wrote, "the fact that power exists in the

36. Theodore Sorensen, *Watchmen in the Night: Presidential Accountability after Watergate* 92 (1975).

37. 7 Op. Atty. Gen. 453, 470.

38. Myers v. United States, 272 U.S. at 177 (dissenting opinion). Justice Louis D. Brandeis wrote in dissent in the same case: "The President performs his full constitutional duty, if, with the means and instruments provided by Congress and within the limitations prescribed by it, he uses his best endeavors to secure the faithful execution of the laws enacted" (at 292).

Government does not vest it in the President. The need for new legislation does not enact it. Nor does it repeal or amend existing law."[39] In constitutional terms the president's responsibility or authority to supervise the executive branch does not extend beyond the degree of control Congress "sees fit to leave within his power."

Nor, in the final analysis, are the legal restrictions on the president's supervisory power all that overwhelming an obstacle to his ability to impose his policy preferences within the executive branch. Ultimately what is required is not that he refrain from giving orders where he is limited to making recommendations, but that his guidance to executive officers—under whatever rubric he couches it—not interfere with their performance of legal duties. Perhaps it would be desirable for more executive functions to be assigned by law directly to the president, with provision for his delegation of them. Even under the present system, in which duties are distributed in rather haphazard fashion, the president is hardly powerless. The most important restriction on his supervisory authority is the most fundamental in our constitutional system—that he govern his actions by the rule of law.

Examples from the Nixon Presidency

The importance of this restriction on presidential conduct was demonstrated during the Nixon presidency. The proposed articles of impeachment against President Nixon included a number of incidents in which he had grossly exceeded his supervisory authority over executive agencies by directing that they engage in illegal or unconstitutional activities: misuse of the IRS for political purposes in violation of the constitutional rights of citizens; improper wiretaps by the FBI and other agencies; interference with the lawful functioning of the CIA, the FBI, the Office of Special Prosecutor, and the Department of Justice as part of the Watergate cover-up. But these were not the only incidents the committee considered where there was apparent misuse of the president's supervisory power. To give four other examples:

• By statute the conduct of litigation to which the United States is a party "is reserved to officers of the Department of Justice, under the direction of the Attorney General," who "shall supervise all [such] litigation."[40] In 1969 the United States brought three civil antitrust ac-

39. Steel Seizure Case, 343 U.S. at 610, 604 (concurring opinion).
40. 28 U.S.C. §§516, 519.

tions against the International Telephone and Telegraph Company (ITT), challenging corporate acquisitions by the conglomerate.[41] After an adverse district court decision in one of these cases, the Justice Department considered whether to file a direct appeal to the Supreme Court. On April 19, 1971, President Nixon telephoned Deputy Attorney General Richard G. Kleindienst, who was acting as attorney general for the ITT litigation because Attorney General John Mitchell had disqualified himself on the ground that his former law firm (also, and incidentally, Nixon's) had represented an ITT subsidiary. President Nixon told Kleindienst:

> The IT & T thing—stay the hell out of it. Is that clear? That's an order. . . . The order is to leave the God damned thing alone. . . . I do not want McLaren [chief of the Antitrust Division] to run around prosecuting people, raising hell about conglomerates, stirring things up at this point. Now you keep him the hell out of that. Is that clear? . . . Don't file the brief [on the appeal to the Supreme Court]. . . . [M]y order is to drop the God damn thing.

Kleindienst postponed the filing of the appeal, instead of dropping it. President Nixon's order was later rescinded on the advice of Attorney General Mitchell, and the appeal was filed. The ITT litigation was settled before the case was heard by the Supreme Court.

• The Agriculture Adjustment Act of 1949 authorizes and directs the secretary of agriculture to make an annual price support available for producers of milk. Under the act as it applied in 1971, the price of milk was to be supported at the level between 75 and 90 percent of parity that the secretary "determines necessary in order to assure an adequate supply." The act further provides that the secretary's determination "shall be final and conclusive."[42]

On March 12, 1971, Secretary of Agriculture Clifford P. Hardin announced his determination that the then-applicable support price for milk would assure an adequate supply for the following marketing year and would be maintained.[43] This determination had been en-

41. Evidentiary material on this incident appears in Statement of Information, Book V. See also Impeachment Inquiry, Book II, 997 (June 4, 1974).

42. 7 U.S.C. §§1446(c), 1426. The statute has since been amended.

43. Evidentiary material on this incident appears in Statement of Information, Book VI. See also Summary of Information 149–50.

dorsed by the president's economic advisors and approved by President Nixon. On March 25 Secretary Hardin rescinded the earlier determination and announced that the price support would be increased. He later stated in an affidavit that he had reevaluated the price support level and that the decision to increase it was "based entirely on a reconsideration of the evidence on the basis of the statutory criteria."

President Nixon provided a different explanation. Responding to allegations that the increase resulted from a promise of campaign contributions by dairy cooperatives, President Nixon acknowledged that he had made the decision to increase the price support, reversing Secretary Hardin's earlier determination. President Nixon stated that he reached his decision primarily on the basis of political considerations, especially because of intensive congressional pressure for a higher price support. The tape recording of the meeting between President Nixon and his advisors at which the president's decision was made indicates that the major factor they discussed was the likelihood that Congress would enact legislation requiring a higher price support, which President Nixon would not be able to veto without risking the loss of political support among farmers.

- The 1972 Amendments to the Federal Water Pollution Control Act authorized appropriations not to exceed $5 billion for fiscal 1973, $6 billion for fiscal 1974, and $7 billion for fiscal 1975 for grants for municipal water treatment facilities. The statute directed that the "[s]ums authorized to be appropriated" for each fiscal year "shall be allotted by the Administrator" of the Environmental Protection Agency (EPA) among the states.[44] President Nixon vetoed this legislation primarily on the ground that the authorization levels it contained exceeded his budget requests and were inflationary, but Congress overrode the veto. In November 1972, after the amendments became law, President Nixon wrote EPA Administrator William D. Ruckelshaus, stating:

> I direct that you not allot among the States the maximum amounts provided by [the statute]. No more than $2 billion of the amount authorized for the fiscal year 1973, and no more than $3 billion of the amount authorized for fiscal year 1974 should be allotted.

44. 86 Stat. 816 *et seq.*, 33 U.S.C. §1251 *et seq.*

Ruckelshaus complied with the president's directive, issuing regulations announcing that he was limiting the amount allotted for fiscal 1973 and 1974 in accordance with the president's letter.[45]

The Supreme Court unanimously held in February 1975 that the administrator's action was illegal. The Court said that the statute does not permit the administrator to allot less than the full amounts authorized for appropriation and that the president's letter and administrator's consequent withholding of authorized funds "cannot be squared with the statute."[46]

- By statute all functions of officers, agencies, and employees of the Department of Justice (with certain specified exceptions) are vested in the attorney general, who is authorized to make such provisions as he considers appropriate to delegate any of them. In addition, the head of each executive department, including the attorney general, is authorized by statute to prescribe regulations for the government of the department, the conduct of its employees, and the distribution and performance of its business.[47] Using this statutory authority, Attorney General Elliot L. Richardson issued a regulation on May 31, 1973, establishing the Office of Watergate Special Prosecution Force, under the direction of a special prosecutor appointed by the attorney general.[48] The special prosecutor was given "full authority for investigating and prosecuting" federal criminal offenses related to Watergate and other matters, including "full authority" in "[d]etermining whether or not to contest the assertion of 'Executive privilege' or any other testimonial privilege." The regulation provided:

> In exercising this authority, the Special Prosecutor will have the greatest degree of independence that is consistent with the Attorney General's statutory accountability for all matters falling within the jurisdiction of the Department of Justice. The Attorney General will not countermand or interfere with the Special Prosecutor's decisions or actions. . . . The Special Prosecutor will not be removed from his duties except for extraordinary improprieties on his part.

45. 37 Fed. Reg. 26,282 (1972).
46. Train v. City of New York, 420 U.S. 35, 47 (1975).
47. 28 U.S.C. §§509, 510; 5 U.S.C. §301.
48. Evidentiary material on this incident appears in Statement of Information, Book IX. See also Nixon Impeachment Report 124.

The regulation also provided that the special prosecutor "will carry out these responsibilities, with the full support of the Department of Justice," until in his judgment he had completed them or until a date mutually agreed upon by the special prosecutor and the attorney general.

On October 19, 1973, President Nixon wrote Attorney General Richardson instructing him "to direct Special Prosecutor Archibald Cox . . . that he is to make no further attempts by judicial process to obtain tapes, notes, or memoranda of Presidential conversations." The next day Richardson wrote the president, urging that a further effort be made to reach an accommodation with Cox on this issue. In a televised press conference, Cox rejected the president's directive. President Nixon ordered Richardson to discharge Cox. Rather than comply with the order, Richardson resigned as attorney general. Deputy Attorney General Ruckelshaus was then asked to carry out the order; "you know what it means when an order comes down from the Commander-in-Chief and a member of his team cannot execute it," General Alexander Haig, assistant to the president, said to Ruckelshaus. Ruckleshaus knew, and he too submitted his resignation. Solicitor General Robert H. Bork became acting attorney general. Bork indicated his willingness to comply with the president's order, and President Nixon wrote him:

> In his press conference today Special Prosecutor Archibald Cox made it apparent that he will not comply with the instruction I issued to him, through Attorney General Richardson, yesterday. Clearly the Government of the United States cannot function if employees of the Executive Branch are free to ignore in this fashion the instructions of the President. Accordingly, in your capacity of Acting Attorney General, I direct you to discharge Mr. Cox immediately and to take all steps necessary to return to the Department of Justice the functions now being performed by the Watergate Special Prosecution Force.

Bork discharged Cox as special prosecutor and abolished the special prosecution force.

Within two weeks Acting Attorney General Bork, with the president's approval, issued a new regulation reestablishing the Office of Watergate Special Prosecution Force and appointed Leon Jaworski to be special prosecutor. The new regulation was identical to the original one in most respects, except that discharge of the special prosecutor required a "consensus" of designated congressional leaders (as well as "extraordinary improprieties"), as did any limitation of his jurisdiction. The legal effect of this new regulation was discussed by the Supreme Court in *United States v. Nixon,* in holding that the special prosecutor's trial subpoena to President Nixon involved a justiciable controversy rather than an "intra-branch" dispute in which the courts could not intervene.[49] Writing for a unanimous Court, Chief Justice Burger noted that "Congress has vested in the Attorney General the power to conduct the criminal litigation of the United States" and "to appoint subordinate officers to assist him in the discharge of his duties." Bork's regulation had delegated the authority to represent the United States in Watergate cases to "a Special Prosecutor with unique authority and tenure." While "it is theoretically possible for the Attorney General to amend or revoke the regulation," Chief Justice Burger wrote, "[s]o long as this regulation remains in force the Executive Branch is bound by it, and indeed the United States as the sovereign composed of the three branches is bound to respect and enforce it."[50]

These examples, arranged in more or less ascending order of flagrancy, illustrate the continuing relevance of constitutional limits on the president's supervisory power. The first two were investigated by the Judiciary Committee because of allegations that bribery was involved. The evidence on this point proved incomplete or unconvincing,[51] and the legality of President Nixon's actions should therefore be considered without reference to the bribery charges. The order to drop the ITT appeal—ignoring the unproved bribery allegation—is close to the borderline between permissible presidential guidance of a discretionary function and impermissible interference with the exercise of discretion vested in an inferior officer. It is a close question not because of the outcome, but because of the nature of the attorney general's prosecutorial discretion; President Nixon's order may have involved no impropriety at all. The price support increase—again, ignoring the bribery question—seems to involve illegal interference

49. The discharge of Special Prosecutor Cox had itself been held illegal by a district court because Acting Attorney General Bork had relied simply on the president's instruction and had not purported to make a finding of "extraordinary impropriety," as required by the regulation. Nader v. Bork, 366 F. Supp. 104 (D.D.C. 1973).

50. 418 U.S. at 694, 696.

51. See Nixon Impeachment Report 189 n. 1.

with the exercise of a duty vested by statute in the secretary of agriculture and abuse of the discretion provided by the statute.[52]

The orders not to allot waste treatment authorizations and to discharge Special Prosecutor Cox were clearly illegal. The Supreme Court held as much about President Nixon's letter to EPA Administrator Ruckelshaus and implied it about the orders to a succession of attorneys general, including Ruckelshaus, to dismiss Cox. The Cox firing is, of course, the most notorious of the four examples. Popularly termed the "Saturday Night Massacre," the removal of the special prosecutor and the resignation of two attorneys general in quick succession precipitated the impeachment inquiry, though not because of any general recognition that President Nixon might have overstepped the bounds of his supervisory power. The Cox firing, too, was encompassed within the proposed articles of impeachment, though not as a separate specification and not necessarily on this theory.[53] Nevertheless, this incident and the other three examples point up the continuing significance of recognizing the constitutional limitations of the president's power to control the actions of executive officers.

The President's Duty of Supervision

The Nixon impeachment inquiry stressed President Nixon's own actions—his own violations of the law, his directions to subordinates to engage in unlawful conduct, his ratification of their illegal acts. The charges in the committee's proposed articles of impeachment focused primarily on violations of the president's take-care duty of the most fundamental type, violations by commission rather than omission. The exception was Paragraph 4 of Article 2. That paragraph charged that President Nixon failed to take care that the laws were faithfully executed by "failing to act when he knew or had reason to know that his close subordinates endeavored to impede and frustrate lawful inquiries by duly constituted executive, judicial, and legislative entities." In its report on this paragraph, the committee stated:

52. See Summary of Information 150.

53. Article 1, paragraph 4 included "interfering or endeavoring to interfere with the conduct of investigations by . . . the Office of Watergate Special Prosecution Force"; Article 2, paragraph 5 included knowing misuse of the executive power "by interfering with agencies of the executive branch, including . . . the Office of Watergate Special Prosecution Force."

> The President's duty to take care that the laws be faithfully executed imposes an affirmative obligation upon him to take reasonable steps to insure that his close subordinates, who serve at his pleasure and rely on his authority in the conduct of their positions, do not interfere with the proper functioning of government.

The report observed that this obligation "must be reasonably construed, especially in the context of a presidential impeachment. The President cannot personally attend to the faithful enforcement of each provision of the Federal criminal code against every violator, nor can he supervise the activities of even his closest subordinates in every particular." Paragraph 4 was limited to specified instances in which President Nixon actually knew or had reason to know of "activities by his close subordinates, conducted for his benefit and on his behalf, to obstruct investigations into wrongful and criminal conduct within his administration."[54]

Neither Paragraph 4 nor the articles of impeachment as a whole sought to define the full extent of the president's supervisory responsibility or of his accountability, through impeachment, for failure to meet that responsibility. As a question of law, the scope of the take-care duty remains undefined; the president's accountability through impeachment for serious misfeasance in the executive branch remains untested.

What follows is an attempt, necessarily tentative and general, to suggest what the president's supervisory responsibility entails. It should be reiterated that it is not a catalogue of possible grounds for impeachment; many, if not most violations of the president's take-care duty, taken singly or together, will not be sufficiently grave to warrant consideration of impeachment. But the take-care clause itself, independent of any substantiality requirement applicable in an impeachment proceeding, suggests that there are limits on the president's supervisory duty. It is these limits that are examined here.

The president's legal responsibility for failure to meet his obligation to oversee the execution of the laws and to superintend the actions of executive officers and employees does not involve the imposition of vicarious liability, by which the wrongdoing of others is attributed to the president in the manner that the torts of a servant are imputed to his

54. Nixon Impeachment Report 171.

master or the contractual violations of an agent are imputed to his principal, but rather a breach of a legal duty imposed upon the president alone. Executive officers are not simply the servants or agents of the president. To varying degrees, they are responsible to Congress and the courts as well as the president. Even when they are performing functions delegated by the president, they are accountable to law and not just to him, for they cannot exceed the legal authority he has the power to delegate. Separation of powers and the rule of law imply a more complex system of accountability than to impute all mistakes or misconduct in the execution of the laws to the chief executive.

Whatever the source of executive officers' authority, whether it is delegated to them by the president relying upon his constitutional or statutory powers or assigned to them by Congress using its legislative powers, it is a practical impossibility for the president to supervise its exercise in every particular. The president cannot be expected or required to "become the administrative officer to every department and bureau," the Supreme Court said in 1843, both because this would "absorb the duties and responsibilities of the various departments of the government in the personal action of one executive officer" and "for the stronger reason, that it is impracticable—nay, impossible."[55] Although, as the Court said in the same opinion, the president's duty "in general requires his superintendence of the administration," there must be limitations on the president's legal responsibility for the conduct of executive officers. It would be unrealistic to seek to hold the president accountable for every act of malfeasance by an executive officer no matter how little the president knows about its occurrence or even about the function of the officer who committed it. The president's take-care duty must be reasonably construed, with recognition of his inability to keep abreast of every action of members of the executive branch.

The President's Duty to Respond to Misconduct

One element of the president's obligation to take care that the laws are faithfully executed is that he is required to take positive steps in response to wrongful action by executive officers. Just as he cannot use his powers, such as the pardon power, to prevent detection or prosecution of wrongdoing in which he is involved, so he cannot fail to take

55. Williams v. United States, 42 U.S. (1 How.) 290, 297 (1843).

action when wrongdoing by executive officers comes to his attention. Both points were emphasized by James Madison.

In the Virginia ratifying convention, George Mason suggested that the president might frequently use his pardoning power to "pardon crimes which were advised by himself" or, before indictment or conviction, to "stop inquiry and prevent detection." Madison responded that this use of the pardon power would be impeachable, for the president could be impeached if he were "connected, in any suspicious manner, with any person, and there be grounds to believe he will shelter him."[56]

In the removal power debate, Madison suggested that the president would be impeachable "if he suffers [executive officers] to perpetrate with impunity high crimes or misdemeanors against the United States, or neglects to superintend their conduct, so as to check their excesses."

This remark, which came to be known as the "Madison superintendency theory" during the Judiciary Committee's deliberations on articles of impeachment against President Nixon (and has already been discussed in that connection), suggests a broad conception of the president's obligation to superintend. At other points in the removal power debate, Madison referred to the possibility that "an unworthy man [might] be continued in office by an unworthy President" and that the president might "join in a collusion with [an] officer, and continue a bad man in office." As Corwin has written, Madison regarded the removal power "as primarily a power to get rid of malfeasant subordinates."[57]

The existence of a presidential duty to respond to misconduct was noted by Attorney General Wirt in his 1823 opinion for President Monroe. The Constitution, Wirt wrote,

> places the officers engaged in the execution of the laws under [the president's] general superintendence: he is to see that they do their duty faithfully; and on their failure to cause them to be displaced, prosecuted, or impeached, according to the nature of the case.[58]

Whatever obligation the president has to superintend the conduct of executive officers to prevent wrongdoing or to ferret out information

56. 3 Elliot 497, 498.
57. Annals 1st Cong., 1st Sess., 372–3, 498, 379; Corwin 370 n. 45.
58. 1 Op. Atty. Gen. at 625.

about its occurrence, it is clear that he has a duty to respond when he learns of misconduct or has substantial reason to suspect it. His failure to remove the wrongdoer, to initiate an appropriate investigation, or (in some circumstances) to remedy the wrongful action is similar to acquiescence or ratification of it. By failing to act, the president in effect "join[s] in a collusion with [the] officer," as Madison said. In these circumstances, the president has failed to perform his constitutional duty.[59]

Misconduct Set in Motion by the President

Although the president cannot be considered personally responsible for every action undertaken in his name and based on his authority, in some circumstances he would seem to have an obligation to oversee specific actions by executive officials pursuant to his directive. When he directs that activity be undertaken that involves a significant possibility of wrongdoing, it is reasonable to conclude that he has a duty to implement suitable procedures to insure that it is carried out by legal means. If illegal conduct does result, the president should be considered responsible for his failure to provide proper guidance on how the activity was to be performed and proper supervision while it was underway.

Without seeking to propose definitive guidelines in an area that necessarily turns upon the circumstances of particular presidential directives and the actions that result from them, among the factors that might be taken into account in determining the extent of the president's duty to oversee are the following: the relationship of the president to the official to whom the function is delegated, with a greater oversight responsibility for those, such as presidential staff assistants, who are his personal subordinates; the availability of other means of superintendence, so that, for example, a directive made in confidence and to which executive privilege applies carries a greater degree of presidential supervisory responsibility than a formal, published delegation of authority to an officer subject to congressional oversight; and the nature of the delegated function, with more presidential super-

59. For an interesting compilation of incidents of this type before the Nixon administration, see C. Vann Woodward, ed., *Responses of the Presidents to Charges of Misconduct* (1974), a study done at the request of the Impeachment Inquiry Staff of the Judiciary Committee. Woodward suggests that presidential offenses described in the study "usually lay in negligence or in indecision about correcting the offensive practice or discharging the accused" (at xxvi).

vision required for those activities to be performed in secret and without acknowledgement of executive involvement than for those performed openly. Perhaps these factors are more applicable to yesterday's problems than to tomorrow's; in any event, they are intended merely to be suggestive.

The relationship of executive privilege to presidential responsibility is worth noting. Aside from the separation of powers, the constitutional bases for executive privilege are "[t]he President's need for complete candor and objectivity from advisers" and "the necessity for protection of the public interest in candid, objective, and even blunt or harsh opinions in presidential decision-making."[60] The privilege exists to aid the president in the exercise of his duties; it presupposes that the decisions for which free and unfettered advice is needed are to be his decisions, not those of his personal aides or department or agency heads. Because it is a presidential privilege, its invocation should carry a coextensive presidential responsibility for the fruits of the decision-making process it is designed to protect. There may very well be a constitutional presumption of personal presidential accountability for any action undertaken by an individual (such as a presidential staff assistant) who is not himself directly accountable to congressional oversight or for any action, by whomever undertaken, to which executive privilege is claimed to apply.

Other Wrongdoing by Executive Officials

Undoubtedly the largest, and unquestionably the most perplexing, category of wrongdoing by executive officials involves misconduct of which the president has no knowledge. More precisely, it involves misconduct for which evidence of presidential direction or ratification is lacking and for which there is no reason to impose a special standard of supervision upon the president. It is the category for which presidential responsibility, if it is to be imposed at all, rests on neglect, inattention, or negligence—on a culpable failure to prevent the wrongdoing or to discover it and take action. Whether the president has violated his duty involves nothing more or less complicated than, literally, whether he has failed to take care that the laws be faithfully executed. The application of this test resembles the application of negligence doctrines in general, with due allowance for the nature of

60. United States v. Nixon, 418 U.S. at 706, 708.

the presidency and the competing demands upon a president's attention. A particular instance of misconduct must be assessed in terms of expectations concerning the supervision that would be expected of a reasonable president in the circumstances. It is difficult to devise any very enlightening definition of the scope of the president's supervisory duty, though it is possible to suggest some considerations that should be kept in mind. First, the president—especially in a government of the size and complexity of the present-day federal establishment—cannot be held responsible for each and every act of wrongdoing within the executive branch. A president cannot be expected to prevent every act of misconduct or even to learn of it upon its occurrence and institute measures to prevent its repetition. If a president has established an administrative system reasonably calculated to keep him apprised of what executive departments and agencies are doing and to oversee the legality of their actions, he should not be held responsible for actions that escape his notice, even if he might be held to account for failure to respond to wrongdoing in a reasonable fashion after it comes to his attention through his own oversight machinery or otherwise. Second, the president should not be held legally responsible—which ultimately would mean accountable through impeachment—for bad policy judgments by executive officers, whatever political consequences such bad judgments might properly have for him. His legal responsibility, again to quote Attorney General Wirt, is to see that laws are executed faithfully—"that is, honestly: not with perfect correctness of judgment, but honestly."[61] It is important to distinguish between the political ramifications for a president of poor or misguided management of programs and his legal responsibility for failure to see that the laws are faithfully enforced and legal duties faithfully performed. A legally proper exercise of administrative discretion may be politically damaging; in our system of government, the President's political accountability for such political mistakes does not depend on the extent of his knowledge or involvement in them. The officials directly responsible are his appointees, and their replacement depends initially upon his initiative and ultimately upon his own replacement by the electorate. By contrast, his legal accountability results from a breach of his constitutional duty, not the unpopularity of the actions of his administration. Third, because misconduct by executive officials carries both political and

61. 1 Op. Atty. Gen. at 626 (emphasis omitted).

legal accountability, the president must be given reasonable latitude in dealing with it, recognizing the nature of his position and his political role. For this reason, doctrines borrowed from other areas of law, involving private duties and private actions, cannot be literally applied to define the president's responsibility. Because his position is unique, so too is the scope of his constitutional duty of supervision.

Conclusion

In summary, there are four distinct ways in which misconduct by executive officials may involve the president's violation of his own constitutional duty to take care that the laws be faithfully executed. First, if the president directs or seeks to induce an official to engage in illegal action, he is responsible for his endeavor to have the law violated or ignored rather than faithfully administered. Second, when the president knows of or has substantial reason to suspect misconduct, he has an obligation to take steps to respond in an appropriate fashion. Third, if the president directs an official or aide to engage in activity involving a substantial risk of misconduct, he is required to supervise the activity in a reasonable manner. Finally, the president is required to oversee the execution of the laws as a whole and is responsible for misconduct by executive officials, even if it occurred without his actual knowledge, if a reasonable president should have known about it and could have taken steps to prevent or rectify it. In no case is the illegal action of subordinates simply imputed to the president; rather, their misconduct triggers an assessment of the manner in which he has performed his own constitutional duty.

5. *THE SOLE POWER OF IMPEACHMENT*

"The sole power of impeachment," vested in the House of Representatives by Article I, section 2, of the Constitution, confers authority on the House to initiate removal proceedings against presidents and other civil officers and to conduct investigations to determine whether to exercise this authority. Before the Nixon inquiry, the meaning of "the sole power of impeachment"—how sole and how powerful it (and the investigative authority it implies) might be—had not been seriously tested.

In considering the issues that arose during the Nixon inquiry, it is essential to recognize some contextual factors. For 105 years, since the conclusion of the Johnson trial, presidential impeachment had been regarded as an antiquated relic in the Constitution. As presidential power had grown, the notion of presidential accountability—especially through impeachment—had waned, and the responsibility of the president, so much stressed by the framers of the Constitution, had become more and more attenuated. Clauses of the Constitution intended to impose limits on presidential power—notably, the oath and the take-care clause—were more frequently interpreted by presidents, and occasionally by courts, to confer power, as they reasoned that the president could not perform his duties if denied the means necessary to accomplish them. The "heaped-up powers on the Chief Magistrate" had not rendered him more responsible; instead, as predicted in 1789, they seemed to place him beyond accountability.

Attitudes about the president had also changed. Alexander Hamilton had written in *The Federalist* No. 67 that it was absurd to magnify "[t]he authorities of a magistrate, in few instances greater, in some instances less, than those of a governor of New York . . . into more than royal prerogatives." Hamilton castigated those who attempted to portray the office of president under the proposed Constitution "not merely as the embryo, but as the full-grown progeny, of that detested parent," monarchy:

> He has been decorated with attributes superior in dignity and splendor to those of a king of Great Britain. He has been shown to us with the diadem sparkling on his brow and the imperial purple flowing in his train. He has been seated on a throne surrounded with minions and mistresses, giving audience to the envoys of foreign potentates, in all the supercilious pomp of majesty. The images of Asiatic despotism and voluptuousness have scarcely been wanting to crown the exaggerated scene. We have been taught to tremble at the terrific visages of murdering janizaries, and to blush at the unveiled mysteries of a future seraglio.[1]

One hundred eighty-five years later, Hamilton's description did not seem quite so caricatured. In their brief to the Supreme Court in *United States v. Nixon*, for example, President Nixon's counsel thought it necessary to add a footnote to the otherwise unremarkable assertions that a "great role [is] entrusted to the presidency [*sic*] by the Constitution" and "the President alone is representative of the whole country." The footnote (with only the citations omitted) stated:

> Lest the President's position be misunderstood, it must be stressed we do not suggest that the President has the attributes of a king. Inter alia, a king rules by inheritance and for life.[2]

One would have thought the list of differences might be slightly longer.

But it was not just President Nixon and his lawyers who made sweeping claims of "more than royal prerogatives" for the office. "Taken by and large, the history of the presidency is a history of aggrandizement," Edward S. Corwin wrote in the 1950s,[3] and the aggrandizement—and popular acceptance of it—accelerated after he wrote. Our "strong" presidents were considered our best presidents, activists who had dealt with crises boldly and decisively, sometimes ig-

1. *The Federalist* No. 67 at 436–7.
2. Brief for the Respondent, Cross-Petitioner Richard M. Nixon, President of the United States, United States v. Nixon 59, n. 43 (filed June 21, 1974).
3. Corwin 29–30.

noring constitutional and legal constraints in the process. The president, and the president alone, was the national leader expected to set policy, cure domestic ills, and safeguard the nation from foreign threats. There was, to be sure, a reaction, stemming primarily from the Indochina War, where heaped-up presidential powers had been applied to an objective that ultimately proved unacceptable to the people, and it had become fashionable to rail against the imperial presidency.[4]

The point here, however, is not that the presidency was (or, for that matter, still may be) too powerful or too imperial. Rather, it is that the power of the president and popular respect for the office, coupled with the unfamiliarity and historical disrepute of the constitutional mechanism for removal, made presidential impeachment seem a process akin to regicide.

For one thing, as President Nixon's counsel suggested, the president alone is considered to be the representative of the whole country. That was not exactly what the framers of the Constitution had in mind when they created a single executive, for they regarded the members of the House, not the president, as the immediate representatives of the people. But the president was a single person and the House a numerous assembly that represented the people only in a collegial capacity. Even though it requires a vote of a majority of the people's representatives to initiate removal proceedings against the president (and removal requires a vote of two-thirds of the Senate, also now popularly elected, contrary to the framers' scheme), impeachment seemed antidemocratic. Impeaching and removing an elected president would, it was suggested, defeat the will of the electorate. The argument had a certain validity, since the president might represent one political party while the opposition party controlled Congress, as was the situation after the 1972 election (though the election of a president is not necessarily properly regarded as a popular mandate, except perhaps in a negative sense, as the 1972 election also suggested). In any case, the point was repeatedly made that even the people's representatives must be extremely wary of frustrating the people's choice. As a note of caution, this was an appropriate warning, but it sometimes carried the implication that any questioning of the president's conduct was somehow illegitimate.

4. See especially Schlesinger, *The Imperial Presidency* (1973).

Another reason that the president's removal from office seemed virtually unthinkable was that it was cruel and unusual—indeed, unprecedented—political punishment. It seems unlikely that the framers of the Constitution had the slightest inkling that presidential impeachment would be a once-a-century undertaking or that it would be 185 years before a president left office by any means other than death or the expiration of his term. They did perceive that removal from office was punitive in its effect. A court of impeachment, Hamilton wrote in *The Federalist* No. 65, had "the awful discretion . . . to doom to honor or to infamy," to sentence a convicted officer to "perpetual ostracism from the esteem and confidence, and honors and emoluments of his country."[5] It is one thing for a president to retire from office at the end of a term, even after defeat at the polls, and quite another for him to be forced to leave after conviction of high crimes and misdemeanors.

Modern elected officials, it is fair to say, do not feel particularly comfortable in an accusatory or condemnatory role. Especially those members of the House who might have had to prosecute President Nixon in a Senate trial if he had been impeached would probably have found it an uncongenial undertaking. Impeachment is a procedure grounded in a different conception of statesmanship than modern legislators are apt to endorse. It is not an attack upon the office of president or an effort to restructure or redefine the presidency. Rather, it is extremely personal: Richard Nixon was suspected of wrongdoing, might be prosecuted, and conceivably could be ousted from office in disgrace. However much a member of the House or Senate might conceive of his function in constitutional terms, the fact remained that the Constitution required him to consider advocating or imposing a political death sentence upon a fellow elected official.[6]

5. At 426.

6. Some of the more flamboyant rhetoric of the Johnson trial concerned what should be done with a convicted president. Manager George S. Boutwell made this suggestion to the Senate: "Travellers and astronomers inform us that in the southern heavens, near the southern cross, there is a vast space which the uneducated call the hole in the sky, where the eye of man, with the aid of the powers of the telescope, has been unable to discover nebulae, or asteriod, or comet, or planet, or star, or sun. In that dreary, cold, dark region of space, which is only known to be less than infinite by the evidences of creation elsewhere, the Great Author of celestial mechanism has left the chaos which was in the beginning. If this earth were capable of the sentiments and emotions of justice and virtue, which in human mortal beings are the evidences and the pledge of our Divine origin and immortal destiny, it would heave and throw, with the energy of the elemental forces of nature, and project this enemy of two races of men into that vast region, there forever to exist in a solitude eternal as life, or as the absence of life,

And impeachment was an adjudicative proceeding to be conducted by a body without much recognized competence in such matters. The observation had been frequently made (not necessarily fairly) that the Senate proved to be a prejudiced and inexpert court in the Johnson impeachment trial. The performance of the House in the Johnson impeachment was, if anything, even more severely criticized. The framers of the Constitution might not have been particularly shocked or offended by the Johnson impeachment—they fully expected the House to display partisan excesses in the exercise of the impeachment power, a danger to be remedied through trial in the Senate—but historians and legal commentators were less understanding. "[T]he verdict of history," according to the Committee on Federal Legislation of the Association of the Bar of the City of New York, writing in January 1974, "is that the Johnson impeachment demonstrates the perils of treating impeachment as an invitation to purely political retribution."[7] A corollary of this criticism—mingled with the reappearance of the criminality argument—was that impeachment was supposed to be a purely judicial process in which political considerations, partisan or otherwise, should play no part. Legislative bodies were not considered to have the expertise or regard for fairness required to perform functions (like impeachment and trial of a president) essentially judicial in character. "Legislative justice" was thought to be a contradiction in terms.[8]

---

emblematical of, if not really, that 'outer darkness' of which the Saviour of man spoke in warning to those who are the enemies of themselves, of their race, and of their God." Recognizing that his oratorical flight sounded a bit punitive, Boutwell immediately added that the Senate's function was "to relieve, not to punish" (2 Johnson Trial 116–7). Later, sporting with the proposal of "the honorable and astronomical manager," defense lawyer William S. Evarts suggested that it was legal and logical, since the Constitution said "removal from office" but "put no limit to the distance of the removal" (2 *ibid*. 297–8).

A more earthbound proposal was made by another of the defense counsel. If Johnson were guilty of any of the charges, he suggested, not only should he be removed, "but a whip should be put in every honest hand to lash him around the world as a man unworthy of the notice of gentlemen and unfit for the association of any of his race; he should be pointed at everywhere and shown as a monster; he should be banished from society; his very name should become a word to frighten children with throughout the land from one end of it to the other, so that when one should meet him his sight would cause—'Each particular hair to stand on end / Like quills upon the fretful porcupine' " (2 *ibid*. 119 [Nelson]).

7. *The Law of Presidential Impeachment* 7.

8. See Roscoe Pound, "Justice According to Law," 14 *Colum. L. Rev*. 1, 7–11 (1914), quoted in Note, "The Trial of Presidential Impeachments: Should the Ghost Be Laid to Rest?" 44 *Notre Dame Law*. 1089, 1098 (1969).

In the Johnson trial in 1868 the managers could give short shrift to the argument that the Supreme Court was the proper tribunal to decide disputes between Congress and the president largely because the Court, a decade after the *Dred Scott* decision,[9] was at the nadir of its reputation. By the time of the Nixon impeachment inquiry, things had changed, and the Court was accepted as the ultimate arbiter of constitutional questions. Where Hamilton had doubted that the Court would possess "the degree of credit and authority" that might be indispensable to reconcile the people to a decision in an impeachment proceeding contrary to the views of the people's representatives,[10] by the time of the Nixon inquiry many conceived of the Court as the sole repository of constitutional wisdom. It was largely for this reason that some (most notably Raoul Berger) argued that courts could review impeachment convictions.[11] The legal reasoning in support of judicial review of impeachment cases is dubious, at best. What is more interesting is the premise, generally unstated, on which the argument rests: impeachment is an adjudicative proceeding, and only the Supreme Court can provide legitimacy to a legal judgment.

Another point related to this and to the punitive and personal aspects of impeachment was that there was an overarching requirement of fairness to the president in an impeachment proceeding. The proceeding was one against the president, and his right to procedural fairness had to be recognized. In part, the importance of fairness to the president (or the presidency) stemmed from the repeated invocation of the concept on President Nixon's behalf. But it also had more important and deeper roots. Procedural fairness had become a prominent feature on the legal landscape. In the criminal law, a "due process revolution" had occurred, largely in the previous decade, and many of the constitutional reforms applied to pretrial proceedings, analogous in some respects to an impeachment inquiry. Whether or not impeachment is a "criminal" proceeding, it is an accusatory one, and comparisons to a criminal prosecution had both an historical foundation and a contemporary application (especially with respect to those elements of the charges against President Nixon that were also the subject of investigation by the special prosecutor and grand juries). In addition, fairness in congressional investigations had itself become a subject of

9. Dred Scott v. Sanford, 60 U.S. (19 How.) 393 (1857).
10. *The Federalist* No. 65 at 425.
11. See Berger, *Impeachment* 103–21.

concern to civil libertarians, dating back to the McCarthy era. The witch-hunts of the 1950s had resulted in judicial recognition of the constitutional rights of witnesses in congressional investigations, as well as reinforcement of perceptions that congressional committees could be insensitive to the requirements of the Bill of Rights.

Finally, and perhaps most critical of all, the Nixon impeachment inquiry was the first in our constitutional history resisted by the official under investigation. Only once, nearly a century earlier, had an official whose impeachment was under consideration dared to suggest that "the sole power of impeachment" did not require him to cooperate fully with an investigation by a House committee. President Nixon did not merely suggest it, but argued that evidentiary demands in an impeachment inquiry might themselves violate the Constitution. Not only, according to President Nixon, did he have constitutional rights in an impeachment inquiry that had to be recognized, but also as president he had constitutional powers, to which the House had to defer. The "sole power of impeachment," so long unused and so little understood, had to confront executive power that was both well developed and assertive.

Accordingly, despite James Iredell's assurance to the North Carolina ratifying convention in 1788 that the House would "be ready enough to make complaints,"[12] the impeachment process did not seem so simple when the investigation of President Nixon began. The House was invoking a moribund procedure that involved unusual investigative power. It was engaging in the unfamiliar task of scrutinizing a president's conduct for evidence of wrongdoing, and it was potentially casting itself in the uncongenial role of prosecuting a case not just for his ouster from office, but for his political disgrace. And it was undertaking the task in a far different legal and political context than the framers knew or anticipated.

These and other factors influenced the manner in which the Nixon inquiry was conducted and the procedural decisions that were made during it. An impeachment investigation in the House, and especially one involving the president, is a political as well as a legal proceeding. Popular conceptions of fairness, much more than technical legal doctrines, are likely to govern procedural decisions in a presidential impeachment inquiry for two reasons. First, the conduct of the investiga-

12. 4 Elliot 32.

tion may itself become an issue in House consideration of the recommendation (whether for or against impeachment) that emerges from it. If the inquiry appears to have been conducted in a biased manner, this provides an argument against House agreement to the recommendation of the investigating committee and invites further proceedings to postpone decision in the House. Second, technical rules of law cannot govern the conduct of a presidential impeachment inquiry because on many important points no applicable rules exist. Legal arguments must be based on analogies to other proceedings (grand jury investigations, administrative hearings), none of them very apt, or on past practice in impeachment investigations, none of it very persuasive. The Nixon inquiry raised a number of procedural issues on which little or no guidance was available from past impeachment investigations; and, even on issues that had been encountered before, past practice was of limited use. Most prior investigations had involved district judges, were conducted by small subcommittees of the Judiciary Committee, and had occurred more than three decades previously. Even when procedural attributes of these investigations could be determined—and it was not easy to locate, much less to analyze, the relevant materials from past investigations, especially those before 1900—they hardly seemed to have much precedential significance for a presidential impeachment inquiry in a far different context, involving much more substantial stakes.

Initiating the Inquiry

The Nixon impeachment inquiry began in rather haphazard fashion. After the "Saturday Night Massacre" in October 1973, various members of the House introduced resolutions calling for the impeachment of President Nixon or for an investigation to determine whether he should be impeached. Speaker of the House Carl Albert referred the impeachment resolutions to the Judiciary Committee, which had traditionally conducted impeachment inquiries,[13] and the resolutions calling for an investigation to the Rules Committee. Under the precedents of the House, the reference of a bill to a committee by the Speaker, even if erroneous, in effect confers jurisdiction on the committee to consider it—a doctrine presumably equally applicable to im-

13. Impeachment investigations became the province of the Judiciary Committee because virtually all of them involved the conduct of federal judges.

peachment resolutions.[14] Jurisdiction, however, does not mean subpoena power or investigative authority, which is conferred on committees by House resolution. The resolution giving investigative authority to the Judiciary Committee in the Ninety-third Congress empowered it to issue subpoenas for investigations and inquiries within its jurisdiction as set forth in the rules of the House,[15] and the rule describing the committee's jurisdiction made no mention of presidential impeachment, although it did include "[p]residential succession."[16] At the time the impeachment resolutions were referred to it, the Judiciary Committee was investigating the nomination of Gerald R. Ford to be vice president on the basis of its jurisdiction over presidential succession, and it could be argued that an inquiry into whether the incumbent president should be impeached and removed from office had just as much relationship to presidential succession as an investigation of the qualifications of his possible successor for appointment as vice president. If so, the Judiciary Committee had jurisdiction to conduct an impeachment investigation.

The House seemed to endorse this view by authorizing the committee to spend an additional million dollars to meet the expenses of investigations and studies pursuant to its general authorizing resolution. These funds, the committee report accompanying the resolution indicated, were "for use by the Committee on the Judiciary in carrying out its responsibility of reviewing and investigating charges that the President of the United States should be impeached."[17]

The upshot was that the committee had jurisdiction over the impeachment inquiry either because it was within its general jurisdiction or because of the reference of impeachment resolutions to it by the Speaker. The more important issue was whether the committee had subpoena power for its impeachment inquiry. That was not merely a question of House procedures and potential conflicts among committees, but a matter that might lead to disputes with recalcitrant wit-

14. Rules of the House of Representatives, Rule XXII, cl. 4, annot. §854 (1971).

15. 93d Cong., 1st Sess., H. Res. 74 (Feb. 28, 1973).

16. Rules of the House of Representatives, Rule XI, cl. 13. This clause lists nineteen areas of committee jurisdiction. Others that might have been construed to encompass some of the allegations against President Nixon were "judicial proceedings, civil and criminal generally" (13a) and "civil liberties" (13d). "Presidential succession" was 13p.

17. 93d Cong., 1st Sess., H. Res. 720 (Nov. 15, 1973). The resolution authorized the additional funds for "the further expenses of the investigations and studies to be conducted pursuant to H. Res. 74." 93d Cong., 1st Sess., H. Rept. No. 93–641, at 2 (Nov. 14, 1973).

nesses, executive agencies, courts, and President Nixon himself.

The argument that "presidential impeachment" was encompassed by "presidential succession" and that the House had conferred investigative authority when it authorized funds posed some problems. There was little basis for arguing that the House meant to confer subpoena power when it authorized expenditures because (among other reasons) the committee could expend a million dollars on an impeachment inquiry without issuing subpoenas, as subsequent events showed. Furthermore, "the sole power of impeachment," as the committee later contended, implies far more extensive investigative authority than do ordinary legislative powers. It is improbable that the House would routinely confer these powers as part of a general authorizing resolution, especially when no presidential impeachment inquiry had been undertaken by a House committee for more than a century. And, with a few exceptions, past impeachment investigations had been authorized by a specific resolution conferring subpoena power, and therefore House precedent ran counter to the argument that impeachment investigative powers were to be conferred on a committee by inference or indirection.[18] Finally, and most important, if the Judiciary Committee indeed had continuing authority to launch impeachment investigations of presidents by virtue of its general jurisdiction, then all that would ever be required to defeat a claim of executive privilege by the president would be to convince a majority of the Judiciary Committee to subpoena the witness or material for whom or which privilege was claimed. This followed from attributes of the impeachment power later claimed by the committee. Impeachment, the committee contended, is an exception to the separation of powers, a constitutional method—really the only method—for scrutinizing the president's con-

18. See generally 3 Hinds' and 6 Cannon's. The most recent impeachment inquiry was among the exceptions (the others, mostly in the 1860s and 1870s, involved misconduct discovered by committees authorized to investigate executive departments, where the committee considered or recommended impeachment of an official as an outgrowth of its discoveries). A special subcommittee of the Judiciary Committee had conducted an inquiry into the conduct of Justice William O. Douglas in 1970, claiming investigative authority on the basis of its jurisdiction over federal courts and judges and authority to investigate judicial personnel. The subcommittee issued no subpoenas because all potential witnesses cooperated. 91st Cong., 2d Sess., House, Comm. on the Judiciary, Special Subcomm. on H. Res. 920, *Associate Justice William O. Douglas, First Report by the Special Subcomm. on H. Res.* 920, at 1 (June 20, 1970). The Douglas inquiry was the first impeachment investigation in twenty-five years, and deviation from the older procedural pattern was not surprising.

duct and calling him to account. Because this is so, executive privilege is inapplicable. Privilege based on separation of powers is irrelevant to a procedure that is a constitutional bridge between the legislative and executive branches. The public interest in the confidentiality of presidential deliberations is outweighed by the public interest in holding the president responsible for his actions. Moreover, the impeachment power is vested solely in the House, and only the House can decide how to conduct an impeachment inquiry. If it has delegated its authority to a committee, then the committee's decisions concerning the need for evidence or information are binding, and failure to comply may itself be grounds for impeachment. Accordingly, a majority of the Judiciary Committee could, at any time, confront the president with the risk of impeachment if he invoked executive privilege through the simple expedient of introducing an impeachment resolution, launching an investigation under its general impeachment investigative authority, issuing a subpoena for the information, and recommending impeachment for disobedience.

This power to initiate a constitutional confrontation—and other sweeping attributes of impeachment investigating authority—seemed to be more than the House meant to confer on the Judiciary Committee through the general language of its rules or by convention. There was much to be said—on the basis of precedent, principle, and policy—for requiring the House to invoke its impeachment power explicitly and directly, especially because the Nixon inquiry involved the first invocation of the impeachment power against a president in more than a century and the first in the nation's history in which there was from the beginning a likelihood (later fulfilled) that the president would resist evidentiary requests and subpoenas. Whatever legal theories could be spun out to argue that the Judiciary Committee had all the investigative authority it needed, it was far preferable for the House to confer the authority expressly.

In early February 1974 the House did just that, enacting a resolution by a vote of 410 to 4 authorizing and directing the Judiciary Committee "to investigate fully and completely whether sufficient grounds exist for the House of Representatives to exercise its constitutional power to impeach Richard M. Nixon, President of the United States of America."[19] The resolution conferred subpoena power to ob-

19. 93d Cong., 2d Sess., H. Res. 803, §1 (Feb. 6, 1974). The resolution was drafted in broad terms to avoid any implications about the reach of the impeachment power or

tain evidence the committee deemed necessary to the investigation.[20] The legislative history of the resolution indicated that the full, complete, and unqualified investigative authority of the House incident to the power of impeachment was conferred on the committee, unrestricted as to the subjects it could investigate and the persons (including the president) whom it could compel to produce evidence.[21] This resolution, especially because it received overwhelming bipartisan support, put the Nixon inquiry on a firm footing. It also established an important procedural point: impeachment investigations, because they involve extraordinary power and (at least where the president is being investigated) may have extraordinary consequences, are not to be undertaken in the same manner as run-of-the-mill legislative investigations. The initiation of a presidential impeachment inquiry should itself require a deliberate decision by the House.

Conducting the Inquiry: Participation by the President's Counsel

There are two procedural models for impeachment investigations by House committees.[22] The first, patterned after a grand jury proceeding, is an *ex parte* investigation in which the target of the investigation has no right to appear, confront and cross-examine witnesses, or adduce evidence in his own defense. The earliest impeachment investigations by House committees were conducted in this manner, and the role of the House in impeachment was frequently analogized to that of a grand jury.

The analogy, however, was deficient in several respects. There was no prosecutor to present evidence before the investigating committee. Instead, impeachment investigations came to be instituted as a result of allegations made by a private citizen, a member of the House, or some other advocate of impeachment. The investigating committee,

---

the evidentiary standard to be applied by the committee or the House. Previous resolutions authorizing impeachment investigations generally called for an inquiry into the official conduct of the officer to determine if he had been guilty of high crimes and misdemeanors requiring the interposition of the constitutional powers of the House.

20. It also provided that the funds made available under H. Res. 720 could be used for the impeachment investigation.

21. 93d Cong., 2d Sess., H. Rept. No. 93–774 (Feb. 4, 1974). See also Nixon Impeachment Report 6.

22. This description is based upon Impeachment Inquiry Staff Procedures Memo.

which generally had no firsthand knowledge of the official or his conduct, often invited the proponent of impeachment to present evidence in support of the allegations. But, because the proponent and his witnesses might also be unknown to the committee, it needed a way to test the evidence. If it recommended impeachment, the committee had to be able to defend its recommendation to the House; if impeachment was voted, members of the House had to prosecute the case in the Senate. The committee, therefore, much more than the proponent of impeachment, resembled a prosecutor; if anything, its task was more analogous to a prosecutor's preparation of the evidence to be presented to a grand jury than to the grand jury's own proceedings.

In these circumstances it was not surprising that investigating committees began to permit the official under investigation to present his side of the case, to question adverse witnesses, and to be represented by counsel. His participation was not simply a question of fairness to him. It provided additional information that enabled the committee to assess the case and to anticipate the issues that would arise if there was a trial.

By the late nineteenth century a second model of impeachment investigations had emerged: an adversarial proceeding in which a proponent of impeachment brought forward charges and adduced evidence in support of them and the official against whom the charges were made—the "respondent," as he was called—sought to refute the charges through examination of adverse witnesses and presentation of evidence in his own defense. The committee (usually a subcommittee of the Judiciary Committee) was cast in a more or less adjudicative role, though the rules of evidence and other formal attributes of trials did not apply.

It was evident from the outset that the Nixon impeachment inquiry would fit neither of these patterns. There was no single proponent of impeachment and no mechanism available for selecting one. Even if there had been, the divisiveness of an adversarial proceeding before the Judiciary Committee would have had serious political ramifications. If the committee had recommended against impeachment after such a proceeding, the argument might have been made that the committee had short-circuited the constitutional process, which provides for trial by the Senate and not by a House committee. If, on the other hand, an adversary proceeding had led to a recommendation of impeachment, which the House accepted, then the issues would have had to be relitigated in a trial in the Senate. Acquittal there might also have had divisive consequences. Similarly, if the committee had recommended against impeachment, but the House voted it and the Senate convicted, then the different outcome of the two adversary proceedings might have undermined the apparent legitimacy of the Senate judgment. In short, an adversary proceeding before the committee would have appeared to be an initial trial, and trying a president is a function reserved to the Senate under the Constitution.[23] An *ex parte* proceeding would have seemed bizarre and fundamentally unfair; it would have done little to legitimate the unfamiliar remedy of presidential impeachment, a function the Judiciary Committee's inquiry had to perform for a recommendation of impeachment to be accepted by the House and the nation.

The committee never considered the possibility of either of these approaches. Instead, it sought to insure thoroughness, expedition, and fairness in its inquiry by hiring a special counsel and a staff pledged to conduct a professional, objective sifting of the evidence for presentation to the committee. In addition to the reputation of Special Counsel Doar, a number of attributes of the inquiry staff helped to assure that it would gather and present evidence in an impartial manner. Members of the staff were hired on this understanding of their function. The staff was bipartisan, so that there were built-in checks against bias in one direction or the other. The staff was isolated from committee members, the press, and the public, so that its professional obligations were constantly reinforced. Finally, the staff was hired for, and committed to, the impeachment inquiry and not the general work of the committee or the House. As a result, it had an organizational single-mindedness not found in previous impeachment inquiries or most congressional investigations.

23. This is not to suggest that an adversary proceeding before the Judiciary Committee would have been unconstitutional. The House's sole power of impeachment carries with it the exclusive authority to decide how to conduct its own impeachment proceedings. A trial to decide whether to impeach is hardly the same as a trial of an impeachment—that is, a trial to decide whether to remove. The division of accusatory and adjudicative functions between the House and Senate implies nothing, as a matter of constitutional law, about how the accusatory function is to be performed. It does provide a practical and rather compelling argument in support of the proposition that the House would be ill-advised to conduct a triallike investigation in a case (especially one involving a president) where impeachment is a likely outcome. An adversary proceeding before a House committee is useful only as a mechanism to exonerate a president.

Beyond these characteristics of the staff itself, other factors helped to insure that its work would be objective and unbiased. The committee included both political supporters and opponents of the president, who would criticize partiality in one direction or the other, and many members who were quick to protect their own authority to reach conclusions and make judgments about the president's conduct. President Nixon and his aides, moreover, stood ready to attack the work of the committee and its staff.

While fairness was built into the impeachment inquiry, President Nixon and his counsel argued that this was not sufficient.[24] James St. Clair contended that he had a right to represent the president in the committee's inquiry—to receive notice of the charges against the president, to cross-examine witnesses, and to present evidence on the president's behalf. He made a number of arguments in favor of this claim, some more compelling than others.

The less persuasive arguments included the proposition that an impeachment inquiry was analogous to a preliminary hearing for a criminal defendant, an adversarial proceeding in which the acused has a right to representation by counsel. The analogy was not particularly apposite since a preliminary hearing focuses on specific charges, while specific charges are not formulated until the conclusion of an impeachment inquiry (and then only if impeachment is recommended). St. Clair also suggested that there was a due process right of participation in any proceeding that might affect an individual's property or reputation—an assertion that was much too sweeping, as the purported right does not apply to any number of governmental actions (ranging from a prosecutor's decision to initiate a criminal investigation to prehearing investigations by administrative agencies) that pose a risk of potentially adverse consequences. These actions, which do not involve final adjudications, are similar in some respects to an impeachment inquiry, though this analogy too is far from exact. St. Clair also pointed to the risk of adverse publicity. To the extent that this argument was intended to cover damage to President Nixon's reputation independent of his possible impeachment, it also seemed overdrawn, since St. Clair suggested at the same time that the integrity and

24. James D. St. Clair et al., "Memorandum in Support of the President's Request for the Right to Have the President's Counsel Participate in the Impeachment Proceedings Conducted by the Committee on the Judiciary of the United States House of Representatives" (c. March 31, 1974) (hereafter St. Clair Participation Memo).

fairness of a proceeding in which the president was not represented could be legitimately attacked. If this were so, it was hard to see how the proceeding could damage President Nixon's reputation, at least in any irremediable way. And, in any event, he was no ordinary citizen being accused in a headline-grabbing congressional witch-hunt; he had ample means to set the record straight, including unique ability to command television time and press coverage. St. Clair proffered one other unconvincing argument—that disclosure of inaccurate or incomplete information from the impeachment inquiry might influence members of the Senate, who would be biased toward conviction no matter what occurred in a subsequent trial. The problem with this contention was that it in effect denied the ability of senators to abide by their constitutionally prescribed oath to "do impartial justice according to the Constitution and laws" in an impeachment trial.

In addition to these dubious arguments, St. Clair made two more compelling points. The first was that participation by the official under investigation had been permitted in past impeachment inquiries, particularly under the "modern practice" (meaning inquiries less than a century, though more than thirty years, previously). As has been mentioned, the reason for the modern practice was that impeachment inquiries had developed into something approaching adversarial proceedings, with a proponent bringing charges and the respondent defending himself against them. The Nixon inquiry lacked a proponent; it was not adversarial because there was no advocate of impeachment; and the modern practice was therefore inapplicable, a point the impeachment inquiry staff made on the basis of an analysis of the records of past impeachment investigations.[25] Nevertheless, St. Clair's argument appeared to have precedent on its side and, more significantly, to accord with the more recent (and presumably more enlightened) trend.

The most persuasive argument in favor of permitting President Nixon's counsel to participate in the impeachment inquiry, however, was that it would help insure fairness and completeness—the very goals the committee sought to achieve. No matter how impartial or objective the inquiry staff was, it could not represent the president's interests as well as the president's own counsel. His participation pro-

25. Impeachment Inquiry Staff Procedures Memo 11, 14–8.

vided an additional assurance, not merely of due process, but of "due process quadrupled," as Rep. Barbara Jordan (D., Tex.) put it.[26]

Despite some misgivings—prompted in part by the president's refusal to provide evidentiary material sought by the committee at the same time he demanded the right to have his counsel participate in the committee's proceedings to insure a full and complete record—the Judiciary Committee ultimately adopted procedural rules that permitted St. Clair to participate in its evidentiary hearings. Chairman Peter W. Rodino, Jr., emphasized (as had past committee chairman, in all those not very apposite precedents) that his participation was a privilege conferred by the committee, and not a right, and was subject to limitations included in the procedural rules and to the control of the committee.[27]

The manner in which St. Clair was permitted to participate reflected the committee's procedures for receiving evidentiary material. The basic evidentiary presentation was made by the Impeachment Inquiry Staff in the form of a "statement of information" on matters the staff considered pertinent to the inquiry, with supporting evidentiary material from testimony before congressional committees, grand jury testimony, affidavits, official records, and other sources. The statement of information—there were more than 650 paragraphs, supported by some 7,200 pages of evidentiary material, presented to the committee over a six-week span—was factual in content and neither reached nor implied conclusions. (Where recordings of President Nixon's conversations were involved, the statement of information did not summarize the content or indicate the relationship of the conversation to other evidence. Instead, the committee heard the full recording and was given a complete transcript.) If evidence conflicted, that was pointed out in the statement of information; exculpatory evidence and even self-serving public statements by President Nixon were included in the presentation. St. Clair attended (but could not interrupt) the presentation of the staff's statement of information to the committee and was permitted to respond and supplement it, in like manner, at its conclusion.

The procedural rules called for the committee to determine what

26. Impeachment Inquiry, Book I, 349 (April 25, 1974).

27. *Ibid.*, 305–6 (April 11, 1974), 377–401 (May 1, 1974), 467–541 (May 2, 1974). The procedural rules appear in Impeachment Inquiry, Book III, Appendix VI, 2251–2.

witnesses should be asked to testify after the conclusion of the staff presentation of evidentiary material. Because of the nature of the evidentiary material the staff had assembled, it desired to call very few witnesses before the committee. (Most of the important figures had testified before the Senate Select Committee on Presidential Campaign Activities the previous year, as well as elsewhere, and their previous testimony was included in the statement of information.) St. Clair was permitted to propose witnesses to appear before the committee, and all those he proposed were invited to appear.[28] He was also permitted to question all witnesses who testified before the committee.[29] Finally, at the conclusion of the inquiry, St. Clair was invited to make both an oral and a written summation on President Nixon's behalf.

Only after the committee's evidentiary hearings were completed and St. Clair had presented his summation did Special Counsel Doar present a summary of the case against President Nixon. Doar was joined in his views by Albert E. Jenner, Jr., who had served as special counsel to the minority during the inquiry, a position from which Republican members of the committee sought his removal when he reached the conclusion that the evidence established a case for President Nixon's impeachment. Nevertheless, the staff arguments were still not one-sided; Samuel Garrison III, formerly the deputy special counsel to the minority, presented an argument against impeachment to the committee.

The Nixon impeachment inquiry, therefore, was conducted as an investigative proceeding, with heavy reliance on a bipartisan staff. Fairness to the president was further buttressed by permitting his counsel to participate in each phase of the committee's evidentiary proceedings.[30] Whether St. Clair's participation was truly necessary to insure

28. H. R. Haldeman, one of the witnesses St. Clair proposed, was not subpoenaed because he informed the committee that he would invoke his fifth amendment privilege against self-incrimination. See 93d Cong., 2d Sess., House, Comm. on the Judiciary, *Testimony of Witnesses, Hearings . . . Pursuant to H. Res. 803*, Book II, 118 (July 10, 1974) (statement by Chairman Rodino). St. Clair's other proposed witnesses did testify before the committee.

29. In keeping with precedent, cross-examination of the type used in trials was not permitted in the impeachment inquiry, a limitation that appears to have had little impact on the questioning.

30. One privilege St. Clair sought was not granted—the opportunity to participate in the staff investigation before evidentiary material was presented to the committee. There

fairness to the President is debatable. As a political matter President Nixon's case would undoubtedly have been strengthened if participation had been denied, a point St. Clair made none too subtly when he argued that participation was necessary to "guard against any potential attack on the integrity or impartiality of the proceedings."[31] Any arguments and evidence the president sought to put before the committee could have been introduced in another manner or simply gratuitously offered to the committee and the public (as, for example, was the explanation of President Nixon's actions that accompanied the edited transcripts he submitted to the committee and made public in response to its first subpoena).

Participation of the official under investigation is not so much a legal or constitutional issue as a question of the committee's needs. In impeachment investigations before the Nixon inquiry, investigating committees had permitted the official to participate because the information and perspective he could provide would supplement the record before the committee. In the Nixon inquiry, participation by his counsel was permitted because to deny it might have damaged the credibility of the committee's investigation.

The Standard of Proof

Participation by President Nixon's counsel was an issue that arose early in the impeachment inquiry and had to be resolved before the Judi-

---

was no precedent for participation by the official under investigation prior to the committee's hearings, but neither was there precedent for such an extensive staff investigation as was being conducted in the Nixon inquiry.

The resolution authorizing the impeachment inquiry empowered the Judiciary Committee to subpoena witnesses to testify by deposition at a proceeding at which no committee members need be present. This deposition authority was without modern precedent, though depositions had been used in the very first impeachment investigation, in conjunction with the preparation of articles of impeachment against Senator William Blount in 1798.

Only one deposition was taken by the impeachment inquiry staff under this authority. The use of the deposition authority was abandoned by the staff on the stated ground that it was not an efficient way of preparing for the initial presentation. Its abandonment came amid demands that the president's counsel be permitted to question witnesses being deposed and obviated the need for the committee to decide that question. Voluntary affidavits were used in a few instances as evidentiary material in support of statements of information presented to the committee by the inquiry staff.

31. St. Clair Participation Memo 5.

ciary Committee began its evidentiary hearings. A related issue, which was not addressed until after the evidentiary hearings, was the standard of proof the committee should apply in determining whether the evidence warranted a recommendation that President Nixon be impeached.

The relationship between the two issues reflects the constitutional division of the accusatory and adjudicative functions in a presidential removal proceeding—the House's sole power of impeachment and the Senate's sole power to try impeachments. As already suggested, a full-blown adversarial proceeding before the House committee might seem to be an arrogation of the Senate's power to try the president. Similarly, if the House used a standard of proof identical to or more stringent than that applicable in the Senate trial—if, for example, it required proof beyond a reasonable doubt before voting impeachment, a standard that itself suggests an adversarial proceeding in which the president's counsel would have great latitude to suggest doubts—then the House would effectively be deciding the same questions the Senate would have to decide after trial, either duplicating the Senate's function or preventing it from having the accusation presented to it.

On the other hand, there were undesirable consequences if the House voted impeachment on the basis of one-sided or incomplete information or insufficiently persuasive evidence. Subjecting the Senate, the president, and the nation to the uncertainty and potential divisiveness of a presidential impeachment trial is not a step to be lightly undertaken.[32] While the formal consequence of an ill-advised impeachment would merely be acquittal after trial,[33] the political ramifications could be much more severe.

Accordingly, whether it is considered a constitutional requirement or a matter of sound policy, the House should not vote impeachments that are unlikely to succeed in the Senate nor should it screen out impeachments on evidentiary grounds where a substantial likelihood exists that trial would result in conviction and removal from office. The standard of proof applied in the House should reflect the standard of proof in the Senate, though it may not be identical with it. In the

32. See Nixon Impeachment Report, Minority Views 380.

33. It is inconceivable that the Senate would dismiss an impeachment before trial—its only available sanction—because it disapproved of the procedures or standard of proof used by the House. More than that, a dismissal on this ground arguably would be an unconstitutional interference by the Senate with the power vested solely in the House, though the House would have no remedy for it.

Nixon inquiry, practically all those involved—Doar, St. Clair, Garrison, the members of the committee who voted for impeachment (at least by implication from their report), and the members who voted against—agreed that the appropriate standard of proof in the House was "clear and convincing evidence."[34]

Only the committee members who voted against impeachment sought to analyze the standard of proof that would be applicable in the Senate, concluding that proof beyond a reasonable doubt would be required for conviction after trial. These members recognized that the Senate had neither promulgated a rule nor formally decided the point in past cases, but asserted that "the overwhelming weight of opinion from past impeachment trials favors the criminal standard" of proof beyond a reasonable doubt.[35] They contended that this standard was appropriate because there is a "fundamental similarity" between an impeachment trial and an ordinary criminal trial, the constitutional provisions pertaining to impeachment are "couched in the language of the criminal law," the framers conceived of removal from office as punishment,[36] and an impeachment trial is a grave undertaking that may have drastic consequences. They asserted:

34. Impeachment Inquiry, Book III, 1927 (Doar), 1890 (St. Clair), 2040 (Garrison); Nixon Impeachment Report 33–4, 136, 141, 146, 157, 172, 180; Nixon Impeachment Report, Minority Views 381.

35. *Ibid.*, 378–9. This assertion is debatable. A more accurate assessment of past impeachment trials is that each senator applied his own standard of proof and only a small fraction of senators left any record of the standard they had used. If the minority meant to suggest that, among those senators writing opinions discussing the standard of proof, a preponderance favored proof beyond a reasonable doubt, the point may be accurate but is of limited significance.

One of the few legal commentators to mention the issue of standard of proof, Alexander Simpson, wrote in 1916 that it had been "many times decided" that "[a] reasonable doubt of the respondent's guilt must result in his acquittal." Simpson made the rather odd argument that, because the Senate acted as a court in impeachment trials, this standard must apply because it is "necessary for the just trial of causes," completely ignoring civil trials in which less stringent evidentiary standards are routinely employed. His citations, moreover, referred only to state court decisions and legal treatises. See *A Treatise on Federal Impeachments* 29 and n. 71 (1916) and "Federal Impeachments," 64 *U.Pa.L.Rev.* 651, 675 and n. 71 (1916).

36. Nixon Impeachment Report, Minority Views 378–9. In support of this contention, the minority cited four statements made in the Constitutional Convention: "Mason favored '*punishing* the principal' for 'great crimes'; Franklin thought that the Constitution should provide for 'the regular *punishment* of the executive'; Randolph stated 'guilt wherever found ought to be *punished*'; and [Morris] said that the executive should be '*punished* only by degradation from his office.' " Each of these statements was made during the debate of July 20, 1787, when it was decided to retain the provision making the executive removable by impeachment. At the time of this debate, the con-

> The removal of a President by impeachment in mid-term . . . should not be too easy of accomplishment, for it contravenes the will of the electorate. In providing for a fixed four-year term, not subject to interim votes of No Confidence, the Framers indicated their preference for stability in the executive. That stability should not be jeopardized except on the strongest possible proof of presidential wrongdoing.[37]

The argument, then, was that too lenient a standard of proof in the Senate would be potentially unfair to the president and the electorate. Removal from office by conviction on impeachment, Charles L. Black, Jr., wrote, is "a stunning penalty, the ruin of a life"; more important, it "unseats the person the people have deliberately chosen for the office." This punishment and frustration of the popular will should not be imposed when substantial doubt of guilt remains, he suggested.[38]

Unlike the committee minority, however, Black recognized that too stringent a standard—and, in particular, the criminal standard of proof beyond a reasonable doubt—also posed problems. It "could mean, in

---

vention had not yet decided to exclude criminal sanctions from the impeachment process. State constitutions were split on this issue. Some (like that of New York, 5 Thorpe 2635) limited judgment on impeachment to removal and future disqualification from office; others (including that of Pennsylvania, the state both Franklin and Morris represented, 5 Thorpe 3088), were silent on the point; still others (including that of Virginia, the state Mason and Randolph represented) provided for criminal punishment. The Virginia constitution of 1776 provided that if found guilty on an impeachment an officer "shall be either forever disabled to hold any office under government, or be removed from such office *pro tempore* or subjected to such pains or penalties as the laws shall direct" (7 Thorpe 3818). The statements in the July 20 debate must be read with this fact in mind.

A provision restricting judgment on impeachment to removal from office and disqualification from future office was included in the draft constitution prepared by the Committee on Detail and reported to the convention on August 6 (Art. XI, §5, 2 Farrand 187). Inclusion of this provision had not been previously discussed by the delegates, and it was never debated by the convention.

Morris's statement (attributed to Mason in the minority report through a typographical error) deserves closer scrutiny. What he said, quoting more fully, was, "The Executive ought . . . to be impeachable for treachery; corrupting his electors, and incapacity were other causes of impeachment. For the latter he should be punished not as a man, but as an officer, and punished only by degradation from office" (2 Farrand 69). Rather than supporting the contention that removal from office is similar to the imposition of criminal sanctions, the statement draws a distinction between punishment as a man—that is, criminal punishment—and punishment only by dismissal from office.

37. Nixon Impeachment Report, Minority Views 379–80.

38. Black 17.

practice, that a man could remain president whom every member of the Senate believed to be guilty of corruption" simply because the proof did not reach this high level. Some lesser standard, between a mere preponderance of the evidence and proof beyond a reasonable doubt, was required, Black concluded, though it was difficult to articulate. He offered "overwhelming preponderance of the evidence" (which has a close affinity to "clear and convincing evidence") and suggested that some "unique rule, not yet named by law" might emerge "in the terrible seriousness of a great case." Lacking any authoritative guidance, senators must find their own standard, Black acknowledged; the important consideration is that they do so conscientiously, with due recognition of the risks of being influenced by partisanship or personal dislike of a president.[39]

Both the minority's argument in favor of the criminal standard and Black's discussion may oversimplify a difficult question, which is closely tied to the nature of grounds for impeachment and especially to the requirement that impeachable wrongdoing be serious. A standard of proof cannot be applied until it is determined what facts must be proved—that is, what would justify conviction and removal on a given charge or aggregation of charges—and that determination must be made individually by each senator. Even if there were agreement on the appropriate standard of proof, senators might be applying it to different sets of factual issues because they may have different conceptions of the nature and magnitude of the wrongdoing that must be proved to support a guilty vote.

Consider, for example, the first proposed article of impeachment against President Nixon. It charged that he had, in violation of his constitutional oath and take-care duty, "prevented, obstructed, and impeded the administration of justice," specifying that after the Watergate break-in he had "engaged personally and through his subordinates in a course of conduct or plan designed to delay, impede, and obstruct the investigation of such unlawful entry; to cover up, conceal, and protect those responsible; and to conceal the existence and scope of other unlawful covert activities." The article listed nine means, one or more of which, it alleged, were "used to implement this course of conduct or plan." What would have had to have been proved under this article in order to remove President Nixon is open to argument—

39. *Ibid.*, 17–8.

not because the article was ambiguous, but because the elements of the charge that would justify conviction would have to be determined by each senator after trial. Some might have decided that the article charged more than was needed; they could appropriately have treated the unnecessary portions as surplusage. Even if every element of the charge had to be proved—that is, that President Nixon did engage in a course of conduct or plan, implemented by one or more of the listed means, for the stated objectives—judgmental issues remained. For instance, the article did not specify when Nixon entered into the course of conduct or plan, except to say that it was subsequent to the break-in. Each senator would have had to decide that for himself and also decide whether President Nixon's participation began early enough to justify his removal from office. That it was possible to have different views on this point and nonetheless consider that President Nixon's conduct constituted grounds for impeachment was demonstrated in the Judiciary Committee. At the time of the committee's deliberations and vote to recommend this article, members who supported the article were not in full agreement about when President Nixon's culpable involvement in the cover-up began.[40]

Because different fact finders in an impeachment trial may be adjudicating different factual issues, it is not very useful to think in terms of a fixed standard of proof. This is all the more true because a standard of proof is itself a judgmental abstraction, which is intended to convey the fact finder's subjective sense of how well established a fact is or how convinced he is of its probable truth.

Another, perhaps more intelligible, though artificial way to make the same point is to suggest that there is no single standard of proof applicable to all impeachment trials, but that the standard will vary with the seriousness of the charge or aggregation of charges involved. If a president were charged with conduct amounting to treason, for example, it seems highly unlikely that a senator would insist on proof of treason beyond a reasonable doubt before he would vote for the president's removal from office. A mere preponderance of the evidence, perhaps even a strong suspicion, would probably be considered sufficient. On the other hand, a greater quantum of proof might be required for less flagrant wrongdoing. The reason this is an artificial way of looking at the problem is that one can never know whether a

40. See Nixon Impeachment Report, "Concurring Views of Messrs. Railsback, Fish, Hogan, Butler, Cohen, and Froelich" 281.

lower standard of proof is being applied to assess guilt of treason or a lesser included offense is the basis for a vote to convict. Evidence giving rise to a suspicion of treason might very well provide clear and convincing proof or proof beyond a reasonable doubt of a serious violation of a constitutional duty, itself justifying removal from office.[41]

The treason example, moreover, points up another consideration that must be taken into account in evaluating the standard of proof. Whether or not removal from office is punishment—and it certainly is true that the effect of a conviction on impeachment would be disgrace and a sort of political banishment—the purpose of impeachment is not punitive, but remedial. The reason for removing an unfit man from office is not vindictiveness toward him but rather the need to replace him with a successor who is not unfit and who will protect the interests of the people. Senator Charles Sumner of Massachusetts wrote in his opinion in the Johnson trial that the object of an impeachment trial "is not punishment, not vengeance, but the *Public Safety*." He proposed a standard of proof, based on this conception, that is radi-

41. A similar point applies to one of Raoul Berger's arguments about judicial review of impeachment convictions. He wrote, "The Senate may convict for 'treason'; by Article III, §3, 'treason' is defined as levying war against the United States or giving aid and comfort to its enemies. Suppose the Senate convicts the President of treason on the ground that he attempted to subvert the Constitution, a favorite formula of Parliament. Whether this be labeled as a 'construction' or a 'factual determination,' it plainly amounts to an attempt to add an omitted category to the Constitutional definition. . . . To impeach for 'treason' on grounds that are outside the constitutional definition, therefore, lies beyond the powers conferred." Berger contended that the Supreme Court could reverse a conviction on these grounds, just as it declared Adam Clayton Powell's exclusion from the House on grounds other than the constitutional standards to be beyond the power of the House. *Impeachment* 106, citing Powell v. McCormack, 395 U.S. 486 (1969) (footnotes omitted).

Berger's hypothetical example is unrealistic, since the House has no need to charge and the Senate no need to judge that attempted subversion of the Constitution is treason. It is enough that it falls within "other high crimes and misdemeanors," as it surely does. There is a substantial difference between the constitutional qualifications for a member of the House—age, citizenship and residence—each of which is independent of the other, and the constitutional standard for impeachment—treason, bribery, or other high crimes and misdemeanors—all of which fall within the category of high crimes and misdemeanors, obviating any need for taxonomic choices.

Indeed, in the Humphreys impeachment trial in 1862, the managers acknowledged that one article charged the elements of treason but contended that it was unnecessary to call two witnesses to testify to an overt act of treason, as constitutionally required in a criminal trial for that offense—Cong. Globe, 37th Cong., 2d. Sess., 2943 (1862). The Senate apparently agreed and found Humphreys guilty of "the high crimes and misdemeanors as charged in this article" by a vote of 33 to 4 (at 2950).

cally different from any articulated during the Nixon impeachment inquiry. The ordinary rule of evidence should be reversed in an impeachment trial, he contended, because the rationale for it—better that many guilty men go free than one innocent man be punished—was inapplicable to a trial to test the issue of whether a president's claim to his office had any continuing validity. Sumner suggested to his fellow senators:

> If on any point you entertain doubts, the benefit of those doubts must be given to your country; and this is the supreme law. When tried on an indictment in the criminal courts Andrew Johnson may justly claim the benefit of your doubts; but at the bar of the Senate on the question of his expulsion from office, his vindication must be in every respect and on each charge beyond a doubt. He must show that his longer continuance in office is not inconsistent with the *Public Safety*. . . . Anything short of this is to trifle with the Republic and its transcendent fortunes.[42]

Sumner's standard of proof, placing the burden of persuasion on the impeached president to prove his innocence of the charges beyond a reasonable doubt, may be considered too extreme. But his argument provides an important counterbalance to concerns about the punitive consequences of impeachment and its interference with the will of the electorate. Impeachment was included in the Constitution as a mechanism for safeguarding the government. The delegates to the Constitutional Convention referred to it as punishment primarily in their discussion of the appropriateness of making the chief executive impeachable along with his ministers—Mason favored "punishing the principal as well as the Coadjutors"; Randolph asserted that "[g]uilt wherever found ought to be punished." And it is fair to infer that even in this context their concern was not so much with punishing wrong-

42. 3 Johnson Trial 255. Sumner, it must be acknowledged, has never been considered an authority on the law of impeachment. He was an outspoken foe of Johnson, who wrote in his opinion that if the rules of the Senate permitted he would have voted guilty of all the articles "and infinitely more" (at 278), and compared acquittal to the *Dred Scott* decision, calling it "another chapter in the Barbarism of Slavery" (at 280). Berger, echoing the opinion of most historians, writes that Sumner was "utterly unfitted by his fanatical commitment to sit in judgment on Johnson" and that his "implacable ruthlessness . . . recalls the Grand Inquisitor who burned deviants from the 'truth' at the stake" (*Impeachment* 269, 270). While this characterization may be justified, Sumner's opinion in the Johnson trial, invective and passion apart, provides an incisive analysis of impeachment as a political trial.

doing after the fact as with deterring it by providing for direct and personal accountability. A good magistrate would not fear impeachments, Elbridge Gerry contended, but "[a] bad one ought to be kept in fear of them." Among the delegates, only Benjamin Franklin stressed the theme of fairness to the executive, arguing that the alternative to a formal mechanism for bringing the chief magistrate to public justice when he rendered himself obnoxious had been assassination, by which "he was not only deprived of his life but of the opportunity of vindicating his character." Impeachment, in addition to providing for the "regular punishment of the Executive when his misconduct should deserve it," would permit "his honorable acquittal when he should be unjustly accused." [43]

The major purpose of impeachment, however, is to rid the government of a chief executive whose past misconduct demonstrates his unfitness to continue in office. Impeachment is a prospective remedy for the benefit of the people, not a retributive sanction against the offending officer.[44] It is a provision, as James Madison contended, "for defending the Community agst the incapacity, negligence or perfidy of the chief Magistrate," whose loss of capacity or corruption "might be fatal to the Republic."[45] If removal of the president was intended to be a remedial step—and, even if it could fairly be said that the framers had something else in mind, that is surely the procedure's current function—there is little justification for contending that absolute certainty of guilt, or proof beyond a reasonable doubt, should be required to bring it into play. Rather, the test must be whether there is sufficient evidence of past wrongdoing meeting the constitutional criteria for grounds for impeachment to demonstrate the unfitness of the president to remain in office. The test must recognize that the

43. 2 Farrand 65, 67, 66, 65.

44. This point is illustrated both by the abandonment of the impeachment proceeding against Richard Nixon after his resignation as president and by the outcome of the one impeachment that was voted against an official who had resigned. In 1876 William W. Belknap resigned as secretary of war just hours before the House was to consider his impeachment for improprieties bordering upon or constituting bribery. The House nevertheless unanimously voted his impeachment, and the Senate rejected the argument that Belknap was no longer amenable to impeachment because of his resignation by a vote of 37 to 29. After trial, however, Belknap was acquitted, with from 35 to 37 senators voting guilty on each of the five articles and 25 senators voting not guilty. Of those voting not guilty, 22 explained that they felt the Senate lacked jurisdiction. See Impeachment Inquiry Staff Grounds Memo 49–50.

45. 2 Farrand 65–6.

degree of future risk from continuing a president in office is directly related to the nature and seriousness of his past misconduct.

The remedial function of impeachment also suggests an answer to concerns that removal of a popularly elected chief executive frustrates or interferes with the will of the electorate. It does so in the sense that it ousts the person the people chose to serve for four years, but it countermands the decision of the electorate for the protection of the people and only on the basis of information of wrongdoing not available to the electorate when it made its choice. The will of the electorate surely does not extend to giving a president a license to engage in the kind of serious wrongdoing that provides grounds for impeachment and removal from office, and a president who commits such wrongdoing has, in effect, violated a pledge that was a condition of election.

The argument that removal interferes with the will of the electorate does not really relate to the standard of proof at all. Looking again at the minority's argument in the Nixon inquiry, the contention was that removal of a president "should not be too easy of accomplishment" and that the stability the framers preferred "should not be jeopardized except on the strongest possible proof of presidential wrongdoing." The issue the minority's contention raised, however, involved the definition of grounds for impeachment, not the standard of proof when impeachable wrongdoing is charged. The minority quite rightly asserted that a president should not be removed from office for partisan reasons, disagreement with his policies, or loss of popularity. But that says nothing at all about the quantum of proof that should be required when he is charged with serious wrongdoing contravening his oath of office or violating his constitutional duties. That issue, to repeat the point made earlier, must be determined with reference to the interests of the people.

The power of impeachment, Joseph Story wrote in the 1830s, is intended "for occasional and extraordinary cases, where a superior power, acting for the whole people, is put into operation to protect their rights, and to rescue their liberties from violation." [46] In those unusual instances in which the issue arises, it is likely that the question of the appropriate standard of proof will, as Black suggested, answer itself on the basis of the nature of the case and the circumstances in which it is tried.

46. 2 Story §749.

6. *THE PRESIDENT'S NONCOMPLIANCE WITH IMPEACHMENT INQUIRY SUBPOENAS*

President Nixon was the first subject of an impeachment investigation to claim a privilege by virtue of his office to withhold evidence from a House committee. Not only was his claim contrary to the logic of the Constitution—as a number of his predecessors, beginning with George Washington, had recognized, though only rhetorically—but it turned out to have been advanced in such bad faith as to vastly diminish the possibility that a similar contention would be made again in the near future. Whatever the merits of President Nixon's claim might have appeared to be, the fact was that he claimed a right to withhold evidence in the hope of preventing discovery of his own wrongdoing, and this amounted to an intolerable interference with the exercise of the power of impeachment constitutionally vested in the House of Representatives alone.

On August 5, 1974, six days after the Judiciary Committee finished its deliberations on articles of impeachment against President Nixon, District Judge John Sirica, following the mandate of the Supreme Court in *United States v. Nixon*, provided the special prosecutor with transcripts of three conversations between President Nixon and H. R. Haldeman, his chief staff assistant, held on June 23, 1972. On the same day President Nixon issued a public statement about these conversations. He said:

> On April 29, in announcing my decision to make public the original set of White House transcripts, I stated that "as far as what the President personally knew and did with regard to Watergate and the cover-up is concerned, these materials—together with those already made available—will tell it all."

> Shortly after that, in May, I made a preliminary review of some of the 64 taped conversations subpoenaed by the Special Prosecutor.
>
> Among the conversations I listened to at that time were two of those of June 23 [1972]. Although I recognized that these presented potential problems, I did not inform my staff or my Counsel of it, or those arguing my case, nor did I amend my submission to the Judiciary Committee in order to include and reflect it. At the time, I did not realize the extent of the implications which these conversations might now appear to have. As a result, those arguing my case, as well as those passing judgment on the case, did so with information that was incomplete and in some respects erroneous. This was a serious act of omission for which I take full responsibility and which I deeply regret.

The June 23 transcripts established that six days after the Watergate break-in President Nixon, knowing that his campaign committee was responsible, directed Haldeman to have the Central Intelligence Agency block an investigation by the Federal Bureau of Investigation. In his statement President Nixon acknowledged that "portions of the June 23 conversations are at variance with certain of my previous statements" and ordered that the transcripts be made available to the Judiciary Committee "so that they can be reflected in the Committee's report, and included in the record to be considered by the House and Senate."[1] Three days later he resigned from office.

On behalf of the Judiciary Committee, Special Counsel Doar had initially requested the recordings of the June 23 conversations from the president's counsel by letter on April 19, 1974. On May 15 the committee had approved a subpoena for these three recordings, along with recordings of eight other conversations and related materials, by a vote of 37 to 1. In response President Nixon had written Chairman Rodino on May 22 that he refused to produce any of the materials specified in the May 15 subpoena or any other materials "allegedly dealing with Watergate" that might be called for in future subpoenas. Although ac-

1. 10 Weekly Comp. of Pres. Doc. 1008 (1974). President Nixon, conceding that his impeachment by the House was "virtually a foregone conclusion," also stated that he would make available to the Senate for his impeachment trial those portions of the sixty-four conversations subpoenaed by the special prosecutor that Judge Sirica decided should be produced for use in the criminal case against six of President Nixon's former aides and associates (at 1009).

cording to his statement of August 5 he had listened to two of the June 23 conversations before preparing this letter, President Nixon wrote:

> The Committee has the full story of Watergate in so far as it relates to Presidential knowledge and Presidential actions. Production of these [eleven] additional conversations would merely prolong the inquiry without yielding significant additional evidence.[2]

On May 30, again by a vote of 37 to 1, the committee subpoenaed tape recordings of forty-five more conversations, as well as Watergate-related papers contained in the files of five former White House employees. President Nixon refused to comply with this subpoena as well, stating in a letter of June 9:

> [T]he voluminous body of materials that the Committee already has—and which I have voluntarily provided, partly in response to Committee requests and partly in an effort to round out the record—does give the full story of Watergate, insofar as it relates to Presidential knowledge and Presidential actions. . . . Simply multiplying the tapes and transcripts would extend the proceedings interminably, while adding nothing substantial to the evidence the Committee already has.

President Nixon concluded this letter, which contained his most extensive explanation of his claim of privilege not to produce materials subpoenaed by the committee, by writing:

> A proceeding such as the present one places a great strain on our Constitutional system, and on the pattern of practice of self-restraint by the three branches that has maintained the balance of that system for nearly two centuries. Whenever one branch attempts to press too hard in intruding on the Constitutional prerogatives of another, that balance is threatened. From the start of these proceedings, I have tried to cooperate as far as I reasonably could in order to avert a Constitutional confrontation. But I am determined to do nothing which, by the precedents it set, would render the Executive branch henceforth and forevermore subservient to the Legislative branch, and would thereby destroy the Constitutional balance.[3]

2. *Ibid.*, 538.
3. *Ibid.*, 592–3.

The asserted basis for President Nixon's claim of executive privilege became clear over the course of the impeachment inquiry. The Judiciary Committee issued its first subpoena, for tape recordings and other materials related to forty-two conversations involving the president that it considered necessary for its investigation of the Watergate cover-up, on April 11, 1974. On April 29 President Nixon announced his response to the subpoena on nationwide television. He agreed to produce and to make public edited transcripts of the recordings of thirty-one of the forty-two conversations, together with other materials not subpoenaed by the committee. He explained:

> I've been well aware that my effort to protect the confidentiality of Presidential conversations has heightened the sense of mystery about Watergate and, in fact, has caused increased suspicion of the President.
>
> Many people assumed that the tapes must incriminate the President, or that otherwise he wouldn't insist on their privacy. But the problem I confronted was this: Unless a President can protect the privacy of the advice he gets, he cannot get the advice he needs.

This principle was recognized in the doctrine of executive privilege, President Nixon said, a doctrine that he contended had been defended and maintained by every president since Washington and recognized as inherent in the presidency. He told the nation that he considered it his constitutional responsibility to defend this principle. Three factors, he said, persuaded him that a major, unprecedented exception to the principle was necessary in this instance. First, the House "must be able to reach an informed judgment about the President's role in Watergate." Second, it was necesary to restore the principle of confidentiality "by clearing the air of the central questions that have brought such pressures upon it" and providing the evidence that would allow the matter to be brought to a prompt conclusion. Third, the people and Congress were entitled to have "not only the facts but also the evidence that demonstrates those facts," so that no question would remain about "the fact that the President has nothing to hide in this matter." An impeachment trial in the Senate, whatever its outcome, would be "a wrenching ordeal," one that the nation had endured only once in its history and "never since America became a world power with global responsibilities." Its impact would be "felt throughout the world," and it would "have its effect on the lives of all Americans for many years to come." He asserted that the "basic question at issue today"—"whether the President personally acted improperly in the Watergate matter"—had to be, and would be, answered by the transcripts he was making available.[4]

In his letter of May 22, following the issuance of two additional Watergate subpoenas (including the one calling for the June 23, 1972, conversations along with others), President Nixon contended that continuing demands would damage the office of president:

> [I]t is clear that the continued succession of demands for additional Presidential conversations has become a never-ending process, and that to continue providing these conversations in response to the constantly escalating requests would constitute such a massive invasion into the confidentiality of Presidential conversations that the institution of the Presidency itself would be fatally compromised. . . . [C]ontinuing ad infinitum the process of yielding up additional conversations in response to an endless series of demands would fatally weaken this office not only in this Administration but for future Presidencies as well.[5]

On May 30 Chairman Rodino wrote President Nixon. The letter, approved by the committee by a vote of 28 to 10, stated that the committee regarded President Nixon's refusal to comply with its subpoenas as "a grave matter." Under the Constitution, "it is not within the power of the President to conduct an inquiry into his own impeachment, to determine which evidence and what version or portion of that evidence, is relevant and necessary to such an inquiry." These matters were within the sole power of the House to decide, Chairman Rodino asserted. He informed the president that, in meeting their constitutional responsibilities, members of the committee would be "free to consider whether your refusals warrant the drawing of adverse inferences concerning the substance of the materials and whether your refusals in and of themselves might constitute a ground for impeachment."[6]

4. Statement of Information, Appendix I, "Presidential Statements on the Watergate Break-in and Its Investigation," 84–5.

5. *Ibid.*, 103.

6. Impeachment Inquiry, Book II, 901–13 (May 30, 1974); Nixon Impeachment Report 194.

President Nixon's letter of June 9, in which he stated his determination to do nothing that would set a precedent unfavorable to the executive branch, was in reply to Chairman Rodino's letter. President Nixon wrote that the question was not who conducts the inquiry, "but where the line is to be drawn on an apparently endlessly escalating spiral of demands for confidential Presidential tapes and documents." The committee was asserting that it should be "the sole judge of Presidential confidentiality," a doctrine neither he nor any president could accept and one that had never before been seriously asserted. Executive privilege is "part and parcel of the basic doctrine of separation of powers," he contended; each branch "historically has been steadfast in maintaining its own independence by turning back attempts of the others, whenever made, to assert an authority to invade, without consent, the privacy of its own deliberations." He continued:

> If the institution of an impeachment inquiry against a President were permitted to override all restraints of separation of powers, this would spell the end of the doctrine of separation of powers; it would be an open invitation to future Congresses to use an impeachment inquiry, however frivolously, as a device to assert their own supremacy over the Executive, and to reduce Executive confidentiality to a nullity. . . . [P]reserving the principle of separation of powers—and the Executive as a co-equal branch—requires that the Executive, no less than the Legislative or Judicial branches, must be immune from unlimited search and seizure by the other co-equal branches.

Once the committee "embarked on a process of continually demanding tapes whenever those the Committee already has fail to turn up evidence of guilt, there would be no end unless a line were drawn somewhere by someone. Since it is clear that the Committee will not draw such a line," he declared, "I have done so."

President Nixon further contended that to draw adverse inferences would "fl[y] in the face of established law on the assertion of valid claims of privilege": "a claim of privilege, which is valid under the doctrine of separation of powers, must be accepted without adverse inferences—or else the privilege itself is undermined, and the separation of powers nullified." [7]

7. 10 Weekly Comp. of Pres. Doc. 592–3.

President Nixon's argument may have been correct in a number of respects, but none of them was particularly helpful to his case. If the claim of privilege was valid, his contention that no adverse inferences should be drawn from its assertion was certainly plausible. But the validity of the claim—the availability of executive privilege in a presidential impeachment inquiry—was the basic issue. Similarly, President Nixon's contention that executive privilege had a constitutional basis closely linked to the separation of powers was later supported by the Supreme Court in its decision on his claim of absolute executive privilege in judicial proceedings. While denying that the privilege was absolute, the Court acknowledged that it "can be said to derive from the supremacy of each branch within its own assigned area of constitutional duties," "is fundamental to the operation of government and inextricably rooted in the separation of powers under the Constitution," and "is constitutionally based." [8] But this meant merely that the applicability of the doctrine of the separation of powers to a presidential impeachment inquiry by the House had to be determined. Finally, President Nixon was correct in suggesting that if executive privilege was inapplicable to impeachment investigations the House conceivably could destroy presidential confidentiality by instituting frivolous or politically motivated investigations of presidents. But this argument proved nothing, under the established rule of constitutional construction that the possibility that a power might be abused is not an argument against its existence.[9]

Two separate questions were involved in the dispute about President Nixon's refusal to comply with the Judiciary Committee's subpoenas. The first, and more basic, was whether the claim of executive privilege was valid. If it was, that was probably the end of the matter with respect to drawing adverse inferences. Whether or not the analogy was controlling as a legal matter, it probably would have been considered just as improper to draw adverse inferences from the valid assertion of executive privilege as it is to draw adverse inferences from a criminal defendant's refusal to testify on the basis of his fifth amendment privilege against self-incrimination. The second question was whether the

8. United States v. Nixon, 418 U.S. at 705, 708, 711.

9. See Martin v. Mott, 25 U.S. (12 Wheat.) 19, 32 (1827): "It is no answer, that such a power may be abused, for there is no power which is not susceptible of abuse" (Story, J.); Luther v. Borden, 48 U.S. (7 How.) 1, 44 (1849): "It is said that this power in the President is dangerous to liberty, and may be abused. All power may be abused if placed in unworthy hands" (Taney, C.J.).

invocation of executive privilege by President Nixon might provide grounds for his impeachment. The answer to that question did not necessarily depend upon whether executive privilege could, in the abstract, be validly claimed in a House impeachment investigation of a president, for even if President Nixon had the power he might be impeached for abusing it.

Should Executive Privilege Apply to Presidential Impeachment Investigations?

Viewed simply as a matter of constitutional law, without regard to whether impeachment (or, for that matter, anything else) is an available sanction, the question whether a president subpoenaed to produce evidence in an impeachment inquiry may assert executive privilege would appear to be readily answerable: he may not. It seems inconceivable that a president should have the power to decide what evidence should be made available to a House committee charged with determining whether to recommend that he be prosecuted for removal from office and thereby to thwart its efforts to exercise its constitutional powers.

In response to a similar objection to his contention that executive privilege was absolute in all congressional proceedings, including a House impeachment inquiry and Senate trial, Attorney General Kleindienst said in April 1973:

> If the only evidence necessary to impeach the President was contained in the bosom of his confidential adviser, I think his impeachment proceeding might not be predicated upon evidence. You do not need facts to impeach the President, because the Congress, if it has the votes, is the sole judge. The House passes a resolution, the Senate tries it, he is impeached, and there is no appeal. That is the end, with or without facts.[10]

Kleindienst was speaking hypothetically, in defense of the most sweeping assertion of the scope of the executive privilege doctrine made during the Nixon administration. His argument confused the question of

10. 93d Cong., 1st Sess., Senate, Comm. on Government Operations, Subcomm. on Intergovernmental Relations, and Comm. on the Judiciary, Subcomm. on Separation of Powers and Administrative Practice and Procedure, *Executive Privilege, Hearings . . . on S. 1142* [*et al.*] 45 (1973).

raw power—whether Congress could remove the president without "facts" —with the question of legality—whether it would be constitutional for Congress to do so. Congress has the power because no other branch of government can reverse its decision. The propriety and constitutionality of a removal not predicated upon evidence would be quite another matter, as was evident a year later when the issue was no longer hypothetical. Impeachment, everyone then acknowledged, was not simply a matter of votes. The House, in directing that the impeachment inquiry be undertaken, and the Judiciary Committee, in conducting it, were determined that the impeachment power should be exercised only if the evidence established grounds for prosecuting a case for the removal of President Nixon. President Nixon, through his counsel, argued that clear and convincing evidence was needed to impeach.

President Nixon's actual claim concerning executive privilege was, in a way, even more assertive than Kleindienst's hypothetical argument. Kleindienst was contending that the president had the power to refuse to produce any evidence at all in an impeachment proceeding. President Nixon, by contrast, regarded executive privilege as a power, vested exclusively in the president, to decide what information to release and what to withhold. He claimed the power to select the evidence within his control that the committee could consider—to provide what he called "the full story of Watergate" (and only of Watergate)—and then to "draw the line" against the production of any additional evidence. Had President Nixon been withholding all evidence (which circumstances made impossible, since he had previously permitted his subordinates to testify and had produced some tape recordings and documents), Kleindienst's prediction conceivably might have proved accurate, even though his rationale was insupportable. President Nixon might have been impeached and removed not on the basis of "facts" about his conduct, but for totally defying criminal, legislative, and impeachment investigations of that conduct.

Because the confidentiality of some presidential conversations had been breached, President Nixon was, in effect, trying to capitalize on the limited disclosures of information that had been made to the impeachment inquiry. He was, in the vernacular of the Nixon White House, using a "modified limited hang-out" strategy rather than "stonewalling" absolutely. It was not a new approach. Indeed, the most extensive lessons on how it could be applied were found in the

White House transcripts, the raw materials of the limited hang-out for the impeachment inquiry. President Nixon understood that through partial disclosure he could at least affect, and perhaps control, the outcome of an investigation. On March 20, 1973, he explained to John Dean why he wanted Dean to prepare a general statement on the involvement of White House staff members in Watergate:

> You've got to have something where it doesn't appear that I am doing this in, you know, just in a—saying to hell with the Congress and to hell with the people, we are not going to tell you anything because of Executive Privilege. That, they don't understand. But if you say, "No, we are willing to cooperate," and you've made a complete statement, but make it very incomplete. See, that is what I mean.[11]

Executive privilege would enable the president both to withhold potentially damaging evidence from an investigation and to produce evidence that would aid his cause (or, at a minimum, confuse the issue), thereby distorting the investigative process. As a matter of common sense, it is difficult to see why a president—as the subject of an impeachment investigation—should have such a power.

The constitutional roots of executive privilege are, first, the separation of powers and, second, the need for confidential communications to enable the president to perform his duties effectively. Separation of powers does not support the claim of executive privilege in an impeachment inquiry. The doctrine, the Supreme Court said in *United States v. Nixon*, does not make each branch independent, but envisions "a workable government."[12] If presidential removal from office is to remain a part of the scheme or workable government, the House must have the power to conduct a thorough investigation to determine whether a president should be impeached. Every power conferred by the Constitution is to be interpreted so that "it will attain its just end and achieve its manifest purpose"[13] rather than in a manner that would "render it unequal to the object for which it is declared to be competent."[14] As was stated on the floor of the House as early as

11. *Submission of Recorded Presidential Conversations to the Committee on the Judiciary of the House of Representatives by President Richard Nixon, April 30, 1974* at 186 (1974).

12. 418 U.S. at 707.

13. Prigg v. Pennsylvania, 41 U.S. (16 Pet.) 539, 611 (1842).

14. Gibbons v. Ogden, 22 U.S. (9 Wheat.) 1, 83 (1824) (Marshall, C.J.).

1796, the power of impeachment "certainly implie[s] a right to inspect every paper and transaction in any department, otherwise [it] could never be exercised with any effect."[15] In 1843 a committee of the House engaged in a dispute with President John Tyler about the production of documents for a legislative investigation (documents Tyler ultimately produced) reiterated the point:

> The House of Representatives has the sole power of impeachment. The President himself, in the discharge of his most independent functions, is subject to the exercise of this power—a power which implie[s] the right of inquiry on the part of the House to the fullest and most unlimited extent. . . . If the House possess the power to impeach, it must likewise possess all the incidents of that power—the power to compel the attendance of all witnesses and the production of all such papers as may be considered necessary to prove the charges on which the impeachment is founded. If it did not, the power of impeachment conferred upon it by the Constitution would be nugatory. It could not exercise it with effect.[16]

Presidents, too, have recognized the broad sweep of the House's investigative power incident to the power of impeachment. The first occasion, also in 1796, was when President Washington refused to provide the House materials concerning the negotiation of the Jay Treaty that he had previously provided the Senate in connection with its deliberations on ratification of the treaty. In his message to the House Washington explicitly acknowledged that the House's right to the documents would be different if it had sought them for an impeachment proceeding.[17] Subsequent presidents, refusing or protesting demands for information for legislative investigations, drew the same distinction. The statement most often quoted during the Nixon inquiry was made by President James Polk. In an 1846 message to the House Polk "cheerfully admitted" the right of the House to investigate the conduct of all government officers with a view to the exercise of its impeachment power. In such an investigation, Polk wrote, "the safety of the Republic would be the supreme law, and the power of the House in the pursuit of this object would penetrate into the most secret recesses

15. Annals 4th Cong., 1st Sess., 601 (1796).
16. 27th Cong., 3d Sess., H. Rept. No. 271 at 4–6.
17. Annals 4th Cong., 1st Sess., 760–2 (1796); 1 Richardson 187.

of the Executive Departments." The House "could command the attendance of any and every agent of government," "compel them to produce all papers, public or private, official or unofficial," and require them "to testify on oath to all facts within their knowledge." When the House thought it proper to institute an inquiry, as the grand inquest of the nation, into malversation by a public officer,

> all the archives and papers of the Executive Departments, public or private, would be subject to the inspection and control of a committee of their body and every facility in the power of the Executive be afforded to enable them to prosecute the investigation.[18]

On the only previous occasions on which the question had been of more than rhetorical concern—the Johnson impeachment investigations and trial—no power to withhold information had been claimed by the president or on his behalf. The Judiciary Committee in 1867 conducted an investigation of President Johnson that lasted eleven months. The investigation covered a wide range of allegations, including scurrilous charges for which there was no evidentiary basis (among them the allegation that Johnson, as vice president, might have been involved in the assassination of President Lincoln). The committee requested and obtained records from the files of executive departments and the Executive Mansion. It questioned cabinet officers and presidential advisors about conversations with the president and decisions by the president, including the vetoing of legislation, the drafting of presidential messages and orders, the issuance of pardons, and the prosecution of Jefferson Davis. Only one witness in the hearings, Jeremiah Black, an advisor to President Johnson, protested against being asked to disclose the deliberations involved in the preparation of a veto message. But Black acknowledged that "a witness sworn to testify before any tribunal is bound in conscience to answer a question which that tribunal declares he ought to answer." When the committee pressed the point, Black responded to its questions about his conversations with President Johnson.[19]

18. 4 Richardson 434–5.

19. 40th Cong., 1st Sess., H. Rept. No. 7 at 183–578 (1867). The Black testimony is at 271. This incident is recounted in Nixon Impeachment Report 207, which states that Black was one of Johnson's attorneys at his impeachment trial. An appearance was entered for Black at the trial, but he withdrew from the case before President Johnson's answer was filed.

Not only did President Johnson make no claim of confidentiality in the impeachment investigation, either for the deliberations leading up to his decisions or for his records or those of executive departments, but he did not object even to the production of his personal bank records. The cashier of Johnson's bank had informed the president that he had been asked to produce the records. He described President Johnson's reaction to the Judiciary Committee:

> He smiled, and said he had no earthly objection to have any of his transactions looked into; that he had done nothing clandestinely, and desired me to show them anything I had relating to his transactions.[20]

Novelty was not the only attribute of President Nixon's claim of executive privilege that raised doubts about its compatibility with "a workable government." Impeachment had been written into the Constitution despite repeated arguments that it would violate the separation of powers and make the president dependent on Congress. In the debate of July 20, 1787, in the Constitutional Convention, the principle of the separation of powers was one of the major grounds advanced against making the executive removable through impeachment. It would be "destructive of [the executive's] independence and of the principles of the Constitution," Rufus King contended; if the legislature had the impeachment power, Charles Pinckney asserted, it would hold impeachment "as a rod over the Executive and by that means effectually destroy his independence."[21] Despite this argument and the importance the delegates attached to the doctrine of separation of powers, the provision for impeachment of the executive was retained by a considerable margin.

As Alexander Hamilton explained in *The Federalist* No. 66, separation of powers is "entirely compatible with a partial intermixture" of departments for special purposes—an intermixture that is "in some cases, not only proper but necessary to the mutual defence of the several members of the government against each other." The "powers relating to impeachments" involve such a case, for they are "an essen-

20. 40th Cong., 1st Sess., H. Rept. No. 7 at 182–3, quoted in Nixon Impeachment Report 207, n. 6.
21. 2 Farrand 67, 66.

tial check in the hands of [the legislative] body upon the encroachments of the executive."[22]

James Madison wrote in *The Federalist* No. 51 that preservation of the separation of powers required these provisions for self-defense:

> [T]he great security against a gradual concentration of the several powers in the same department, consists in giving to those who administer each department the necessary constitutional means and personal motives to resist encroachments of the others. The provision for defence must in this, as in all other cases, be made commensurate to the danger of attack.

But, Madison continued, "it is not possible to give each department an equal power of self-defence. In republican government, the legislative authority necessarily predominates. The remedy for this inconveniency is to divide the legislature into different branches," as little connected with each other as possible.[23] Hamilton observed in his discussion of impeachment that this principle had been applied; the division of the powers relating to impeachment between the House and Senate "guards against the danger of persecution from the prevalency of a factious spirit in either of these branches."[24]

In our early constitutional history the House was often called "the grand inquest of the nation." It was not simply an ostentatious title, but a term carried over from English parliamentary practice, where it described the power of the House of Commons to investigate all government actions and officers. This inquisitorial power had originated in the power of impeachment, though it extended to investigations without this express purpose. Relying on the history of legislative inquisitorial power in England and this country, Raoul Berger has argued that executive privilege is a "constitutional myth"—a view the Supreme Court rejected when it held executive privilege to be "constitutionally based." Nevertheless, the origins of the inquisitorial power of the House, as Berger describes them, refute the argument that executive privilege, even if it has a constitutional foundation, could have been intended to apply to an impeachment investigation of a president's conduct—the purest example of the House's assertion of its authority to act as "the grand inquest of the nation." The "true spirit" of

22. At 429–30.
23. At 337–8.
24. *The Federalist* No. 66 at 430.

impeachment, Hamilton wrote in *The Federalist* No. 65, is that it is "designed as a method of national inquest into the conduct of public men," an inquest initiated by the House as the direct representatives of the people.[25]

The other asserted basis for executive privilege in an impeachment inquiry is the need for confidentiality in the conduct of the presidency. In *United States v. Nixon* Chief Justice Warren Burger, writing for a unanimous Supreme Court, included the need for confidentiality among "the considerations justifying a presumptive privilege for presidential communications" and making it "fundamental to the operation of government." He wrote:

> The expectation of a President to the confidentiality of his conversations and correspondence, like the claim of confidentiality of judicial deliberations, for example, has all the values to which we accord deference for the privacy of all citizens and added to those values the necessity for protection of the public interest in candid, objective, and even blunt or harsh opinions in Presidential decision-making. A President and those who assist him must be free to explore alternatives in the process of shaping policies and making decisions and to do so in a way many would be unwilling to express except privately.

The interest in preserving confidentiality is "weighty indeed and entitled to great respect," Burger wrote. But it could be outweighed by other interests, including "the demands of due process of law in the administration of criminal justice." The general interest in the confidentiality of presidential conversations would not "be vitiated by disclosure of a limited number of conversations preliminarily shown to have some bearing on the pending [Watergate cover-up] criminal cases," the Court held:

> [W]e cannot conclude that advisers will be moved to temper the candor of their remarks by the infrequent occasions of disclosure because of the possibility that such conversations will be called for in the context of a criminal prosecution.

In the "analogous context" of jury deliberations in criminal cases, the Chief Justice noted, the Court had "recognized that isolated inroads

25. *Executive Privilege: A Constitutional Myth* 15–47 (1974); *The Federalist* No. 65 at 424 (emphasis omitted).

on confidentiality designed to serve the paramount need of the criminal law would not vitiate the demands served by secrecy." The Court had observed that a juror "of integrity and reasonable firmness" would not expect "to be shielded against the disclosure of his conduct in the event that there is evidence reflecting upon his honor"; it had found "[t]he chance that now and then there may be found some timid soul who will take counsel of his fears and give way to their repressive power" to be "too remote and shadowy to shape the course of justice."[26]

Analysis of the probabilities that disclosure might affect the nature and results of deliberations provides an even more compelling argument against the availability of executive privilege in an impeachment inquiry involving the president himself than in a criminal prosecution involving his former aides and associates. The interest in confidentiality that the Supreme Court stressed was the president's interest in receiving candid advice from others. It is difficult to see how this interest could be substantially imperiled by an impeachment investigation of the president's conduct. The constitutionally protected interest in confidentiality operates prospectively; as President Nixon himself put it, the reason for protecting the advice a president gets is to insure that in the future presidents may continue to get the advice they need. But it is highly improbable that an advisor will temper his remarks to a president because the president's conduct might later be the subject of an impeachment investigation—about as "remote and shadowy" a contingency as can be imagined. If anything, an advisor with that possibility in mind is likely to be more resolute and outspoken in urging the president to conduct himself properly or in warning him of the possible consequences of a proposed course of action. In this respect the possibility that a president's conduct might later be investigated increases rather than reduces the likelihood that he will receive "the advice he needs."

The likelihood of the breach of the confidentiality of advice given the president in an impeachment investigation is even less than that of its breach in a criminal prosecution of subordinates, the situation before the Supreme Court in *United States v. Nixon.* As the Judiciary Committee's report stated in response to President Nixon's claim that

26. 418 U.S. at 708, 711–3. The juror case quoted by the Court is Clark v. United States, 289 U.S. 1, 16 (1933).

requiring him to produce information in the impeachment inquiry threatened the ability of future presidents to meet their responsibilities,

> The President's statements . . . exaggerate both the likelihood of such an inquiry and the threat to confidentiality from it. Only two Presidents (including President Nixon) out of thirty-seven have ever been the subject of impeachment investigations. It can scarcely be contended that the far-reaching inquiry into the deliberations between President Andrew Johnson and his cabinet appointees and aides resulted in any impediment of the communications between Presidents and their advisors. There is no more reason to believe that this impeachment inquiry will have that effect.[27]

The history of the Constitution also supports the conclusion that executive privilege founded on the president's need for candid advice should not apply to impeachment proceedings. The framers recognized the need of the president to obtain advice; the primary issue they considered in this regard was whether a council of advice or privy council should be established. The Constitutional Convention overwhelmingly rejected the only proposal for a privy council that came to a vote, but a vestige of this institutional arrangement survived in the form of the clause empowering the president to obtain opinions in writing from the heads of executive departments on any matter respecting the duties of their departments.[28] James Iredell discussed this provision in the North Carolina ratifying convention:

> It is . . . much to be desired, that a man who has such extensive and important business to perform [as the president] should have the means of some assistance to enable him to discharge his arduous employment. The advice of the principal executive officers, which he can at all times command, will, in my opinion, answer this valuable purpose. He can at no time want advice, if he desires it, as the principal officers will always be on the spot. Those officers, from their abilities and experience, will probably be able to give as good, if not better, advice than any counsellors would do.

27. Nixon Impeachment Report 210.
28. 2 Farrand 541–3; Constitution, Art. II, §2, cl. 1.

Iredell stressed the importance of requiring the advice to be written. "[T]he necessity of their opinions being in writing, will render them more cautious in giving them, and make them responsible should they give advice manifestly improper"; "the solemnity of the advice in writing, which must be preserved, would be a great check upon them."[29]

The framers recognized the possibility that the president would be given bad advice. Roger Sherman, for example, several years after the convention explained the reason that the president should not be permitted to choose his own counsellors without the advice and consent of the Senate. If he could do so,

> he would be surrounded by flatterers, who would assume the character of friends and patriots, though they had no attachment to the public good, no regard to the laws of their country, but influenced wholly by self-interest, would wish to extend the power of the executive, in order to increase their own; they would often advise him to dispense with laws, that should thwart their schemes, and in excuse plead, that it was done from necessity to promote the public good—they will use their own influence, induce the president to use his, to get laws repealed, or the constitution altered, to extend his powers and prerogatives, under pretext of advancing the public good, and gradually render the government a despotism.

"This seems to be according to the course of human affairs," Sherman concluded gloomily, "and what may be expected from the nature of things."[30]

The president was not empowered to shield executive officers from the consequences of their actions, presumably including the giving of

29. 4 Elliot 108–10. Some of the proposals for a council of advice to the president expressly provided that the counsellors would be responsible for bad advice. For example, Gouverneur Morris and Charles Pinckney proposed a council composed of the chief justice and the heads of designated executive departments, whose advice would not be binding on the president. Their proposal, later altered by the Committee on Detail and never voted upon by the convention, provided that each officer "shall be responsible for his opinion on the affairs relating to his particular Department" and "liable to impeachment and removal from office for neglect of duty malversation, or corruption" (2 Farrand 342–4).

A constitutional amendment proposed in the New York ratifying convention called for a council to advise the president in the appointment of officers. It provided that the council "should keep a record of their proceedings, and sign the same, and always be responsible for their advice, and impeachable for malconduct in office" (2 Elliot 408).

30. Quoted in 3 Story §1528, n. 1 at 386.

bad advice. The Constitution expressly provides that the president's pardon power does not extend to cases of impeachment. Justice Joseph Story explained the reason for this limitation in his *Commentaries on the Constitution:*

> The power of impeachment will generally be applied to persons holding high offices under the government; and it is of great consequence, that the President should not have the power of preventing a thorough investigation of their conduct, or of securing them against the disgrace of a public conviction by impeachment, if they should deserve it. The constitution has, therefore, wisely interposed this check upon his power, so that he cannot, by any corrupt coalition with favourites, or dependents in high offices, screen them from punishment.[31]

The power of the president to obtain advice from executive officers, their responsibility for the advice they give, and his lack of power to screen them imply that the framers did not consider the president's need for candid advice to be a bar to the disclosure of the advice he received. To the contrary, the provision for written opinions, though it has proved meaningless in practice, suggests that the framers foresaw a need to preserve evidence of executive deliberations in order to insure accountability.

And it was not just the accountability of the president's advisors that the framers considered. While executive officers were to be responsible for the advice they gave, their advice was not to bind the president or diminish his own responsibility. Again to quote Iredell:

> You surely would not oblige him to follow their advice, and punish him for obeying it. If called upon on any occasion of dislike, it would be natural for him to say, "You know my coun-

31. 3 *ibid.* § 1495; see also 1 James Kent, *Commentaries on American Law* * 184 (6th ed. 1848). Story argued similarly in support of his contention that the president had no power to pardon persons held in contempt by either house of Congress. The main object of the legislative contempt power "is to secure a purity, independence, and ability of the legislature adequate to the discharge of all their duties. . . . If the executive should possess the power of pardoning any such offender, they would be wholly dependent upon his good will and pleasure for the exercise of their own powers. Thus, in effect, the rights of the people entrusted to them would be placed in perpetual jeopardy" (3 Story § 1497).

Taken together, these arguments imply that the House is to be supreme in its own sphere—specifically, that its power to investigate the conduct of executive officers and to compel the production of evidence for this purpose cannot be limited by the president.

> cil are men of integrity and ability: I could not act against their opinions, though I confess my own was contrary to theirs." This . . . would be pernicious. In such a situation, he might easily combine with his council, and it would be impossible to fix a fact upon him. It would be difficult often to know whether the President or counsellors were most to blame. A thousand plausible excuses might be made, which would escape detection. But the method proposed in the Constitution creates no such embarrassment. It is plain and open. And the President will personally have the credit of good, or the censure of bad measures; since, though he may ask advice, he is to use his own judgment in following or rejecting it.[32]

The leading argument against an executive council was essentially evidentiary; it might, as Iredell said, make it "impossible to fix a fact upon [the president]." That was the conclusion that the Committee of Eleven, consisting of one delegate from each state, reached near the end of the Philadelphia convention. The committee "judged that the Presidt. by persuading his Council—to concur in his wrong measures, would acquire their protection for them." Hamilton argued the point at length in *The Federalist* No. 70. Multiplicity in the executive, he wrote, "adds to the difficulty of detection" for the purpose of imposing censure or punishment:

> It often becomes impossible, amidst mutual accusations, to determine on whom the blame or the punishment of a pernicious measure, or series of pernicious measures, ought really to fall. It is shifted from one to another with so much dexterity, and under such plausible appearances, that the public opinion is left in suspense about the real author. The circumstances which may have led to any national miscarriage of misfortune are sometimes so complicated that, where there are a number of actors who may have had different degrees and kinds of agency, though we may clearly see upon the whole that there has been mismanagement,

32. 4 Elliot 110. The proposals for a council of advice made during the Constitutional Convention had provided that the president would not be bound by the advice offered. The proposal by Morris and Pinckney stated that the president "shall in all cases exercise his own judgment, and either Conform to such opinions or not as he may think proper" (2 Farrand 343–4). The Committee on Detail's revision of this proposal stated, "their advice shall not conclude him, nor affect his responsibility for the measures which he shall adopt" (2 Farrand 367).

> yet it may be impracticable to pronounce to whose account the evil which may have been incurred is truly chargeable.

And, Hamilton pointed out, "if there happen to be collusion between the parties concerned, how easy it is to clothe the circumstances with so much ambiguity, as to render it uncertain what was the precise conduct of any of those parties." He concluded,

> A council to a magistrate, who is himself responsible for what he does, are generally nothing better than a clog upon his good intentions, are often the instruments and accomplices of his bad, and are almost always a cloak to his faults.[33]

In the context of a presidential impeachment inquiry, the "candid advice" rationale for executive privilege is nothing more than a variant of the proposals the framers rejected. It would screen the incumbent president from responsibility—provide "a cloak to his faults"—not on the basis of the advice he actually received, but rather in order to preserve a structural arrangement by which he and his successors could receive free and unfettered advice. This rationale for executive privilege, at least as applied to a presidential impeachment proceeding, is deficient in two respects. First, it is not at all clear that the framers intended that advice given the president be protected from disclosure; the constitutional provision for written opinions suggests that their intention was the opposite. Even if, as the Supreme Court has held, the expectation of confidentiality is normally to be accorded constitutional recognition, a presidential impeachment proceeding is surely among the extraordinary instances in which the need for confidentiality is outweighed by the need for revelation. Second, the very reason that the framers rejected proposals for an executive council strengthens the argument against executive privilege in an impeachment proceeding, for the candid advice rationale in effect postulates that the need for secret advice to future presidents is more important than probing the conduct of the incumbent. The rejection of an executive council, James Wilson wrote, meant that "our first executive magistrate is not obnubilated behind the mysterious obscurity of counsellors." [34] But, if a president is empowered to withhold information from an impeachment investigation of his own conduct of office, his responsibility is

33. 2 Farrand 542; *The Federalist* No. 70 at 459–60, 462–3.
34. 1 Wilson 319.

beclouded by something far more mysterious—a conjectural assumption that, if the confidentiality of his deliberations is compromised (except as he chooses to compromise it), then advisors to future presidents will not give those presidents the candid advice they require for fear that their advice, too, might be revealed in a presidential impeachment proceeding. That the available evidence on the views of the framers does not explicitly refute this rather arcane argument is hardly surprising. That evidence, however, is so incompatible with the "candid advice" rationale for executive privilege in an impeachment proceeding as to suggest that the privilege should not apply.

Is It Fair to Compel a President to Produce Evidence in an Impeachment Proceeding against Him?

Whatever conclusion one reached about the applicability of executive privilege in an impeachment proceeding against a president, there was a separate ground for contending that President Nixon should not have been required to produce the evidence called for in the Committee's subpoenas. It was that it was fundamentally unfair to require him to provide evidence that might serve as the basis for an accusation against him.

Although never fully articulated during the Nixon inquiry, this argument appeared to go considerably beyond the contention (itself debatable) that fifth amendment privilege against self-incrimination applies directly to an impeachment proceeding.[35] Fifth amendment

35. Two precedents are pointed to in support of the contention that fifth amendment privilege may be invoked in an impeachment proceeding. The first, involving the 1879 investigation of George Seward, former counsul general in Shanghai, is ambiguous. The Committee on Public Expenditures in the State Department, investigating Seward's conduct, issued a subpoena directing him to produce certain books and records. Seward refused to comply and invoked his fifth amendment privilege; the committee recommended that he be held in contempt of the House. The House referred the issue of contempt to the Judiciary Committee, which concluded that Seward's claim of privilege against self-incrimination was valid (and also that the records, if official documents, should have been requested from the State Department, not Seward personally) and that he should not be held in contempt—see 45th Cong., 3d Sess., H. Rept. No. 141 (1879). The Committee on Expenditures, meanwhile, had reported a resolution of impeachment against Seward, including noncompliance with its subpoena among the charges against him described in its report—45th Cong., 3d Sess., H. Rept. No. 134 (1879). The House adjourned without acting on either committee's recommendation; see 3 Hinds' §§1699–1700.

The second precedent, this one from a Senate trial, is also inconclusive. In the 1905 trial of Judge Charles Swayne, the House managers sought to introduce testimony

privilege, as normally interpreted, is not automatic; to receive constitutional protection, a witness must explicitly invoke the privilege. President Nixon, of course, did not invoke it; for him to have done so would have had substantial political repercussions. Although, as a legal matter, no inference of guilt may be drawn from a claim of privilege against self-incrimination, public opinion obviously would be influenced to the detriment of a president if he relied upon fifth amendment privilege in an impeachment inquiry. That might have been particularly true in the case of President Nixon, whose previous assurance that he was "not a crook" had itself caused adverse public reaction.

If a privilege against self-accusation applied to an impeachment proceeding because fundamental fairness required it, therefore, it might well be a privilege that did not have to be expressly invoked. One could legitimately question the fairness of requiring a president to acknowledge that he was refusing to produce subpoenaed evidence in order to protect himself from impeachment and removal from office. Fairness to the president could be argued to require the investigating committee to interpolate a claim of self-accusation privilege on his behalf when he refused to produce evidence or, in President Nixon's case, to treat his claim of executive privilege as a euphemistic equivalent of that privilege.

Swayne had voluntarily given to the subcommittee that had conducted the impeachment investigation of his conduct. By statute, testimony given by a witness before a congressional committee could not be used as evidence "in any criminal proceeding against him in any court, except in a prosecution for perjury committed in giving such testimony." The objection was made that Swayne's testimony before the House subcommittee was inadmissible under the statute. Senator Orville H. Platt, presiding at the trial, sustained the objection, stating, "[W]ithout deciding technically whether this is testimony which was given by a witness before a committee, or whether it is proposed to use it in a criminal proceeding, or in a court, the Presiding Officer thinks that the intention of the statute is such as to make this evidence inadmissible." The Senate affirmed this ruling by a considerable margin; see 3 Hinds' §2270. It is usually considered to be a determination by the Senate that an impeachment trial is a "criminal proceeding," though Senator Platt's explanation did not go that far. If the trial is a criminal proceeding, then the privilege against self-incrimination would be applicable to it and to the House inquiry preliminary to it.

There is no question that fifth amendment privilege may be invoked as it applies to subsequent criminal prosecutions in the courts. A president (or anyone else) subpoenaed in an impeachment inquiry may claim this privilege as a basis for refusing to provide evidence or to testify. If a claim of privilege is made, the investigating committee may nonetheless compel the production of the subpoenaed evidence or testimony by granting use immunity—that is, preventing the use of the evidence (or evidence derived from it) in any subsequent criminal prosecution.

Even apart from the mechanics of claiming it, the putative privilege against self-accusation in an impeachment proceeding would have to differ from fifth amendment privilege in other ways, as well, at least for it to have been of any value to President Nixon. One, perhaps a corollary of the manner in which it would be interposed, is that normal waiver doctrines could not apply. The special prosecutor argued to the Supreme Court in *United States v. Nixon* that President Nixon had waived executive privilege through partial disclosure of presidential conversations and other materials. His argument was founded upon a supposed analogy between executive privilege and other testimonial privileges, most particularly the privilege against self-incrimination. In opposition to this view, the president's counsel argued that the analogy was misplaced; executive privilege was a presidential power, not a testimonial privilege, and doctrines of waiver did not apply. Although it avoided the issue, the Supreme Court's opinion implicitly supported the president's argument.[36] For a privilege against

36. The special prosecutor, citing court cases and the Uniform Rules of Evidence, asserted in his brief to the Supreme Court that the general principle is that "the privilege holder's offer of his own version of confidential communications constitutes a waiver as to all communications on the same subject matter." He argued, "[T]he President cannot have it both ways. He cannot release only those portions he chooses and then stand on the privilege to conceal the remainder. No privilege holder can trifle with the judicial search for truth in this way" (Brief for the United States, United States v. Nixon 122 [filed June 21, 1974]).

In reply the president's counsel contended that "the separation-of-powers notions that underlie . . . 'executive privilege' are such that ordinary common law notions of waiver are inapplicable here. The privilege refers to the power of the president to decide whether or not the public interest permits disclosure of particular information." He quoted Alexander M. Bickel, who had written that the "nature and reason of the privilege are . . . to repose in the President and in him alone the subjective judgment whether to maintain privacy or release information—and which, and how much, and when, and to whom. Far from being waived, the privilege . . . is as much exercised when information is released as when it is withheld." A constitutionally based privilege that exists only so that the president can function effectively hardly vanishes because "little mousetraps of 'waiver' are sprung," the president's counsel contended, quoting Charles L. Black, Jr. See Reply Brief for the Respondent, Cross-Petitioner Richard M. Nixon, President of the United States, United States v. Nixon 27–8 (filed July 1, 1974) (hereafter Reply Brief).

The Supreme Court did not reach the waiver issue, holding instead that there was no absolute and unqualified privilege, at least where diplomatic and military secrets are not claimed to be involved. The Court's reasoning, however, supports the view that the privilege may be considered a power to choose whether to release or withhold information, subject to court review in limited circumstances. It implicitly rejects the argument that selective release of information, as in the Watergate investigations, constitutes a waiver of executive privilege for additional information on the same subject.

self-accusation in an impeachment proceeding to have been of benefit to President Nixon, it, too, would have had to have been nonwaivable; the partial disclosure or production of evidence, either before or during the impeachment inquiry, could not have affected it. Similarly, and again like executive privilege and unlike the privilege against self-incrimination, it would have had to extend to materials that were arguably public property, such as the recordings of President Nixon's conversations made at public expense and on a recording system installed and maintained by the Secret Service, and to materials that were not personal to the president, such as documents in the files of his former staff assistants. The privilege against self-accusation in an impeachment proceeding would have had to reach all materials pertaining to the president's conduct of his office that were within his custody or control—in short, all materials that the president chose to withhold from the impeachment inquiry.

While the scope of such a self-accusation privilege would be substantially the same as that of executive privilege, its recognition would have been even more detrimental to the impeachment process. The argument for executive privilege in an impeachment inquiry was, in essence, that it was not intended to protect the incumbent president, but rather the expectations of confidentiality that would permit presidents in the future to receive the candid advice they needed. This argument, as previously discussed, should not prevail in an impeachment proceeding because both the logic and the constitutional history of the impeachment remedy militate against it. A privilege against self-accusation in an impeachment proceeding would be more irreconcilable with executive accountability. Unlike executive privilege, it would be intended to protect the incumbent, not the future effectiveness of the office; recognition of the privilege would imply that a president has the right to withhold evidence precisely because he thinks that it is potentially inculpatory. If the privilege applied, a president could probably not be impeached if the evidence that would establish his wrongdoing happened to be within his custody or subject to his control. Unless, contrary to the usual law concerning privileged materials, adverse inferences could be drawn from the assertion or interpolation of this privilege or (and it may amount to the same thing) mere suspicion could serve as the basis for impeaching a president who refused to produce subpoenaed evidence, the self-accusation privilege would make the removal of a president a matter of happenstance or a consequence of tactical blunders by a president in tailoring his evidentiary responses. It would require that much more stress be placed on the testimony of adverse witnesses (such as John Dean in the Nixon case) and would make judgments of their credibility more critical. And it would increase the reliance on whatever evidence a president did choose to produce, whether in response to political pressure before the initiation of the impeachment inquiry, in other proceedings, or in an effort to convince the public he had "nothing to hide" from the inquiry. The most crucial evidence in the Nixon inquiry included the testimony of President Nixon's subordinates before the Senate Select Committee on Campaign Activities, other congressional committees, and grand juries, which was obtained after President Nixon "waived" executive privilege for testimony but not for the production of tangible evidence in the spring of 1973; the material provided to the special prosecutor for his criminal investigations, including tape recordings of conversations produced after the "firestorm" of public reaction to the "Saturday Night Massacre" in October 1973; and the transcripts provided to the Judiciary Committee and released to the public in response to the committee's first subpoena. Without this evidence—all of which was, in President Nixon's view, within his control by virtue of the doctrine of executive privilege—it would have been much more difficult for the Judiciary Committee to recommend impeachment. Although the Nixon inquiry was an extreme case in this respect, both because of the nature of the allegations being investigated and because of the existence of the tape recordings, it is very likely that any investigation of presidential conduct must depend to a substantial extent on evidence obtained from the White House itself. If, as a privilege against self-accusation in an impeachment proceeding would imply, the president has the right to withhold evidence he thinks may be adverse to him, then to a significant and perhaps decisive extent he can dictate the results of the investigation.

A privilege permitting this result would be intolerable. The evidence a president withheld under such a privilege could be assumed to be inculpatory; the more substantial his implicit admission that subpoenaed evidence would establish wrongdoing, the less evidentiary basis the investigating committee would have to recommend his impeachment. This irrational result could be avoided in the Nixon inquiry because President Nixon was claiming a privilege that was not personal and therefore implied nothing about his culpability. It is avoided in normal circumstances where the privilege against self-incrimination is invoked because the doctrine of waiver prevents partial withholding of subpoenaed evidence. Unlike executive privilege or privilege against self-incrimination, a privilege against self-accusation in an impeachment proceeding would carry a strong implication that withheld material was damaging to the president.

At least one modification of the privilege would be necessary to avoid this result: a doctrine of waiver would have to apply. If a president produced some information, he could not be permitted to withhold further information from the investigating committee. He would have to resist all evidentiary requests, at least from the time of the first demand by the impeachment investigating committee.

Can a case be made for this more limited privilege against self-accusation in an impeachment proceeding? The answer depends primarily upon what one conceives to be the primary function of the impeachment process. If it is considered to be prosecutorial in nature—a proceeding directed at the officer personally and intended to punish him by depriving him of his present office and of his capacity to hold future office—then there may be a case for such a privilege, with a scope commensurate with that of the impeachment power. (That is, because a president may be removed for wrongdoing that is not personal or criminal, but violative of constitutional duties and official in character, the privilege might be construed to extend to evidence and materials within his official control.)

This, however, would appear to be nothing more than acceptance of executive privilege under another guise. It has all the flaws of executive privilege in terms of its impact on the impeachment remedy with no semblance of the public policy argument that was made in support of executive privilege. It ignores the public interest in being able to remove an unfit president from office, concentrating entirely on the potentially punitive aspects of removal. In this respect, it resembles other proposals to make the impeachment process like a criminal proceeding—by limiting "high crimes and misdemeanors" to criminal offenses, by requiring proof beyond a reasonable doubt at trial, and so forth. Each of these proposals overlooks the basic purpose of the impeachment mechanism, stated succinctly by Rep. James Bayard, one of the managers for the House in the Blount impeachment in 1799. Bayard told the Senate:

> [I]mpeachment is a proceeding purely of a political nature. It is not so much designed to punish an offender as to secure the

> State. It touches neither his person nor his property, but simply divests him of his political capacity.[37]

To contend that a proceeding to "secure the State" should be stymied out of a sense of fairness to the president under investigation would seem to involve a mistaken perception of priorities. The availability of a privilege against self-accusation in an impeachment proceeding, no matter how procedurally fair it may seem to be to the subject of the investigation, would be unfair—and might even be dangerous—to the people. Like executive privilege, a privilege against self-accusation would seem to be contrary to the fundamental purpose of the impeachment remedy.

To conclude that there is no privilege against self-accusation in an impeachment inquiry does not imply that its assertion should automatically lead to impeachment. All the lack of privilege establishes is that there is no legal right justifying noncompliance with subpoenas. Whether that noncompliance should be included among the charges in an impeachment resolution depends upon a variety of factors involving both the noncompliance and the nature of the rest of the case.

Is the President Impeachable for Refusing to Comply with Subpoenas Issued in an Impeachment Inquiry?

President Nixon's counsel argued to the Supreme Court that executive privilege "refers to the power of the President to decide whether or not the public interest permits disclosure of particular information." This interpretation suggests the availability of impeachment for the abuse of executive privilege, a point the president's counsel came close to conceding in the same brief. He argued that "the President is the executive branch, co-equal to the multi-membered legislative and judicial branches," that preservation of coequality required that the president not be "deprived of his power to control the disclosure of his most confidential communications," and that if the president misuses his powers "he must be proceeded against by the remedy that the Constitution has provided."[38] Thus, even if President Nixon had the constitutional power to invoke executive privilege in an impeachment inquiry, the use of this power in bad faith—to prevent the discovery of

37. Annals 5th Cong., 3d Sess., 2251 (1799).
38. Reply Brief at 40–1.

wrongdoing, rather than to protect the confidentiality of deliberations involving the lawful exercise of presidential power—might have been considered to be a potentially impeachable abuse of power. In this respect, misuse of executive privilege could be treated like misuse of the pardon power or the removal power.[39]

At least one member of the Judiciary Committee relied on this argument in opposing a separate article of impeachment based on President Nixon's noncompliance with the committee's subpoenas. William S. Cohen (R., Maine) said during the committee's deliberations on articles, "[W]e should [not] set in concrete as a matter of law that no future President should ever be able to invoke the doctrines of executive privilege or national security as restraints upon our power." Cohen elaborated on the point in additional views filed with the committee's report:

> While the President's stated reasons for his refusal to comply with our Committee's subpoenas may have had a colorable claim or basis, the evidence before the Committee (even before the release of the June 23, 1972, transcript) was more than sufficient to find that the claim of executive privilege was illegitimately and improperly invoked, not to protect the Office of the President, but to protect a particular President from the disclosure of his personal participation in the obstruction of justice. Accordingly, the President's non-compliance formed an integral part of Article I (and possibly Article II) and rests more soundly and solidly within that factual framework.[40]

39. In the introduction to the reply brief, the president's counsel acknowledged that the president, in exercising discretion vested in him alone, might commit high crimes and misdemeanors and quoted Chief Justice Taft in *Ex parte Grossman* (with reference to abuse of the pardon power): "Exceptional cases like this, if to be imagined at all, would suggest a resort to impeachment rather than to a narrow and strained construction of the general powers of the President" (Reply Brief at 4, quoting 267 U.S. 87, 121 [1925]).

40. Debate on Articles of Impeachment 479 (July 30, 1974); Nixon Impeachment Report, "Additional Views of Mr. Cohen on Article III" 516–7. The resolution of impeachment offered by Harold D. Donohue (D., Mass.) at the beginning of the committee's deliberations on articles, which served as the basis for the committee's debate, contained only two articles; the resolution treated noncompliance with the committee's subpoenas as an abuse of power under its Article 2. (The Donohue resolution appears in Impeachment Inquiry, Book III, Appendix III, 2255–8.) This approach proved unacceptable both to those members who considered noncompliance to be sufficiently serious to warrant a separate article and to those who considered it too insubstantial to be included at all.

To establish that executive privilege had been abused, however, it had to be shown that withheld evidence was necessary to the investigation of the subject matter for which it was sought. With merely a *prima facie* demonstration of need, on the one hand, opposed by the claim of the president (who possessed the evidence) that it was cumulative or irrelevant, on the other, it was difficult to make this showing. Only with convincing evidence of a pattern of wrongdoing having the same objective or motivation was it likely to be inferred that the claim of executive privilege was asserted in bad faith. That inference could be drawn about the Watergate subpoenas issued by the committee for the impeachment inquiry because refusal to comply was part and parcel of the "course of conduct or plan" to obstruct investigations ultimately alleged in Article 1. Invocation of executive privilege was among the methods used to carry out this obstruction, as the materials President Nixon revealed when he yielded in his assertion of privilege demonstrated.

It would have been far more difficult to draw the inference of bad faith concerning the assertion of executive privilege in refusing to comply with subpoenas involving activities other than the obstruction of investigations of the Watergate cover-up and related illegal activities. There were four such subpoenas, authorized by the committee on June 24. They dealt with allegations about the ITT antitrust litigation and Senate hearings on the nomination of Richard Kleindienst to be attorney general (to determine whether President Nixon knew of Kleindienst's incomplete and misleading testimony concerning the president's conversation with him about dropping the Supreme Court appeal of one of these suits); the milk price support decision of 1971 (to determine if there was a relationship between President Nixon's directive to increase the price support and political contributions by certain dairy cooperatives); misuse of the Internal Revenue Service (to determine the extent of President Nixon's knowledge and actions in connection with efforts to use the IRS to harass or obtain information about political opponents); and domestic surveillance (to determine the extent of President Nixon's involvement with the Plumbers). President Nixon refused, completely or in substantial part, to comply with these subpoenas; his refusal hampered the committee's inquiry. Although charges concerning misuse of the IRS, domestic surveillance, and the Kleindienst testimony were eventually included in Article 2, the committee was unable to make a determination on the milk price decision because of the president's noncompliance with its subpoena. Its report noted:

> The evidence before the Committee provided some support for the suspicion that the President's conduct in this matter may have been grounds for his impeachment, but without the subpoenaed materials the Committee lacked the evidence to determine whether there was basis for such a charge.

Even as to other matters, the committee suggested that the president's refusal to comply with its subpoenas was not "without practical import." Had it received the evidence it subpoenaed, the committee wrote in its report, it "might have recommended articles structured differently or possibly ones covering other matters."[41]

Instead of drawing adverse inferences from President Nixon's refusal to comply with its subpoenas—including the inference that executive privilege was invoked in bad faith—the committee majority chose to treat repeated noncompliance as the basis for an independent article of impeachment. As adopted by the committee, proposed Article 3 charged President Nixon with failing "without lawful cause or excuse" to produce the materials called for by the subpoenas and with willfully disobeying them. The proposed article stated that the committee deemed the subpoenaed materials to be necessary "in order to resolve by direct evidence fundamental, factual questions relating to Presidential direction, knowledge, or approval of actions demonstrated by other evidence to be substantial grounds for impeachment of the President." It charged that, in refusing to produce these materials,

> Richard M. Nixon, substituting his judgment as to what materials were necessary for the inquiry, interposed the powers of the Presidency against the lawful subpoenas of the House of Representatives, thereby assuming to himself functions and judgments necessary to the exercise of the sole power of impeachment vested by the Constitution in the House of Representatives.

The committee voted 21 to 17 to recommend this article of impeachment, a significantly narrower margin than for the two other proposed articles. Two Democrats who had voted for the other articles (Walter Flowers of Alabama and James R. Mann of South Carolina) voted

41. Nixon Impeachment Report 194–6, 200–2, 189 n. 1, 189.

against Article 3; only two Republicans (its author, Robert McClory of Illinois, and Lawrence J. Hogan of Maryland) voted for it, compared with six Republicans who voted for Article 1 and seven who voted for Article 2.[42]

In its report the committee majority wrote that President Nixon's conduct had forced the committee to deliberate and make judgments on a record that was incomplete, as he himself had acknowledged in his August 5 statement. The purpose of Article 3, the report stated, was to establish a standard barring similar conduct in future impeachment inquiries:

> There can be no question that in refusing to comply with limited, narrowly drawn subpoenas—issued only after the Committee was satisfied that there was other evidence pointing to the existence of impeachable offenses—the President interfered with the exercise of the House's function as the "Grand Inquest of the Nation." Unless the defiance of the Committee's subpoenas under these circumstances is considered grounds for impeachment, it is difficult to conceive of any President acknowledging that he is obligated to supply the relevant evidence necessary for Congress to exercise its constitutional responsibility in an impeachment proceeding. If this were to occur, the impeachment power would be drained of its vitality. Article III, therefore, seeks to preserve the integrity of the impeachment process itself and the ability of Congress to act as the ultimate safeguard against improper presidential conduct.

Rep. McClory, who had introduced Article 3, wrote of it, "Article III is no make-weight article. For posterity, it is the most important article. It preserves for future generations the power to hold their public servants accountable."[43]

The committee majority and Rep. McClory stressed the precedential importance of Article 3 not simply because President Nixon had resigned and they were writing with an eye to the future. The basic point they were making was that the threat of impeachment for noncompliance with subpoenas issued in an impeachment inquiry was the only sanction the House had to compel a President to produce infor-

42. Debate on Articles of Impeachment 488–9 (July 30, 1974).

43. Nixon Impeachment Report 213, 354 ("Additional Views of Mr. McClory on Article III concurred in by Mr. Daniels and Mr. Fish").

mation. Sanctions available against other individuals who refused to obey subpoenas were inappropriate in the case of a president. While the House could hold the president in contempt, it had no way to enforce that judgment; it could hardly imprison him to compel the production of evidence or send its sergeant-at-arms to the White House to seize subpoenaed materials. Referring the matter to the Justice Department for prosecution as a criminal offense (the usual method of dealing with contempt of congressional committees) was unrealistic, both because it involved reliance on the executive branch to prosecute the chief executive and because there was substantial doubt that an incumbent president could be prosecuted while he remained in office. (Indeed, the Justice Department had argued in opposition to Spiro Agnew's claim that an incumbent vice president could not be prosecuted that the president, unlike the vice president, was immune from indictment. And the special prosecutor had taken a similar position when President Nixon was named an unindicted co-conspirator, rather than being indicted, by the Watergate grand jury.) Court enforcement of the subpoenas was probably not available; in any case, the courts possessed no means to coerce compliance that were not also available to the House. The Supreme Court had noted this point in 1881, observing that when the question of impeachment was before either the House or the Senate, "acting in its appropriate sphere on that subject," it could compel the attendance of witnesses and their answers to proper questions "in the same manner and by the use of the same means that courts of justice can in like cases." The only real sanction for presidential disobedience of a court order enforcing the subpoenas would be impeachment.[44]

Among the objections raised against Article 3 during the committee's debate was that the wrongdoing it charged was not substantial enough to provide an independent ground for President Nixon's impeachment. "If this article were standing alone," Flowers asked, "would we be seriously thinking about impeaching the President of the United States for this charge?" It was "just not sufficient," he said. Tom Railsback characterized the article as "political overkill"; he predicted that its adoption would endanger the "fragile coalition" that

44. 93d Cong., 2d Sess., House, Comm. on the Judiciary, Impeachment Inquiry Staff, "Enforcement of Congressional Subpoenas" 6–11 (April 11, 1974) (unpublished) (hereafter Impeachment Inquiry Staff Subpoena Enforcement Memo); Kilbourn v. Thompson, 103 U.S. 168, 190 (1881).

supported Articles 1 and 2. M. Caldwell Butler, pointing to the House's discretion in deciding whether to impeach and what charges to bring, suggested that the first two articles "placed the issue of Presidential conduct sufficiently before the Senate." He, too, concluded that the conduct charged in Article 3, by itself, was not an impeachable offense; the article was not needed, and it served no useful purpose. More than that, Butler said, the charge offended his sense of fair play. It would "impeach a President for a failure to cooperate in his own impeachment, and to me that is basically unfair."[45]

In its report the committee minority made a similar point. Removing the president "for failure to furnish information to his accusers, as it were," would involve "an element of unfairness, or even circularity." The minority argued that adoption of Article 3 by the House "would have set an unwise and potentially mischievous precedent." It "would have unnecessarily introduced an element of brittleness at the heart of our system of Constitutional checks and balances." A "flat no-privilege rule for impeachment investigations" might lead to misuse of the impeachment power to encroach on executive confidentiality and to the removal of a president "for no other grievance than his refusal to comply with an impeachment committee's subpoena." The potential for abuse of an "automatic impeachment" rule was not fanciful, the minority wrote:

> One might well pause before encouraging a bare majority of any committee looking into a civil officer's performance to recommend that he stand trial for his office because it was not fully satisfied with the completeness of the information he produced. Yet if the rule is laid down that . . . a President can under no circumstances enjoy any privilege to withhold documents or testimony from a duly designated impeachment committee which considers such evidence "necessary" to the conduct of an impeachment inquiry, then the mere attempt to exert such a privilege would afford sufficient grounds for his removal—a sort of default judgment, in the most grave proceeding contemplated by our Constitution.

Such a rule, according to the minority, "would severely and excessively weaken the office of the Presidency"; adherence to it reflected "a

45. Debate on Articles of Impeachment 483, 473, 477 (July 30, 1974).

dangerous rigidity in Constitutional interpretation seldom contemplated by the Framers."[46]

Despite the minority's argument, the committee majority, while it endorsed a "flat no-privilege rule," had not adopted an "automatic impeachment" rule. Article 3, as amended in committee, was expressly tailored to the situation confronted in the Nixon inquiry, specifically President Nixon's refusal to produce subpoenaed materials the committee deemed necessary to resolve questions of presidential involvement in actions demonstrated to be substantial grounds for impeachment. The wording of the article in effect acknowledged that the president would not automatically be impeached if he refused to comply with impeachment inquiry subpoenas. Even though there may be no other sanction for his withholding of evidence, at least until he leaves office (and without a pardon), Article 3 suggested that the president could not be impeached and removed for noncompliance with subpoenas unless, in the context of the particular case, his misconduct met the requirement of substantiality applicable in presidential removal proceedings. As with so much else in the law of the presidency, the impermissible assertion of executive privilege in an impeachment proceeding might be an irremediable wrong because, in the circumstances, the only available sanction is too extreme. A significant legal void exists where, as a practical matter, there is no remedy if the president withholds evidence bearing on his conduct.

The extent of the void is a matter of opinion. The late Alexander Bickel, for one, considered it virtually complete. He suggested that it was difficult to imagine that the House would approve an article of impeachment based on noncompliance with subpoenas without also approving other articles or that the Senate would convict on that charge without also convicting on others. In Bickel's view the noncompliance article would be "a gesture," "a makeweight," serving no real purpose. Others took a contrary position, arguing that noncompliance with impeachment subpoenas would be the most fundamental of all charges. Former Special Prosecutor Archibald Cox, for example, said in late May 1974:

> In my view, the refusal to comply with the Judiciary Committee's subpoenas denies presidential accountability through a constitu-

46. Nixon Impeachment Report, Minority Views 478, 492, 478, 489, 490–1.

> tional process the framers were careful to provide. Failure of the committee to treat the refusal as a major ground for impeachment would go far to concede that presidential wrongdoing is beyond the reach of any form of law.[47]

To impeach the president for failing to comply with impeachment inquiry subpoenas, however, placed the House in the position of asserting its own prerogatives, for purposes that might seem self-serving. The interest of the House in protecting its sole power of impeachment from presidential encroachment might be thought to be no different in kind from the president's interest in protecting the powers of his office. President Nixon's arguments about the consequences for the presidency if his claim of privilege were not honored had a ring similar to the committee's arguments about the consequences for the impeachment power if his claim were permitted to prevail. Although it is fair to say that President Nixon's predictions about the danger to the presidency were disingenuous while the committee was stating a genuine concern in good faith, the distinction may not have been immediately apparent.

And the committee was not merely invoking the constitutional power of the House, but asking it to inaugurate a process that would have substantial consequences, whatever the outcome. What was involved, said Rep. Harold V. Froelich (R., Wis.), was "a classic case in separation of powers," with "two great branches of government involved in a stalemate, both arguing the Constitution." Article 3 involved "a dispute about the scope of intersecting powers," the committee minority wrote.

For that reason the minority contended that the committee should have sought a court decision upholding the validity of its subpoenas before charging noncompliance as a ground for impeachment.

> [W]e do not believe that this or any President should be impeached for acts based on his colorable claim of important Constitutional rights, absent a prior judicial determination that such claim was ill-founded. Where, as here, the situation seemed literally to cry out for an arbiter, we believe that the Committee should have sought an early resolution of the [c]ontroversy by in-

47. Alexander M. Bickel, "Should Rodino Go to Court?" *The New Republic,* June 8, 1974, at 13 (hereafter Bickel); Archibald Cox, "The Lawyer's Profession" 12 (mimeo., May 27, 1974), reprinted as "President vs. the Law," *Newsday*, June 17, 1974, at 4.

voking the aid of the Federal judiciary, the branch of government which tradition and the Constitution have deemed the best suited to undertake the arbiter's role.[48]

It was suggested that President Nixon might well have complied with a judicial decree that he obey the committee's subpoenas, providing the committee with the evidence it sought. Railsback argued that the committee made a mistake in not going to court, and "we certainly should not impeach the President because we made a mistake." If, on the other hand, President Nixon disobeyed a court order, that itself would be grounds for his impeachment. Said the minority, "We are satisfied that any wilful disobedience of lawful judicial process which was duly adjudicated to be a contempt of the court would also have constituted an impeachable offense."

From one perspective, the proposition that the president could be impeached if he disobeyed a court order to comply with the subpoenas amounted to a contention that only a court's compulsory process has any vitality. It ran counter to the minority's own argument that there should be no "automatic impeachment" rule for the withholding of evidence. "Automatic impeachment" would follow from disobedience of a subpoena with only the extra step of obtaining a court order, then impeaching for disobedience of it rather than failure to comply with the subpoenas themselves.[49]

48. Debate on Articles of Impeachment 455, 456 (July 30, 1974); Nixon Impeachment Report, Minority Views 486–7.

49. Debate on Articles of Impeachment 474 (July 30, 1974); Nixon Impeachment Report, Minority Views 487. Perhaps recognizing the implications of this position, the minority put heavy emphasis on the alternative argument that the committee should have asked the House to hold Nixon in contempt, providing him an opportunity to show cause for not complying with the subpoenas before recommending impeachment for noncompliance (at 484–5). This argument, despite the stress opponents of Article 3 placed upon it, was faulty. A contempt citation against President Nixon would have been, as the committee majority wrote, "an empty and inappropriate formality" (Nixon Impeachment Report 212). The president was on notice that the committee might treat his failure to comply with its subpoenas as grounds for his impeachment and had explained his reasons for not complying in his June 9 letter. In addition, his counsel had the opportunity to argue the issue before the committee, though he did not do so. Finally, if the House had voted to prosecute Article 3, Nixon would have had the opportunity to present a full defense in his Senate trial before any sanctions were imposed for noncompliance. The Senate trial unquestionably met due process requirements; furthermore, it would have placed the House's assertion of power before a neutral tribunal, acting in an adjudicative capacity. The minority's contempt argument implied that the House, unlike the committee, was a proper judge because it was not a party to the

More fundamentally, the argument that the committee should have sought judicial enforcement of its subpoenas before recommending an article of impeachment for noncompliance ignored significant practical and constitutional problems that would have been involved in seeking a court ruling. The practical problems began with a technical matter. The jurisdiction of federal courts (apart from the limited original jurisdiction of the Supreme Court) is prescribed by statute. No statute provided a clear jurisdictional basis for a suit by the committee to enforce its subpoenas. Conceivably, jurisdiction existed under the statutory provision for an "action in the nature of mandamus to compel an officer . . . of the United States . . . to perform a duty owed to the plaintiff."[50] But that statute was available only if the president's duty to comply with the committee's subpoenas was mandatory and executive privilege entirely inapplicable. Claiming jurisdiction on this basis would have been pushing the committee's subpoena power to its limits, and perhaps beyond, on the threshold question of jurisdiction. A similar claim of mandamus jurisdiction by the Senate Select Committee on Campaign Activities for its legislative subpoenas against President Nixon had been rejected by the courts, and that committee had ultimately found it necessary to obtain special legislation conferring jurisdiction on the courts to pass upon its subpoenas.[51]

Most of those who considered the problem thought that similar legislation would be needed to enable the Judiciary Committee to seek court enforcement of its subpoenas. But enactment of such legislation would have taken time, as would the conduct of litigation. And jurisdictional legislation itself might have been subject to constitutional attack. It conceivably could have been argued that the House had no constitutional authority to share with the courts its sole power of impeachment or the correlative power to compel the production of evidence for an impeachment inquiry. In *United States v. Nixon* the

---

dispute concerning the subpoenas. But, in fact, the committee was the agent of the House; it was asserting the power of the House, specifically delegated to it by the House.

Although it is difficult to explain the minority's reasons for giving so much emphasis to the lack of a formal contempt finding by the House, one factor may have been that the possibility of a court test was highly remote (and rejected by President Nixon). Another factor, admittedly more conjectural, was a tendency to think of the committee's recommendation of an article of impeachment as though it were a final judgment. Beyond that, the argument may have been something of a makeweight—a rationale for a position that it was difficult to explain on other "principled" bases.

50. 28 U.S.C. §1361.

51. See Impeachment Inquiry Staff Subpoena Enforcement Memo 8–10.

Supreme Court, while affirming its power to "say what the law is," had indicated that powers vested in one branch of government cannot be shared with another:

> [T]he "judicial power of the United States" vested in the federal courts by Art. III, §1 of the Constitution can no more be shared with the Executive Branch than the Chief Executive, for example, can share with the Judiciary the veto power, or the Congress share with the Judiciary the power to override a presidential veto.[52]

There were contrary House precedents, involving the designation by joint congressional resolution of "commissions" composed of members of an expiring Congress. These commissions were authorized to conduct impeachment investigations between Congresses and to report to the incoming House.[53] As precedent for a sharing of the impeachment power, however, these commissions were both obscure and distinguishable from the situation that the committee confronted. More significantly, it could be argued that giving the courts jurisdiction to pass upon the validity of the committee's subpoenas did not involve sharing power at all, but merely the use of the judicial power "to construe and delineate claims arising under express [constitutional] powers" and "to interpret claims with respect to powers alleged to derive from enumerated powers"—a function of the judiciary that the Supreme Court reaffirmed in *United States v. Nixon.*[54] That argument probably would have prevailed in a dispute about the constitutionality of jurisdictional legislation, but it was not clear-cut.

And the jurisdictional hurdle was only the beginning. Even assuming the courts had or could be given jurisdiction, it still could be contended that the validity of the committee's subpoenas in the face of President Nixon's claim of executive privilege was not justiciable—that is, not "the kind of controversy courts traditionally resolve."[55] By itself

52. 418 U.S. at 704–5, quoting Marbury v. Madison, 5 U.S. (1 Cr.) at 177.

53. See 6 Cannon's §§544, 550, 552.

54. 418 U.S. at 704, 696.

55. *Ibid.* at 696. In *United States v. Nixon* the Court confirmed that it had the power to construe the scope of executive privilege, a power of the president. It reaffirmed Chief Justice Marshall's assertion in *Marbury v. Madison* that "it is emphatically the province and the duty of the judicial department to say what the law is" (at 705). But *Marbury v. Madison* was itself a case in which the Court held that it had no jurisdiction, in that instance because it was unconstitutional for Congress to enlarge the Court's original jurisdiction by legislation.

the availability of executive privilege in an impeachment proceeding would not be a nonjusticiable question; the courts could rule on that, just as they ruled on its availability in response to judicial subpoenas. The problem was that the courts would necessarily have been faced with the question of the validity of the committee's subpoenas, as well. Because that question involved the scope of a power that was vested solely in the House and a process from which the judiciary had been deliberately excluded by the framers, it could be contended—and might be decided by the courts themselves—that it was the kind of issue they should not seek to resolve.

The Constitutional Convention decided to exclude the Supreme Court from the impeachment process when it transferred the power to try impeachments from the Court to the Senate. One reason was that the Court, both because of its relatively small size and the manner of its appointment, was thought to be an improper tribunal to try the president—a consideration not necessarily applicable to preliminary evidentiary matters in a House impeachment inquiry. Other reasons, however, involved the nature of impeachment and the proper functioning of the Court itself. Justice Joseph Story, writing in the 1830s, defended the convention's decision; he asserted that an impeachment proceeding involved issues and procedures far different from those in ordinary jurisprudence. His definition of the impeachment power, which reached what he said "are aptly termed, political offences," was part of his argument that the Supreme Court was not a competent tribunal for impeachment proceedings. These offenses, he wrote, related to "the discharge of the duties of political office," duties that "are easily understood by statesmen, and are rarely known to judges." They

> must be examined upon very broad and comprehensive principles of public policy and duty. They must be judged of by the habits, and rules, and principles of diplomacy, of departmental operations and arrangements, of parliamentary practice, of executive customs and negotiations, of foreign, as well as of domestic political movements; and, in short, by a great variety of circumstances, as well those, which aggravate, as those, which extenuate, or justify the offensive acts.

These considerations, he wrote, "do not properly belong to the judicial character in the ordinary administration of justice, and are far removed from the reach of municipal jurisprudence."[56]

56. 2 Story §764.

Yet the reach of the impeachment power—and specifically the determination by the Judiciary Committee that subpoenaed evidence was necessary for deciding whether to recommend impeachment—was among the issues that the courts might have had to pass upon in deciding whether President Nixon had a valid reason or excuse for failing to comply with the subpoenas. Bickel, who believed the committee should have sought court enforcement of its subpoenas, described the issue in a subpoena enforcement proceeding as "whether the evidence sought is relevant to a plausibly stated, but as yet hypothetical, impeachable offense," applying "the farthest, outer limits of the power to impeach, rather than . . . precise and definitive formulations, such as clash with the 'sole' function of Congress."[57] He thought this posed no particular difficulty for the courts:

> [T]he question of whether material under subpoena is relevant to the lawful business of a given accusatory body—grand jury, administrative agency or court—is one that judges decide every day. . . . The issue . . . of what the outer limits of an impeachable offense may be within the meaning of the Constitution can be determined by quite respectable legal standards, drawn as is customary in constitutional cases from historical materials, from prior practice and from ascertainable principles inherent in the structure of the American scheme of government. Would that half the heated political issues enthusiastically disposed of by judges in the past two decades had lent themselves equally well to decision within the accustomed discipline of the judicial process![58]

Applying this approach, Bickel suggested that a court could properly refuse to enforce a committee subpoena for evidence concerning the impoundment of funds because impoundment, although a dubious constitutional practice, did not rise to the level of an impeachable offense.[59]

57. Bickel 12. This statement is not technically precise. The issue for the courts in passing upon a congressional subpoena is not whether the evidence sought is relevant, but rather whether the inquiry for which the subpoena is issued was authorized by the House or Senate in furtherance of a legitimate function and whether the committee's determination that the evidence is needed for its inquiry is a reasonable one. The courts normally accord great deference to decisions by congressional committees that evidence should be subpoenaed. For a recent discussion of court enforcement of congressional subpoenas, see Eastland v. United States Servicemen's Fund, 421 U.S. 491 (1975).

58. Bickel 13–4.

59. *Wall Street Journal*, June 5, 1974, at 8.

Bickel appears to have been contending that judges, too, are capable of making *ex cathedra* pronouncements of what, hypothetically, is and is not an impeachable offense. As Justice Story insisted, however, defining even the outer limits of the impeachment power in an actual case is a much more complex undertaking than that. If all the considerations Story identified were relevant, Bickel may have been correct about the ability of the courts to decide upon the validity of the committee's subpoenas. It would have been easy for them to uphold the committee's determination that it needed subpoenaed material for the impeachment inquiry. The courts need not have decided the relevancy issue at all, but could instead have deferred to the committee's judgment because only legislators were competent to resolve the questions it raised.

But reaching even that conclusion—much less deciding whether specific allegations might or might not be grounds for impeachment—could have seemed to have put the courts squarely in the business of defining "high crimes and misdemeanors." Bickel considered this acceptable, first, because it involved only the "farthest, outer limits" of the impeachment power and, second, because the judicial definition would not be binding upon Congress. On the latter point, he wrote:

> Congress would in no sense put itself in the position of disobeying a judicial decree if it ignored whatever a court did choose to say about the nature of impeachable offenses. The result of the lawsuit, assuming Congress lost, would merely be that the court had declined to enforce a subpoena. Congress could still proceed to impeachment, trial, and conviction, if it wished, on its own theory of the nature of an impeachable offense. . . .
>
> Whatever a judge, and particularly the Supreme Court if it came to that, had seen fit to say about impeachable offenses might influence congressional opinion, even though the judicial pronouncements had no binding effect. But the influence would arise from the intrinsic merit, if any, of the judges' views, and why should Congress be shielded from an influence of that sort?[60]

60. Bickel 12. Ralph K. Winter, Jr., of the Yale Law School, proposed the following standard for judicial enforcement of impeachment inquiry subpoenas: "When the claimed impeachable offense is of a noncriminal nature, subpoenas are nonjusticiable. Where the subpoena charges an offense that is an indictable offense, a court might well say this is like a grand jury subpoena. In the latter case, impeachment of the President is

But the problem was not so much that the courts might influence members of Congress by commenting on the scope of the impeachment power (though dicta by one or another judge, especially on the criminality question, might be accorded more deference than they deserved) as that some judgment, however tentative, about the scope of the impeachment power seemed to be necessary to pass upon the validity of the committee's subpoenas. And this, for the reasons Story articulated, might have been considered by judges themselves to be an improper function for the courts. If they had reached that conclusion, they would have refused to decide the case at all.

Justice Story made another point about the impeachment process and the courts. He contended that their exclusion from the process was appropriate not only to insure that impeachment operated properly, but also to insure the effective functioning of the judicial branch.

> Whatever shall have a tendency to secure, in tribunals of justice, a spirit of moderation and exclusive devotion to juridical duties is of inestimable value. What can more surely advance this object, than the exemption of them from all participation in, and control over, the acts of political men in their official duties?[61]

Limits on justiciability exist in part to protect the courts themselves. For the Supreme Court to have decided that enforcement of the committee's subpoenas involved a justiciable dispute could have had consequences for the future conduct of judicial business, as well as for the impeachment process. That consideration, too, had to be taken into account.

The very reason that a court adjudication of the validity of the sub-

---

a substitute for indictment of a President, and I think the need for enforcement is much greater there" (*Wall Street Journal*, June 5, 1974, at 8). Even assuming Winter's distinction could be drawn (and it would invite argument about whether an allegation was more criminal or noncriminal), it suggests a two-tier ranking of grounds for impeachment—the more serious, criminal grounds, on the one hand, and the less important, constitutional grounds, on the other—that would have mischievous consequences. Winter later recanted, writing: "The determination of whether an impeachable offense has occurred is a question of fact, law and politics in the highest sense, and the institutions entrusted with the power to make it must accept full responsibility for their decision without being either permitted or compelled to share it with an institution whose relation to that decision is wholly incidental. On balance therefore, I think courts ought to decline to intervene in impeachment subpoenas." ("The Seedlings for the Forest," 83 *Yale L. J.* 1730, 1743 [1974]—a review of Berger, *Executive Privilege: A Constitutional Myth.*)

61. 2 Story §764.

poenas was advocated—to induce obedience to them or to provide a ground for impeachment on the basis of disobedience of a court order—reinforced the argument that the judiciary might refuse to consider the case. As previously mentioned, the Supreme Court, in its only statement on the subject, had suggested that in carrying out its impeachment function the House has every means to compel the production of evidence that the courts have. A court decision upholding the committee's subpoenas therefore would have added nothing, in legal terms, to the coercive means already theoretically available to compel compliance. The prediction that President Nixon might have respected judicial power (because of the greater prestige of the courts) when he did not respect the impeachment power of the House may have been valid, but it was hardly a point a court would wish to articulate or rely upon.

The argument may be carried one step further. The proponents of a court test of the subpoenas were really seeking a judicial declaration that President Nixon had violated his constitutional duty and encroached upon the power of the House in his refusal to produce subpoenaed evidence. Such a declaration would have come very close to being an advisory opinion, which the judiciary, limited by the Constitution to deciding cases and controversies, has no power to render.[62] The Constitution is not ambiguous about who is to decide whether the president has violated his constitutional duties and should be removed from office. The question is for the House in determining whether to impeach and for the Senate as the final adjudicative tribunal.

62. See Holtzman v. Schlesinger, 484 F.2d 1307 (2d Cir. 1973), in which the court of appeals held that Rep. Elizabeth Holtzman of New York had no standing to challenge the legality of the bombing in Cambodia simply because she might be called upon to determine whether the president should be impeached because of it. The court said, "The claim that the establishment of illegality here would be relevant in possible impeachment proceedings against the President would in effect be asking the judiciary for an advisory opinion which is precisely and historically what the 'case and controversy' conditions set forth in Article III, Section 2 of the Constitution forbid. . . . The judgment sought could hardly have any subsequent binding effect on those who have the responsibility for such a measure [impeachment]" (at 1311). In another challenge to the continuation of the war in Indochina, Mitchell v. Laird, 488 F.2d 611 (D.C. Cir. 1973), the Circuit Court of Appeals for the District of Columbia held that plaintiff legislators did have standing, in part because a declaration that the defendants acted without constitutional authority "would bear upon the duties of plaintiffs to consider whether to impeach defendants," and that the case was not moot partly for the same reason. The court dismissed the case, however, because it involved the political question of whether President Nixon had tried in good faith and to the best of his ability to bring the war to an end as promptly as was consistent with the safety of those fighting and the interests of the nation.

Not only was it being suggested that the courts be used to buttress the conclusion that the committee had already reached—to give an authoritative answer to a question that the House initially and the Senate finally were required to decide on their own—but it was also being proposed that the judiciary be asked to aid in the first stage of the process when it was unthinkable that the courts should be permitted to intervene at the end. Before and during the Nixon inquiry, the availability of judicial review of an impeachment trial was always discussed from the perspective of the right of a convicted official to seek review of the proceedings that resulted in his removal from office. But if judicial review were available (and it should be added immediately that the case against it is overwhelming), it presumably would be equally available to the House, as improbable as that may seem. The only reason to suggest that a convicted official could seek review of his conviction but the House could not seek review of an acquittal is that impeachment is a criminal prosecution to which rules of double jeopardy apply and prevent retrial on the same charge after acquittal. A strong argument can be made, however, that impeachment is not a criminal proceeding—an argument that has been persuasively presented by the leading advocate of judicial review in impeachment cases, Raoul Berger.[63]

If ever there were an instance in which the House might consider it desirable to seek court review of a Senate judgment on an impeachment, it would be an acquittal on an article that charged interference with its sole power of impeachment by refusing to comply with its subpoenas. Suppose the House had adopted Article 3, the impeachment had gone to trial, and the Senate had acquitted on all articles. Suppose, further, that more than one-third of the Senate had decided (and stated in written opinions) that, as a matter of law, executive privilege was available in an impeachment investigation and that was the reason for their not guilty vote on Article 3. If the House took this legal point to court and the Supreme Court decided that the House was right and the senators wrong, presumably there would have been a second trial, in which the Court's constitutional interpretation would have prevailed.

This bizarre hypothetical case is suggested in order to illustrate the encroachment on the Senate's sole power to try all impeachments—a power that involves deciding issues of law as well as issues of fact—that

63. Berger, *Impeachment* 78–85.

would result from a court decision before impeachment or trial (or before retrial, in the fantasy). The legal issues involved in President Nixon's refusal to comply with the Judiciary Committee's subpoenas were ones that the Senate ultimately had to decide. For the House, the potential prosecutor of an impeachment, to have taken these issues to the judicial branch rather than to the court with jurisdiction over impeachments would have involved going to the wrong forum.[64]

For all these reasons, it was not appropriate to seek a court decision that the committee's subpoenas were valid. Had the committee taken its subpoenas to court, its inquiry would have been delayed and attention diverted, perhaps to no avail. Despite the superficial similarities between the committee's dispute with the president concerning its subpoenas and the special prosecutor's dispute with him concerning the subpoenas for the Watergate cover-up trial, there was a critical legal difference. *United States v. Nixon* and the earlier case of *Nixon v. Sirica*,[65] which involved a grand jury subpoena (and was, in that limited respect, more analogous to the committee's situation), did not raise the question of justiciability because they concerned the exercise

64. In the Nixon inquiry there was no mechanism for reaching the correct forum—the Senate—short of voting an article of impeachment based on noncompliance with the subpoenas. No one suggested that the Senate might determine the validity of the subpoenas as an interlocutory matter before impeachment or trial, and without necessarily also deciding that noncompliance was (or was not) a high crime or misdemeanor warranting President Nixon's removal from office.

No constitutional obstacle exists to such interlocutory determinations by the Senate at the instance either of the House or of the official under investigation. The prohibition on advisory opinions, applicable to Article III courts, may not apply to the Senate in its capacity as the court for impeachments, and the Constitution (Art. I, § 5) specifically provides that "[e]ach House may determine the Rules of its Proceedings." The Senate could provide for a proceeding in which it would decide preliminary legal questions relating to an impeachment investigation in its adjudicative capacity as the tribunal for trying impeachments, permitting both sides of the question to be argued. This proceeding would not have the defects attributed, for example, to the Senate resolution that Andrew Johnson's orders to remove Stanton and install Thomas were unconstitutional and contrary to law—a resolution that was considered and passed by the Senate in its political capacity and was later argued to have made the Senate a biased tribunal for the impeachment trial of this issue.

Among the drawbacks of this procedure—aside from lack of precedent, which is its most serious liability—is that it would place the House in an adversarial posture to the official it is investigating, perhaps prematurely. Most other objections seem ultimately to translate, in one way or another, into a contention that the Senate is not very competent at deciding constitutional and legal questions. Within the current constitutional scheme, in which the Senate has the final responsibility for doing so in an impeachment trial, this objection can carry no weight.

65. 487 F.2d 700 (D.C. Cir. 1973).

of judicial subpoena power.[66] President Nixon was asking the judiciary in these cases to quash its own subpoenas, arguing that his power to control the release of materials to which executive privilege applied overrode the judicial power to compel the production of evidence for the performance of judicial functions. The issue arose in the context of proceedings already before the courts, and it had to be resolved to enable those proceedings to continue.

The equivalent procedure in the impeachment inquiry was for the Judiciary Committee, to which had been delegated the full scope of the investigative power of the House incident to its power of impeachment, to consider President Nixon's claim of privilege, as well as the need for the material it was subpoenaing. The committee did so before it voted to recommend impeachment for noncompliance. The members of the committee who desired to take the matter to court were in effect suggesting that the committee's interpretation of its own power, unlike the courts' interpretation of judicial power, was not sufficiently authoritative to warrant the extreme step of recommending impeachment because President Nixon disregarded it. The final judgment on that question, however, was entrusted by the Constitution not to the courts but to the Senate, if the House agreed with the committee and included defiance of its own constitutional power among the charges in articles of impeachment.[67]

The fundamental question about the wisdom of Article 3 may have been obscured in this discussion, as it was at the time, by consideration of whether President Nixon's claim of privilege had any merit and whether the committee should have sought court enforcement of its subpoenas. Even with those issues resolved, the problem of fairness raised by Rep. Butler remains. Would it have been proper to force the president to defend the powers of his office at peril of losing that office? Should he have been required to make his defense either in the first instance or ultimately in forums whose institutional interests ran counter to the position he was asserting?

These abstract questions must be approached on the assumption

66. President Nixon did contend that these cases were nonjusticiable because the claim of executive privilege was a political question, an argument the court of appeals rejected in *Nixon v. Sirica* and the Supreme Court rejected in *United States v. Nixon*.

67. For this reason, too, later compliance with trial subpoenas (whether issued by the Senate or, in accordance with past practice, by the House itself) would not have purged the wrongdoing charged in Article 3, though it is likely as a discretionary matter that the House would not have pursued the charge.

that the claim of privilege was, at least colorably, made in good faith and for the publicly stated reasons. Considered on this basis, the issue is no easier to resolve than was the similar question posed by Andrew Johnson's defense counsel more than a century ago or than the conundrum confronted by the Constitutional Convention almost two centuries ago when it tried to reconcile separation of powers with an effective mechanism for holding the president accountable.

In the actual circumstances of the Nixon inquiry, the issue was less troubling, whether because, as Rep. Cohen suggested, the evidence revealed a less legitimate motive for President Nixon's failure to comply or because, as both he and Butler suggested, Article 3 was not crucial to the impeachment. At a minimum, the Nixon case made it clear that the claim of executive privilege by a president in an impeachment investigation should be viewed with extreme skepticism. It may have settled more than that, at least for our time, by scuttling the notion that executive privilege may be claimed at all in an impeachment proceeding. Whether as a legal or a political matter, Nixon's assertion of the privilege, given the nature of at least some of the evidence he sought to suppress, will make it very difficult and perhaps impossible for future presidents to take a similar tack from even the best of motives. A different case might possibly have taught a different lesson; even the Nixon case with a different denouement conceivably could have left the issue more in doubt. Despite his professed concern about setting precedents that could weaken the office of president, in the end President Nixon, far more than the Judiciary Committee, appears to have done just that.

7. *IMPLICATIONS FOR THE FUTURE*

The basic issue in presidential impeachment remains the problem that most troubled the delegates to the Constitutional Convention in 1787: how to insure that the president is legally accountable without making him subservient to Congress. The complicated solution the framers devised—selection of the president by electors specially chosen for the purpose, not by Congress; eligibility of the president for reelection; division of the procedure for removing him between the House and the Senate, with a two-thirds vote required in the Senate for conviction and removal—has been altered by both extraconstitutional developments (such as the rise of political parties) and constitutional changes (most notably the two-term limitation of the Twenty-second Amendment). Nevertheless, the most important guarantee of presidential protection from partisan removal from office is still that the procedure requires formal accusation by a majority of the House, an adversary trial, and a vote of conviction by at least two-thirds of the Senate.

The Andrew Johnson impeachment demonstrated how formidable an obstacle the two-thirds requirement can be. Johnson had been elected vice president on a national unity ticket during the Civil War; that he might become president, especially during the critical period of postwar reconstruction, had simply not been contemplated. The Republican majority in Congress was inflated both because southern states were excluded from representation and because the Democratic party had been severely damaged elsewhere as a result of the war. Johnson was impeached by a House of Representatives that was overwhelmingly Republican (and no Republican members of the House voted against his impeachment); he was tried by a Senate that consisted of forty-two Republicans and twelve Democrats. In partisan terms, his acquittal mathematically required defections from the Republican ranks; this highly political impeachment was eventually resolved in a manner that ran counter to the interests of the dominant political party. The recurrence of such a lopsided partisan majority in Congress in opposition to the president is highly improbable. The more typical situation is the one that caused President Nixon to resign rather than go through an impeachment trial. Although the Democratic party controlled both House and Senate in 1974, Nixon's removal from office would have required the votes of some senators who had been politically loyal to him. Their abandonment of him in the face of overwhelming evidence that he was guilty of serious wrongdoing precipitated his resignation.

Far from showing that the constitutional scheme is subject to partisan abuse, therefore, the Johnson trial ultimately demonstrated how strong the safeguard is against the successful use of presidential impeachment as a partisan weapon. Like the Nixon resignation more than a century later, it suggests that the outcome of a presidential removal proceeding will depend much more on whether guilt of serious wrongdoing is established than on partisanship. The two-thirds vote requirement makes it virtually inconceivable that a president could be removed from office through impeachment unless members of his own political party vote for his conviction—an outcome that is scarcely likely to be based on partisan considerations. "[T]he security to innocence" from the two-thirds vote requirement is, as Hamilton wrote, "as complete as itself can desire."[1]

And that, it should be recalled, was the primary safeguard the framers of the Constitution adopted. As discussed in chapter 2 of this book, they recognized that impeachment would be a political process; it is, after all, a proceeding involving a political issue of the most fundamental sort—the constitutional legitimacy of the chief executive's remaining in power. The purpose of a presidential impeachment and the issues in the proceeding differ from those in a criminal prosecution. A president is not removed from office to deter his successors from engaging in wrongdoing, to permit his rehabilitation, or as retributive punishment for his misdeeds. Deterrence and retribution may be among the effects of an impeachment (it is difficult to assign any role to rehabilitation), but they are incidental to the primary objective—to be rid of a chief executive whose past misconduct indicates that he ought to be replaced. And, because presidential impeachment does not have the functions of a criminal prosecution, there is little

1. *The Federalist* No. 66 at 430.

reason to impose restrictions derived from analogies to the criminal law either in defining the grounds for impeachment or in establishing the procedures to be followed by the House and Senate.

Away from the exigencies of a particular impeachment, it is hard to believe that anyone would seriously advocate that a president should be removable from office only if charged with and found guilty of a serious crime in a proceeding with all the procedural requisites of a criminal prosecution. If that is what the framers had intended, it would have been illogical for them to have entrusted the conduct of the proceeding to the House and Senate, which have no particular competence in this regard. One good answer to the contention that impeachment is supposed to be a criminal prosecution for indictable offenses was given by John Randolph in the Chase trial. If that was the intent, he asked, why does the Constitution provide for impeachment at all?

> Could it not have said, at once, that any civil officer of the United States convicted on an indictment, should (*ipso facto*) be removed from office? This would be coming at the thing by a short and obvious way. . . . Whence this idle parade, this wanton waste of time and treasure, when the ready intervention of a court and jury alone was wanting to rectify the evil?[2]

Impeachment and removal are entrusted to the two branches of the legislature because the objectives and the questions to be resolved are political. Edmund Burke's opening argument in the Hastings impeachment trial, much quoted during the Nixon inquiry, makes the essential point. "It is by this tribunal," Burke told the House of Lords,

> that statesmen, who abuse their powers, are accused by statesmen, and tried by statesmen, not upon the niceties of a narrow jurisprudence, but upon the enlarged and solid principles of state morality. It is here, that those, who by abuse of power have violated the spirit of the law can never hope for protection from any of its forms:—it is here that those who have refused to conform themselves to its perfections can never hope to escape through any of its defects.[3]

2. 2 Chase Trial 452.
3. 7 Works of Edmund Burke 13–4 (1839).

Rhetoric apart, there has been substantial difficulty in the American system in conforming impeachment to this model. The limitations the framers imposed on impeachment in their written Constitution and the prohibition of the related devices (constructive treason and bills of attainder) that the English Parliament had used to establish its supremacy, invited the argument that the framers also intended to restrict the causes for impeachment and the method by which it was conducted. Despite the express limitation on the purpose of impeachment—dismissal and disqualification from office—the argument could be made that the framers sought to create a purely adjudicative proceeding, a prosecution more criminallike than the English model from which they borrowed. And, as impeachment came to be a mechanism primarily for investigating and occasionally for trying judges who had misbehaved, its application to the basic purpose for which it was designed—the removal of the president—became more unfamiliar. A procedure invoked against only one president in the first 185 years of our constitutional history obviously did little to solidify principles of state morality.

The Nixon impeachment inquiry, it is to be hoped, began to put presidential impeachment on a stronger footing. Though it involved the use of an unfamiliar procedure and was undertaken in the face of numerous obstacles, the Nixon inquiry succeeded in its immediate objective (a full and complete inquiry into allegations of misconduct against President Nixon and recommendations based on the results of that investigation) and in demonstrating that presidential impeachment and removal can be a workable, if difficult, constitutional remedy.

Two aspects of the Nixon inquiry may pose problems the next time presidential impeachment is considered. The first, probably inevitable in the circumstances, was that the Judiciary Committee may have overemphasized the adjudicative aspects of the function it was performing. For reasons discussed earlier, the impeachment process and the committee's performance were themselves under intense scrutiny. The appearance of partisanship or one-sidedness might well have undermined an eventual recommendation to impeach, just as leaks to the press during the committee's evidentiary hearings resulted in attacks on the work of the committee. The committee reacted to the pressure it confronted by attempting to avoid any appearance of unfairness or partiality; this, in turn, created the risk that its eventual recommendations would be more judgmental than prosecutorial, more in the nature of a reasoned legal decision than of the strongest possible accusation for prosecution in the Senate. Had the proceeding continued, it was conceivable that members of the committee (and even other members of the House) might have had some difficulty adjusting to the accusatory role required of managers in an impeachment trial. In the circumstances of the Nixon case, the problem was not particularly serious. Neither the allegations against President Nixon nor the temper of the times were conducive to the declamatory flamboyance of the great impeachment trials of the past, and a low-key prosecutorial approach would probably have been most successful in the Senate and with the nation. On the other hand, an adjudicative approach to the conduct of an impeachment investigation and the framing of articles of impeachment does postpone consideration of trial strategy and may to some extent limit the options of those who must prosecute the case in the Senate.

The second problem, while exacerbated by the circumstances of the Nixon inquiry, is inherent in the impeachment process. Impeachment is a time-consuming way of getting an unfit president out of office, a point that has been recognized from the beginning. While the Johnson impeachment suggests that the House can act quickly (he issued his orders to remove Stanton and install Thomas on a Friday afternoon and was impeached the following Monday; articles of impeachment were adopted the next week), the Johnson trial was not completed for nearly three months. And the factual simplicity of the Johnson case is as unlikely to recur as are the evidentiary convolutions of the Nixon case, which helped make that impeachment inquiry as long and involved as it was. No future president is likely to be impeached three days later for what he does openly and in writing, just as no president is ever again likely to face impeachment and removal on the basis of such a complex and continuing series of events as were at issue in the Nixon inquiry.

Nevertheless, the length of time presidential impeachment takes is one of its major defects. The Nixon case suggested one method of shortening what Rep. Theodore Sedgwick described in 1789 as "the tardy, tedious, desultory road, by way of impeachment"—resignation by the president to avoid impeachment and conviction. President Nixon was not the first federal official facing impeachment who resigned. Resignation was not that uncommon in the heyday of impeachment investigations of judges and is still the usual result when judges or executive officials are charged with serious misconduct. Their resignations, however, hardly rival that of a president in importance. The Nixon case may eventually be regarded as precedent for forced resignation as an alternative to impeachment and trial, and the political pressure to resign on a future president accused of impeachable wrongdoing may be considerable. Added to that pressure will be personal considerations that may make resignation appear to be an appealing solution to a president facing impeachment and possible removal. It would avoid the even more disgraceful fate of being the first president actually ousted from office, whose name might very well become, as one of Andrew Johnson's counsel put it, a word to frighten children with throughout the land. And it would permit the retention of the perquisites that are given to former presidents, including the retirement benefits given (under current statute) to any former president who has not actually been removed by conviction in an impeachment trial. Resignation is not a bad proposition from the public's standpoint, either; it achieves the basic objective of impeachment while shortening the process and sparing the ex-president the vindictive consequences of an impeachment conviction. Of course, it cannot literally be forced on any president; the decision to resign is his alone.

One other choice is available to a president facing impeachment, which might also reduce the prolonged uncertainty and possible paralysis of the executive branch of the government resulting from presidential impeachment proceedings. Under the Twenty-fifth Amendment, adopted in 1967 for entirely different purposes, the president may declare himself "unable to discharge the powers and duties of the office," which are then temporarily discharged by the vice president as acting president. As a temporary expedient, especially in a case in which a president thinks he is likely to prevail in an impeachment trial, this procedure—also voluntary with the president—may make some sense.[4]

4. The Twenty-fifth Amendment creates another procedure that is not voluntary with the president. It provides that the vice president shall become acting president if he and a majority of the principal officers of the executive departments (or such other body as Congress may by law provide) declare that the president is unable to discharge the powers and duties of his office. If the president thereafter declares that no inability exists, he resumes the powers and duties of his office unless the vice president and a majority of the cabinet (or other designated body) again declare him unable and each House affirms

Impeachment's problem, however, is not only that it is tedious and desultory, but that it may be tardy. No structural change can shorten the length of time it takes to set the impeachment process in motion in the House, although its replacement by a mechanism more akin to a vote of no-confidence would presumably expedite decisions to remove or retain presidents. But a no-confidence system would create problems of its own, not the least of which is that it might invite manipulation by introducing elements of plebiscitary democracy, permitting a president and his supporters to seek a popular mandate for particular actions or policies. The first two uses of the Twenty-fifth Amendment—to replace a vice president who resigned as part of a plea bargain in a criminal prosecution and to replace his successor, who became president after the incumbent resigned to avoid impeachment and removal—are a recent reminder that constitutional mechanisms are likely to have unanticipated uses. Change should not be undertaken lightly.

There has been no clamor to reform the impeachment mechanism itself, despite a few suggestions to provide a more comprehensible listing of grounds for impeachment than the current constitutional catch-all term, "other high crimes and misdemeanors." The case for such an amendment is that it would prevent future claims that impeachment is directed at criminal rather than constitutional wrongdoing. But the likelihood of such claims, in the wake of the Nixon inquiry, seems slim. And the real difficulty in determining what presidential misconduct warrants impeachment is not in defining the misconduct—the constitutional duties of the president provide an appropriate, and appropriately general, definition for purposes of impeachment proceedings—but in assessing whether the wrongdoing, taken together, is sufficiently serious to warrant removal from office. That is not a definitional problem, but a judgmental one, and it can be as readily addressed under the existing constitutional clause as under a lengthier catalogue of impeachable misconduct—perhaps more readily. An effort to be explicit and comprehensive would invite an attempt to solve problems in the abstract that are better considered in the context of a particular case.

Obviously, if one were starting work on a new Constitution, "high

---

their declaration by a two-thirds vote. This complicated procedure, designed for instances of mental or physical incapacity, is ill-adapted to the case of a president facing impeachment, though its terms do not preclude its use in that situation.

crimes and misdemeanors" would be among the phrases that could stand replacement. Preferably, the substitute would be an even simpler and less explicit term—"for cause" or "for serious wrongdoing." But it hardly makes sense to consider a constitutional amendment to update the language of a provision that can be, and in practice has been, interpreted in just that way.

In short, there is little reason to meddle with the impeachment provisions and some risks in trying to change them. More important, the prospect of amendment is practically nil. The next time a president is suspected of wrongdoing or accused by his political opponents, the constitutional procedure for investigating his conduct and seeking his removal will almost certainly be the same as it is today. When the occasion again arises, it will be too late to consider structural change; whether the constitutional system works (and, indeed, how that is determined) will depend on the people who must use it.

The participants in that future proceeding will find it a harrowing enterprise, as anyone who endured the Nixon inquiry can attest. And they will discover that there is a paucity of precedent addressing their problems. The rejection of an impeachment resolution by the House in 1867, an acquittal by the Senate in 1868, and a proceeding short-circuited by resignation in 1974 hardly provide an abundant body of case law. Perhaps the framers of the Constitution did not expect presidential impeachment to be so rare and therefore so awesome as it has turned out to be. For the people through their representatives to seek to remove the chief executive of their government does not seem an event that should lead to great constitutional handwringing. Elected officials, after all, can turn out to be corrupt or maladroit; a procedure for removing them is an unexceptionable device; its use, while obviously not cause for jubilation, would not seem to be an occasion of grave crisis.

If past presidents had been worse or past Congresses more assertive, presidential impeachment might have turned into a relatively routine proceeding. Yet one need not be a constitutional Pangloss, believing that all is for the best in the best of all governmental systems, to understand why presidential impeachment has been so seldom considered and, consequently, is a matter of such great moment when it is. Presidential incompetence usually does not manifest itself in the form of serious constitutional wrongdoing or, at least, as constitutional wrongdoing in which Congress and the public do not have a considerable degree of complicity. To remove a president is, in effect, to declare that the voters made a bad choice in electing him, and that is not an easy message for other elected politicians to convey. Even a misbehaving and unpopular president, moreover, has means of dispelling pressures for his impeachment, including delay and conciliatory measures. For these reasons and others, presidential impeachment is difficult to get under way, much less to carry through to a conclusion. It has been, and remains, a cumbersome and unwieldy weapon; its use is therefore an extraordinary constitutional event.

INDEX